THE BRITISH INDUSTRIAL DECLINE

The decline of British industry in the late Victorian and early Edwardian period is a subject of major concern to economic and modern British historians. *The British Industrial Decline* collects together a rich spectrum of essays from a broad array of perspectives, ranging from controversial cultural readings of industrial decline to sophisticated economic explorations. The book sets out the present state of discussion and introduces the new directions in which the debate about the British decline is now proceeding.

Among other themes, *The British Industrial Decline* examines

- the role of the service sector alongside manufacturing
- the distinctiveness of the British regions
- the state's role in the British decline including an analysis of its responsibility for the maintenance and modernization of infrastructure
- the association of aristocratic values with entrepreneurial vitality
- how British historians have discussed success and failure, with a critique of the literature of decline

The British Industrial Decline is an up-to-date, multi-perspective introduction to this crucial, widely debated topic.

ROUTLEDGE EXPLORATIONS IN ECONOMIC HISTORY

1 ECONOMIC IDEAS AND GOVERNMENT POLICY
Contributions to contemporary economic history
Sir Alec Cairncross

2 THE ORGANIZATION OF LABOUR MARKETS
Modernity, culture and governance in Germany, Sweden, Britain and Japan
Bo Stråth

3 CURRENCY CONVERTIBILITY
The gold standard and beyond
Edited by Jorge Braga de Macedo, Barry Eichengreen and Jaime Reis

4 BRITAIN'S PLACE IN THE WORLD
Import Controls 1945–1960
Alan S. Milward and George Brennan

5 FRANCE AND THE INTERNATIONAL ECONOMY
From Vichy to the Treaty of Rome
Frances M.B. Lynch

6 MONETARY STANDARDS AND EXCHANGE RATES
M.C Marcuzzo, L. Officer, A. Rosselli

7 PRODUCTION EFFICIENCY IN DOMESDAY ENGLAND, 1086
John McDonald

8 FREE TRADE AND ITS RECEPTION 1815–1960
Freedom and trade: Volume I
Edited by Andrew Marrison

9 CONCEIVING COMPANIES
Joint-stock politics in Victorian England
Timothy L. Alborn

10 THE BRITISH INDUSTRIAL DECLINE
Edited by Jean Pierre Dormois and Michael Dintenfass

THE BRITISH INDUSTRIAL DECLINE

Edited by
Jean-Pierre Dormois
and Michael Dintenfass

LONDON AND NEW YORK

First published 1999
by Routledge
2 Park Square, Milton Park, Abingdon, Oxfordshire OX14 4RN

Simultaneously published in the USA and Canada
by Routledge
711 Third Avenue, New York, NY 10017

First issued in paperback 2014

Routledge is an imprint of the Taylor & Francis Group, an informa business

© 1999 editorial matter and selection, Jean Pierre Dormois
and Michael Dintenfass; individual chapters, the contributors

Typeset in Garamond by
The Florence Group, Stoodleigh, Devon

All rights reserved. No part of this book may be reprinted or
reproduced or utilised in any form or by any electronic,
mechanical, or other means, now known or hereafter invented,
including photocopying and recording, or in any information
storage or retrieval system, without permission in writing
from the publishers.

British Library Cataloguing in Publication Data
A catalogue record for this book is available from the British Library

Library of Congress Cataloguing in Publication Data
1. Industries—Great Britain. 2. Industrial Policy—Great Britain.
3. Industrial productivity—Great Britain. 4. Great Britain—Economic
conditions—19th century—Regional disparities. 5. Great Britain—
Economic conditions—20th century—Regional disparities.
I. Dormois, Jean Pierre. II Dintenfass, Michael, 1952–
HC260.I52B753   1998
338′.00941—dc21   98–22609
CIP

ISBN 13: 978-1-138-86822-9 (pbk)
ISBN 13: 978-0-415-17231-8 (hbk)

Publisher's Note
The publisher has gone to great lengths to ensure the quality of this reprint
but points out that some imperfections in the original may be apparent

CONTENTS

Contributors vii
Foreword by Barry Supple xi

Introduction 1

PART I
The literature of decline 5

1 Converging accounts, misleading metaphors and persistent doubts: reflections on the historiography of Britain's 'decline' 7
   MICHAEL DINTENFASS

2 1066 and a wave of gadgets: the achievements of British growth 27
   DEIRDRE N. MCCLOSKEY

PART II
Economic growth and performance 45

3 Industrial performance, the infrastructure and government policy 47
   ROBERT MILLWARD

4 Competitiveness and growth: new perspectives on the late Victorian and Edwardian economy 65
   DAVID GREASLEY AND LES OXLEY

5 Flagging or failing? British economic performance, 1880–1914 85
   B.W.E. ALFORD

CONTENTS

PART III
Technology and industry   101

6   The audit of the Great War on British technology   103
CORRELLI BARNETT

7   The balance of technological transfers 1870–1914   114
JAMES FOREMAN-PECK

8   Regional vs national perspectives on economic 'decline' in late Victorian and Edwardian Britain   139
W.R. GARSIDE

PART IV
Institutions and culture   153

9   Education and economic decline 1870–1914: an innocent suspect?   155
MICHAEL SANDERSON

10   The voice of industry and the ethos of decline: business citizenship, public service and the making of a British industrial élite   175
MICHAEL DINTENFASS

11   The City of London, 1880–1914: tradition and innovation   189
PETER CAIN

PART V
A French perspective on the British 'decline'   205

12   France's experience of industrial retardation during the *Belle Epoque*   207
JEAN-PIERRE DORMOIS

Index of names   231

CONTRIBUTORS

B.W.E. Alford is the author of a number of authoritative books on British economic history, including *Britain in the World Economy since 1880* (Longman, 1992) and *British Economic Performance 1945–1975* (Cambridge University Press, 1996). He has edited with Rodney Lowe *Economic Planning 1945–51* (HMSO, 1991). He heads the department of historical studies at the University of Bristol.

Correlli Barnett CBE, the acclaimed author of *The Lost Victory* (Pan Books, 1995), *The Audit of War: The Illusion and Reality of Britain as a Great Nation* (Pan Books, 1986) and *The Collapse of British Power* (Alan Sutton, 1984) is one of Britain's most distinguished military historians. He served formerly as Keeper of the Churchill Archives Centre at Churchill College, Cambridge.

Peter Cain is research professor of history at Sheffield Hallam University. He is a specialist on economic imperialism. He is the author of *Economic Foundations of British Expansion Overseas* (Macmillan, 1980) and, with A.C. Hopkins, of *British Imperialism 1688–1990* (2 volumes, Longman, 1993).

Michael Dintenfass, an economic and business historian who first studied the British coal industry in *Managing Industrial Decline* (Ohio State University Press, 1993), has also published *The Decline of Industrial Britain 1870–1980* (Routledge, 1992). He is currently associate professor of history at the University of Wisconsin at Milwaukee.

Jean-Pierre Dormois is a junior faculty member in British history at the University of Montpellier. After studying at Harvard, he was Knox fellow at Trinity College Cambridge. He is the author of *Vue d'Amérique* (France-Empire, 1990), *L'économie britannique au XXe siècle* (Hachette, 1994) and *L'économie française face à la concurrence britannique à la veille de 1914* (L'Harmattan, 1997).

James Foreman-Peck, an expert on British technology, is the author of *A History of the World Economy* (Harvester Wheatsheaf, 1991, 2nd edition

CONTRIBUTORS

1994) and co-author (with Robert Millward) of *Public and Private Ownership of British Industry 1820–1990* (Oxford, 1994) as well as the editor of *New Perspectives on the Late Victorian Economy* (Cambridge University Press, 1991). After holding a professorship at the University of Hull, he is now university lecturer at Oxford and Fellow of St Antony's College. He is President-elect of the European Historical Economics Society.

William Garside is professor of economic history at the University of Birmingham. He has published *British Unemployment 1919–1939* (Cambridge University Press, 1990) and edited *Capitalism in Crisis: International Responses to the Great Depression* (Pinter, 1993). He is currently engaged in a study of British and Japanese industrial policy and performance since 1945.

David Greasley is reader in economic history at the University of Edinburgh. Originally interested in the coal industry, he has since tackled various aspects of the British pre-Second World War and interwar economy. His latest publications include 'Unit Roots and British Industrial Growth' (*Manchester School*, 1997) and 'Technological Epochs and British Industrial Production, 1700–1992' (*Scottish Journal of Political Economy*, 1997).

Deirdre N. McCloskey, a well-known advocate of British economic achievements since the publication of *Essays on a Mature Economy* (1971) as well as the initiator of a heated debate on economic rhetoric, is past president of the American Economic History Association. Her latest books include *If You're So Smart* (University of Chicago Press, 1991), *Second Thoughts* (Oxford University Press, 1993) and *Knowledge and Persuasion in Economics* (Cambridge University Press, 1994). She is professor of economics and professor of history at the University of Iowa.

Robert Millward is professor of economic history at the University of Manchester and co-author with James Foreman-Peck, of *Public and Private Ownership of British Industry 1820–1990* (Oxford, 1994). He was recently co-author (with John Singleton) of *The Political Economy of Nationalisation in Britain 1920–1950* (Cambridge University Press, 1995).

Les Oxley is currently professor of economics at the University of Waikato. He has held visiting positions at the Australian National University, Monash University, and the University of Western Australia. He has published widely on applied econometrics and macroeconomic dynamics, and is a joint founding editor of the *Journal of Economic Surveys*.

Michael Sanderson is reader in history at the University of East Anglia in Norwich and the editor of the New Studies in Economic and Social History published by the Economic History Society and Cambridge

CONTRIBUTORS

University Press. His research interests are in theatrical and educational history and in the latter area his recent publications include *The Missing Stratum: The Technical School in England 1900–1990s* (Athlone, 1994) and *Education, Economic Change and Society 1780–1870* (Cambridge University Press, 1995).

Barry Supple, currently director of the Leverhulme Trust in London, one of the prime fund-givers for scientific research in the United Kingdom, held the chair of economic history at the University of Cambridge. He gave his understanding of the theme of the conference in his farewell address as president of the Economic History Society in 1993 (published in the *Economic History Review* in 1994). He has published *The Rise of Big Business* (Edward Elgar, 1992).

FOREWORD

It is a personal as well as an academic pleasure to contribute a prefatory note to this collection of essays on a topic of endless fascination – and endless significance. There has never been an epoch in Britain's history over the last 500 years when some jeremiad concerning the country's failure or regression has not been available for the gratification of pessimists.

This was so, however muted the anguish of a minority, even during the brief moment (whenever that might have been) of the economy's apotheosis. But it has been markedly, and very significantly, the case when Britain's relative economic performance has lagged. The resulting debate, whatever the validity of specific arguments, has an importance which transcends the 'truth' of claim and counter-claim, since it sheds light on the nature of British economic and social and political history, and on the ways in which that history is constructed by those who play a contemporary or retrospective part in it.

In the past, and even now among many popular and political commentators, the fact that Britain's lag is inevitable, unless the economy were to dominate the world for ever, appears to make little impact. However, scholarly study in recent years has woken up to the difference between lagging behind others and lagging behind an economy's intrinsic potential. Further, it has begun to consider anew the crucial question of convergence, and whether Britain is, after all, one unit in a global, or at least an international, system of economic development.

But these are complex and meta-historical issues. For economic historians the two critical questions are, first, whether (or in what sense) Britain actually declined in periods such as the late nineteenth century or the years since the Second World War; and, second, what have been the implications and consequences of the perennial perception of decline which has dogged political and journalistic (and often academic) debate. This collection addresses more the first than the second issue, but obviously is related to both. The pervasive conclusion that there is no evidence of decline until after the Great War might perhaps be tempered by the gloss that 'decline' has a special, and protean, meaning even then. But the precise focus of

FOREWORD

scholarly conclusions is at this stage less important than the fact that the perennial question of the country's economic performance in various critical periods of its history should still give rise to reasoned debate and the interchange of conceptual and empirical argument. There are spurious as well as sensible elements in the controversy concerning Britain's economic performance. Happily, however, there can be no doubt about the utility and liveliness of economic history as it grapples with the problem of understanding and interpretation. This volume bears further witness to that fact.

Barry Supple
Director
The Leverhulme Trust
London, February 1997

INTRODUCTION

Ever since André Siegfried published his resounding *Crise britannique au XXe siècle* in 1931 – an ominous year in Britain's twentieth-century history – the issue of the 'British decline' has been a recurring theme in both academic circles and the media, (de)generating into strong opposition between pessimists stressing Britain's disappointing performance as well as loss of stature and optimists defending its growth record and technical achievements. This volume attempts to re-examine the most strident charges made against the late Victorian economic make-up as well as Britain's path of industrialization after the First World War. It originated in an international conference on the 'Roots of the British "Decline" in the Late-Victorian and Edwardian Period' that Jean-Pierre Dormois convened at the Centre d'Etudes et de Recherches Victoriennes & Edouardiennes at the University of Montpellier in September 1995. The Montpellier meeting was the most recent in a series of historical symposia on the performance of the modern British economy that began with the conference on the 'New Economic History of Britain' at Harvard in 1970 and continued with the 'Anglo-American Conference on the Decline of the British Economy' at Boston University in 1983 and the symposium on 'British Culture vs. British Industry?' at the University of Glasgow in 1986. The published proceedings of each of these meetings possessed a unity of viewpoint that made them landmarks in the field of British economic history. The *Essays on a Mature Economy* that Donald N. McCloskey assembled from the Harvard colloquium demonstrated the applicability of the economist's theory and statistical methods to historical problems, but they were also a monument to the proposition 'that British performance was better than . . . [had] been commonly believed' (McCloskey 1971, p. 5). The contributors to Bernard Elbaum and William Lazonick's *The Decline of the British Economy* agreed that after 1870 Britain had not performed as well economically as it should have, and the explanations they elaborated had a common source in the institutional analysis of Alfred D. Chandler, Jr (Elbaum and Lazonick 1986; Chandler 1980 and 1990; and Chandler and Daems 1980). The papers Bruce Collins and Keith Robbins collected in *British Culture and Economic*

INTRODUCTION

Decline complemented one another by their scepticism towards Martin Wiener's thesis about the adherence of British industrialists to a gentlemanly ethos and by their commitment to an international perspective on British culture and industry (Collins and Robbins 1990; Wiener 1981).

The influence of these works was readily audible in the conversation at Montpellier, and their imprint is clearly visible in this book. Jean-Pierre Dormois's essay on 'France's experience of industrial retardation during the Belle Epoque' continues the comparative initiative that was a hallmark of *British Culture and Economic Decline*, and so too do David Greasley and Les Oxley in 'Competitiveness and growth,' at the same time that they, like McCloskey and company almost thirty years ago, turn new developments in econometric technique to history's advantage. Michael Sanderson's contribution on education and economic decline testifies to the enduring centrality of institutional questions to the argument over British performance.

This volume nonetheless departs from its predecessors in the representation of a broadly consensual vision of modern British economic history. Where they projected a single interpretation, we offer a diversity of views and a freshness of approaches. Whereas in each of the previous collections either an optimistic or pessimistic tone predominated, here both schools of thought find ample expression. Both the arguments in defence of the British record and those critical of it, however, have been largely reconceived. The debate over British decline that emerges in these pages is thus substantially different from the disagreements to which the contributors to the McCloskey, Elbaum–Lazonick, and Collins–Robbins books were party.

The British economy under historical scrutiny here is very much a disaggregated one, and in the chapters of Robert Millward, W.R. Garside and Peter Cain the service sector comes back into the picture alongside manufacturing, and the different regions of Britain recover their distinctiveness. The state's role in the story of British decline is recast as well. So often either the author of monetary, budgetary and commercial policies or the phantom architect of national development programmes, it again assumes, in James Foreman-Peck's essay, responsibility for the regulation of technology and business organization, and in Robert Millward's it regains pride of place in the maintenance and modernization of the country's infrastructure. The culture to which British industry belonged is also imagined anew in this book. Peter Cain examines the association of aristocratic values with entrepreneurial vitality. Michael Dintenfass introduces civic virtue as the principal ideal informing business decision-making.

This collection also stands apart from earlier works in the field by virtue of its self-consciousness about how British historians have talked about success and failure. Part I of the book presents two chapters devoted to the literature of decline. In the first, Michael Dintenfass scrutinizes the chronologies, measurements and metaphors with which narratives of British performance have been constructed to understand why an optimistic reading of the historical

INTRODUCTION

record has failed to win a consensus. In the second, D.N. McCloskey proceeds to a rhetorical critique of the pessimistic story of British decline through a meditation on freedom, creativity and economic ingenuity.

Part II of the book ventures upon the better known ground of economic growth and performance, but the landscape that emerges is only partly familiar. Robert Millward reveals the low productivity of the non-manufacturing components of the economy – transport, communications and public services – as the source of Britain's divergence from Germany and the United States along the path of national income growth, and he suggests that the pressure of urbanization on social overheads severely constrained the formulation of an effective policy response. Employing recent advances in time-series analysis, David Greasley and Les Oxley portray an economy that experienced no sharp discontinuity in growth before 1914 – no 'climacteric' – and converged strongly with the French economy between the late nineteenth century and the late twentieth but only very slowly with that of the United States. Revisiting some old standards of economic storytelling, capital formation, market share and productivity growth, B.W.E. Alford detects already before 1914 signs of the rigidity and inflexibility that were to compromise Britain's bid to meet the requirements of modern economic development after the First World War.

Correlli Barnett, James Foreman-Peck, and W.R. Garside take up questions of technology and industrial organization in Part III. Barnett and Foreman-Peck both express disquiet over Britain's capacity for technological innovation, the one from the vantage point of military history and the other from the perspective of economic history, and both direct critical attention towards British governments. Where Foreman-Peck identifies a regulatory environment that before 1914 was hostile to new British departures in electricity, chemicals and telecommunications, and with baleful effects on the manufacturing trades that supplied them, Barnett laments how the return to *laissez-faire* and the gold standard in the 1920s nullified the burst of innovation that between 1916 and 1918 made up the deficiencies that had accumulated to 1914. Garside emphasizes the success of the manufacturing regions centred on Birmingham, Glasgow and Sheffield in developing flexible structures of production and distribution that, by facilitating the free circulation of ideas, skills, designs and practices, enabled the profitable exploitation of the available resources and market opportunities.

Michael Sanderson opens Part IV on institutions and culture with an audit of the pre-1914 educational system, from which it emerges with the credit of having supplied, after 1890 at any rate, all the schooling and training the economy might have required. Michael Dintenfass follows with a study of the definition of individual distinction in coal mining in the 1920s that suggests it was the nobility of industrial statesmanship and business citizenship, and not the indignity of trade, that governed enterprise management. In another chapter that moves the conversation about culture beyond

INTRODUCTION

Wiener's dichotomies, and the conversation about performance beyond manufacturing, Peter Cain traces the dynamism of the commercial and financial industries of the City of London back to the archaic gentlemanly ways that have been blamed for the sluggishness of the goods-producing sectors of the economy.

We complete our discussion not with a concluding essay that assembles the findings and interpretations of the different contributors into a uniform account of British economic history since 1870 but with an invitation to further inquiry: Jean-Pierre Dormois's consideration of how the weaknesses of the late Victorian and Edwardian economy appear in the light of the economic history of France. The dialogue the volume represents allowed no other ending. When scholars adept at econometric, institutional and rhetorical analysis disclose that services were a great British success and the source of the country's comparatively slower growth, that manufacturing was a site of dynamic innovation and a sector whose capacity for change the state seriously restricted, and that the analytical power of these tales rests on the suitability of military and biological metaphors for economic investigations, there can be no gestures towards closure. The chapters that follow, then, are not the last word in a long-running historical quarrel. Questioning how the participants in the argument have constructed the economy, represented the state and construed the culture, the essays presented here signal the redefinition and reformulation of a venerable controversy. We offer them as an introduction to the new directions in which the debate about British decline is now proceeding.

References

Chandler, Alfred D. (1980). 'The Growth of the Transnational Industrial Firm in the United States and the United Kingdom', *Economic History Review*, 2nd series, XXIII (August), pp. 396–410.
Chandler, Alfred D. (1990). *Scale and Scope*, Cambridge, Mass.: Belknap Press.
Chandler, Alfred D. and Herman Daems (eds) (1980). *Managerial Hierarchies*, Cambridge, Mass.: Harvard University Press.
Collins, Bruce and Keith Robbins (eds) (1990). *British Culture and Economic Decline*, New York: St Martin's Press.
Elbaum, Bernard and William Lazonick (eds) (1986). *The Decline of the British Economy*, Oxford: Clarendon Press.
McCloskey, Donald N. (ed.) (1971). *Essays on a Mature Economy*, Princeton, NJ: Princeton University Press.
Wiener, Martin J. (1981). *English Culture and the Decline of the Industrial Spirit 1850–1980*, New York: Cambridge University Press.

Part I

THE LITERATURE OF DECLINE

1

CONVERGING ACCOUNTS, MISLEADING METAPHORS AND PERSISTENT DOUBTS

Reflections on the historiography of Britain's 'decline'

Michael Dintenfass

The historical record and the historiographical problem[1]

In 1960 Britain came tenth in the Organization for Economic Co-operation and Development's (OECD) league table of real income per capita.[2] This represented a striking change from fifty years earlier when Britain had been the wealthiest nation in Europe and if not the richest country in the world, then behind only the United States and perhaps Canada. That the average Briton in 1960 enjoyed a standard of living that his countrymen of 1910 would hardly have been able to conceive of was certainly true. It was equally true, however, that over the intervening decades real income per head had grown more slowly in Britain than in several other nations.

For the economic historians of the 1960s the past performance of the British economy posed a serious intellectual challenge. Derek H. Aldcroft offered one solution to it in the August 1964 issue of the *Economic History Review*. His argument was that 'Britain's relatively poor economic performance' could 'be attributed largely to the failure of British entrepreneurs to respond to the challenge of changed conditions.' Lacking 'the drive and dynamism' of their 'predecessors of the classical industrial revolution', British businessmen were unable to attain the increases in output, exports and productivity that their American and German counterparts achieved.[3] One year later David S. Landes took up the themes of economic 'decline' and entrepreneurial 'failure' with characteristic vigour in his contribution to *The Cambridge Economic History of Europe*. The evidence and argumentation assembled there were on a scale far larger than Aldcroft had attempted, but the conclusions were fundamentally the same. 'All the evidence agrees', Landes wrote, 'on the technological backwardness of much of British manufacturing industry – on leads lost, opportunities missed, markets relinquished that need not have been.' Responsibility for this lamentable record lay squarely with the owners and managers of Britain's enterprises:

> her merchants, who had once seized the markets of the world, took them for granted. . . . Similarly, the British manufacturer was notorious for his indifference to style, his conservatism in the face of new techniques, his reluctance to abandon the individuality of tradition for the conformity implicit in mass production.[4]

By 1970 Britain had slipped to fifteenth place in the OECD's standings as France, Japan, the Netherlands, Iceland and Finland joined the United States, Sweden, Australia and Germany, among others, on the list of countries with average per capita incomes higher than that of Britain. The lineaments of British performance continued to attract the attention of specialists in economic history, but much more flattering readings of the British story now came to the fore. One of the first to proceed in this direction was Charles Wilson with an essay in the *Economic History Review* of August 1965. Turning his gaze from 'those frontiers of pig iron and cotton stockings' towards 'light industry, distribution, and salesmanship', he found an economy very different from the one about which Aldcroft and Landes had written. 'It was in large measure the economy men wanted, an economy that supplied their needs abundantly and on the whole efficiently.'[5] Four years later Lars G. Sandberg undertook a reconsideration of the frontier of cotton textiles, and he did so equipped with a new analytical tool: the quantitative methods of formal cost-benefit analysis. His results, published in the *Quarterly Journal of Economics* (February 1969), showed that the preference of British cotton masters for spinning mules rather than ring spindles was not a 'sign of technological conservatism' but an economically rational response to the factor costs they faced and the techniques available to them.[6] Where Wilson had concluded that there was 'no evidence that the growth of *new* industries or the development of new territories was inhibited by a lack of entrepreneurial talent', Sandberg suggested that there were no entrepreneurial deficiencies to be found in one of Britain's oldest and largest staple trades either.[7] Less than a year after the appearance of Sandberg's pioneering essay in historical quantification, Donald N. McCloskey, a Harvard-trained member of the economics department at the University of Chicago, pursued the logic of the Wilson–Sandberg view of British economic history to its ultimate conclusion in an article with the provocative title 'Did Victorian Britain Fail?' McCloskey's answer was a resounding no. The economy with which Aldcroft and Landes had found so much fault had grown 'as rapidly as permitted by the growth of its resources and the effective exploitation of the available technology'.[8] The means by which McCloskey redeemed the past performances of British entrepreneurs were as striking as his revisionist conclusion. Foremost among them were a serious of hypothetical calculations. How fast would the country's labour supply have had to have grown in order to sustain the growth rates achieved when Britain was at the height of its industrial pre-eminence? How fast would its capital supply have had to have grown to have maintained these rates of expansion? How much faster would British income have grown if capital markets had been more efficient in allocating investments between home and overseas outlets? By calculating what had not happened, McCloskey arrived at a favourable judgement of what had happened in Britain's economic past.

Over the next two decades, British living standards continued to rise, Britain's relative position among the industrialized countries slipped still further, and the optimistic interpretation of Britain's past record became the prevailing wisdom among scholars specializing in economic history. Roderick Floud, in his contribution to the two-volume economic history of Britain since 1700 that he edited with McCloskey, conceded that Britain had 'certainly lost the predominant position which she had held as the leading or only manufacturing nation', but in his judgement 'this was not because of deficiencies within the British economy. It stemmed, instead, from the increasing complexity of the international economy, and of the national economies within it.'[9] Sidney Pollard, professor of economic history at Sheffield and then the University of Bielefeld, arrived at very much the same conclusion. Britain experienced 'the change-over from solitary pre-eminence in industrial and mining production to being one of several industrial countries', but there had been no 'failure in entrepreneurship as a weakness in British society'. On the contrary, the economy had remained 'fundamentally sound', 'flexible and possessing hidden reserves at least the equal of any other'.[10] In his *Capitalism, Culture, and Decline in Britain 1750–1990* (1993), W. D. Rubinstein, professor of social and economic history at Deakin University, brought the optimistic revision of British economic history to a culmination by standing the findings of Aldcroft and Landes squarely on their heads. What had appeared as the failure of British industry was in reality the intelligent, realistic 'transfer of resources and entrepreneurial energies' away from activities for which Britain was relatively poorly suited 'into other forms of business life', namely 'commerce and finance', where Britain's 'comparative advantage always' had lain.[11]

To be sure, the favourable verdicts of the professors of economic history never succeeded in completely removing the doubts about the quality of Britain's past economic performance, and dissenting voices continued to be heard through the 1980s. Martin J. Wiener maintained in his *English Culture and the Decline of the Industrial Spirit 1850–1980* (1981) that from the late nineteenth century there had been a 'steady and continual erosion of the nation's economic position in the world'.[12] Correlli Barnett made the Second World War the central event of Britain's 'astonishing' and 'protracted decline as an industrial country' in his *The Audit of War* (1986).[13] Bernard Elbaum and William Lazonick gathered together in *The Decline of the British Economy* (1986) a collection of papers concerned with the 'century-long affliction' that had caused Britain to lag 'behind other advanced nations in productivity growth' and to suffer 'continuing decline in industrial competitiveness and its relative level of per capita income'.[14]

None of these critical portrayals of Britain's economic record owed much to the theoretical understandings and statistical practices that were the stock-in-trade of the revisionists who placed Britain's economic history in a more flattering light. Wiener was an intellectual historian and Barnett a military historian. Elbaum and Lazonick were institutional economists openly sceptical of the neoclassical economic doctrines in which Sandberg, McCloskey, Floud and Rubinstein placed their faith. The works that these outsiders produced each won a wide general readership, commanded the attention of opinion and policy-makers and elicited a barrage of hostile comment in the professional economic history journals.

Since 1965 the historiography of British economic performance in the late nineteenth and twentieth centuries has exhibited two divergent tendencies. Among the economic historians who considered the matter 'from the perspective of economic theory and applied statistics' there has emerged an optimistic consensus that Britain performed 'as one would expect a competitive and prosperous economy to perform'. British entrepreneurs were 'on the whole ... responsive to the opportunities available' to them, and the economy grew as rapidly as resources and technologies permitted.[15] Historians outside the domain of economic history, on the other hand, have continued to raise questions about the decisions British businessmen made in the past and to emphasize the disparity between Britain's growth rate and the growth rates of her competitors. Why have the economic historians not been able to allay the doubts of the non-specialists? Why has the pessimists' story of 'failure' and 'decline' persisted in the face of the rigour and sophistication that the professionals brought to the study of British economic history?

The ready answer, of course, is that the specialist tools of the economic historians worked against the acceptance of their positive interpretation of Britain's economic record. Neoclassical theory, after all, is not part of the standard mental equipment of the man in the street, or the professor in his study, and production functions and regression analysis are luxury goods of still narrower distribution. Moreover, the story of steady, uneventful growth that the optimists told was hardly as dramatically satisfying as the pessimists' grim tale of 'decline' and 'failure'. Certainly, it did not make for gripping headlines.

While there is no doubt something in all of this, it cannot be the whole story. The ranks of the professional economic historians prominent in this debate included people of exceptional literary talent and some publicists of the highest quality. They set out their case in the most comprehensible of everyday terms, and it was available in several inexpensive and accessible volumes. Nor was the general ideational climate consistently to their disadvantage. From the middle 1980s at any rate considerable political and journalistic capital was invested in the same favourable judgements of the British economy that the economic historians had long endorsed.

The remainder of this chapter proceeds on the premise that the explanation of the curious history of the debate over Britain's 'decline' lies in large part within that historiography and that an understanding of this scholarly controversy requires an examination of the conduct of the conversation itself. In the next three sections I look in turn at three key aspects of the argument over Britain's economic past: the chronologies of dispute, the measures of descent and the metaphors of controversy. Attention to these features of the debate allows us to specify the exact terms of the disagreement between optimists and pessimists, but it also brings out the considerable common ground between them – common ground that the cut and thrust of scholarly exchange has largely obscured. In the final section of the chapter, I return to the question of the persistence of the pessimist case, and through a consideration of what each side has contributed to the debate thus far, I offer some brief suggestions about its conduct in the future.

The chronologies of dispute

The academic antecedents of the argument over Britain's 'decline' lay in a prior scholarly controversy about a Victorian 'climacteric'. Back in 1952 E.H. Phelps Brown and S.J. Handfield-Jones, in an essay in the *Oxford Economic Papers*, located a deceleration in British productivity growth beginning in the 1890s. D.J. Coppock replied in the pages of the *Manchester School of Economic and Social Studies* four years later that the turning point had actually come in the 1870s, and he soon found himself in dispute with A.E. Musson over the degree to which the British economy had slowed down during the so-called Great Depression of 1873–1896. These exchanges turned to a considerable extent on the identification of the opportunities open to British business, and it was to them that Aldcroft, Landes and Wilson all referred in setting the historiographical stage for their assessments of Britain's economic past.[16]

The preoccupation of this earlier debate with the later years of Victoria's reign was extremely important in setting the temporal boundaries of the controversy over British performance and British entrepreneurship. The original pessimists, Aldcroft and Landes, each extended the endpoint of their analyses further forward in time than the protagonists in the argument over the 'climacteric' had done, but both brought their stories to a conclusion by 1914. Wilson's positive account of the dynamism and vitality at work in Britain's light manufacturing, consumer goods and retailing sectors was very much a tale, as he put it, about 'late Victorian Britain'.[17] In its initial phase, then, the debate about Britain's past economic performance was a debate about the years between 1870 and 1914.

For all that the 'new' economic historians changed the discourse of this debate by their employment of neoclassical theory and applied statistics, they took the chronological parameters of the question of 'decline' very much as they found them. Sandberg limited his original estimation of the costs and benefits of English mules and American rings to 'the period immediately preceding World War I'.[18] McCloskey's calculations of the growth Britain achieved and of the increases in labour and capital supplies that would have been necessary for it to have done better were confined to the years 1870–1914. Indeed, of the twelve papers that appeared in the first anthology of optimistic writings about British economic history, *Essays on a Mature Economy* (1971), just one ventured beyond the eve of the Great War.[19]

With the renewal of a more critical appraisal of Britain's economic past in the 1980s, judgements about the country's progress and the enterprise and efficiency of its businessmen were cast in rather different chronological terms. Wiener's exploration of the cultural origins of British 'decline' began with the late Victorian and Edwardian years, but it extended the period of poor performance into the late twentieth century. For Elbaum and Lazonick too, the slow growth of British output, efficiency and income was a long-term phenomenon that began decades before one world war and continued for decades after the next. Barnett, mindful also of the Victorian roots of the British 'disease', saw the sad history of Britain's economy as very much a twentieth-century event and the 1940s as its most critical moment.

How did the specialist economic historians who had so vigorously defended the rationality and competence of British entrepreneurs before 1914 respond to the neopessimist assertions that 'decline' was a long-term phenomenon and that the short terms that mattered most had occurred after 1918? By and large, they exhibited in the face of these challenges the same sort of conservatism and aversion to innovation that their opponents thought so characteristic of Britain's businessmen. The first (1981) edition of Floud and McCloskey's *The Economic History of Britain since 1700* offered its readers an essay by Sandberg on 'The Entrepreneur and Technological Change' that covered the years 1860–1914 and another by B.W.E. Alford on industry between the wars, as well as general surveys of 1860–1914 and 1900–1945, but this substantial work included no long-term assessment of Britain's economic record from 1860 to the 1970s. Similarly, Pollard's 1989 study of *Britain's Prime and Britain's Decline* confined the discussion of British economic performance to exactly those years with which Aldcroft's original 1964 investigation had been concerned, that is, 1870 to 1914.[20]

It was in fact only in the 1990s that the proponents of a positive account of British economic history broadened the chronological framework of their analyses, and their efforts to do so have yet to match the persuasiveness of their studies of the late Victorian and Edwardian period. In its second edition (1994), Floud and McCloskey's *The Economic History of Britain* expanded to three volumes, but its approach to the problem of performance remained highly episodic. There was now Pollard's 'Entrepreneurship, 1870–1914', James Foreman-Peck on 'Industry and Industrial Organisation in the Interwar Years,' and Barry Supple's reflections about 'British Economic Decline Since 1945', as well as Charles Feinstein's 'Success and Failure: British Economic Growth Since 1948' and Robert Millward's assessment of 'Industrial and Commercial Performance Since 1950'. There was still not, however, a single contribution that matched the theoretical and quantitative resources of the professional economic historian to the long-term perspective on Britain's past performance that Wiener and Elbaum and Lazonick emphasized. For a sustained and self-consciously favourable interpretation of Britain's economic record since the last third of the nineteenth century one has only been able to turn (and only recently at that) to Rubinstein's *Capitalism, Culture, and Decline*. Unfortunately, this work owes more to its author's antipathy to Martin J. Wiener than to the constructive influence of Lars G. Sandberg and Donald N. McCloskey. The bulk of the text is devoted to cultural and social history, and not to economic history. The theoretical underpinnings of its economic analysis are rudimentary at best, and its statistical apparatus, though not insubstantial, bears only haphazardly on the question of how well the British economy performed historically.

The scholarly controversy about the 'decline' of the British economy began as a debate about the late Victorian and Edwardian years. As the argument took shape, however, the later critics of Britain's past performance abandoned their predecessors' fixation on the 1870–1914 period and insisted instead that the slow growth of output, productivity and income was a long-term development, crucial phases of which occurred in the mid-twentieth century. Their protagonists, the specialist economic historians whose labours had rehabilitated Britain's pre-1914 decision-makers, proved slow in systematically deploying their arsenal of analytical techniques along these new chronological fronts. Thus, it has been possible to regard the late nineteenth and early twentieth-century economy as reasonably successful *and* to believe that Britain's record was one of relative 'failure' over the longer term.

Measures of descent

Fluency in the arts of calculation did more than anything else to distinguish the specialist economic historians of the 1970s and 1980s from those who lamented Britain's economic trajectory in the past. It is necessary therefore to look closely at the indices by which each school judged the British record. How different were the figures that the optimists and the pessimists respectively preferred?

The measures of performance on which Aldcroft and Landes based their critical assessments of Britain's economic history were very largely measures of quantities produced and exported. They captured, for the most part, the production and trade of individual British industries, particularly branches of the manufacturing and mining sectors, and not that of the economy as a whole. They were also very much comparative measures, juxtaposing the volumes selected British industries made and exported with the quantities that their German and American equivalents manufactured, mined and traded.[21]

Both of the original pessimists gave pride of place to metal-making in their accounts of Britain's 'decline'. Aldcroft reported that 'between 1886 and 1913 Britain lost her position as leading producer and exporter of iron and steel'. Landes was still more precise. The United States, he reported, 'permanently took over first place in both iron and steel output' in 1890. Germany captured second place with respect to steel in 1893 and with respect to pig iron in 1903, and by the quinquennium 1910–1914 Germany was producing on the average 'almost twice as much iron, more than twice as much steel' as Britain. By the same point in time Germany had also surpassed Britain, 'which had been the leading supplier to the world for a century', in the export of these basic metals.[22]

Aldcroft and Landes also accorded considerable weight to the chemicals industry, and again their concern was with how much Britain and the other industrial nations produced and exported. By 1913 Britain, which according to Aldcroft 'had once been the dominant producer' of chemicals, 'accounted for only 11 per cent of world production compared with 34 per cent for America and 24 per cent for Germany, while Germany's exports of chemicals were nearly twice those of Britain'. As Landes told it, in the space of just thirteen years after 1900 German production of sulphuric acid grew from half of the British total (550,000 tons compared to 1 million) to more than half again as large (1.7 million tons to 1.1 million).[23]

To the extent that Aldcroft and Landes tried to gauge British performance on a scale larger than that of a single trade their attention remained fixed on industrial production and the international trade of manufactured goods. Looking at the years between 1870 and 1913, Landes found that Britain's 'output of manufactured commodities (including minerals and processed foods) slightly more than doubled ... against a German increase of almost sixfold'. Looking at the trade of such goods between 1875 and 1895, he found that 'the value of British exports stood still, though volume rose by some 63 per cent, [and] the value of German exports rose 30 per cent and volume correspondingly more'. In a similar vein, Aldcroft emphasized that while Britain's share of the world trade in manufactures had fallen from 37.1% in 1883 to 25.4% in 1913, Germany's share had increased from 17.2% to 23% and that of the United States from 3.4% to 11%.[24]

Wilson, in his more optimistic rendering of the late Victorian economy, was openly critical of the sorts of indices that Aldcroft and Landes employed, arguing that 'the business of a national "economy" is to serve the needs of society as society sees them and not to perform statistical feats unrelated to what men at any rate *thought* they wanted'. His complaint was not that the pessimists had judged British performance in terms of the output of individual trades or that they had measured competitiveness in terms of the nation's share of particular overseas markets. It was rather that they had selected producer-oriented rather than consumer-oriented industries, and it was the achievement of his article that it reversed this priority. Where Landes and Aldcroft supplied tonnages of metals and chemicals, Wilson informed his readers that the number of Britain's multiple stores had climbed from '1500 odd' in the 1880s to the 11,645 of 1900 and that the Co-Op's sales had increased threefold over the same period.[25]

The introduction of fundamentally different ways of measuring performance into the evaluation of Britain's economic past was the work of the new economic historians whose training included the techniques of applied statistics as well as neoclassical theory. McCloskey's 1970 essay in the *Economic History Review* was very much the landmark in this regard. The numbers with which he rescued the Victorian economy from damnation measured, first, the aggregate ouput of the economy as a whole, and, second, the efficiency with which the British made use of all the resources and techniques available to them. The growth rates that mattered from this perspective were those of real gross national product per annum and real productivity minus increases in capital and labour (or total factor productivity).[26]

The aggregate indices of output and efficiency growth that McCloskey employed provided the enduring statistical foundation for favourable readings of Britain's economic past thereafter. They were recalculated with better data and different assumptions. They were calculated for other periods and extended to cover longer intervals. They formed the basis of comparisons of Britain and other countries. There was never any doubt, however, that they were adequate to meet the challenge that Aldcroft and Landes had posed.[27]

Floud's 1981 survey of the British economy in the period 1860–1914 turned to a large extent upon estimates of the rate of growth of output and of output per person employed and upon a comparison of these figures with the equivalent numbers for Germany and the United States. In the revised version of this essay (1994), he extended these statistics backwards to 1700 and forward to 1973, and he broadened the comparative perspective to include Sweden, France, Italy and Japan in addition to the United States and Germany. Supple's chapter on 'British Economic Decline Since 1945' in the same collection took as its preferred measures of economic achievement the annual growth rate of Britain's gross domestic product 1856–1973, the annual growth rate of GDP per head 1960–1987, the rate of growth of productivity in manufacturing 1960–1985, and the level of GDP 1950–1984, and it compared Britain on these grounds with the United

States, Germany, Japan, Italy, France and the Netherlands. In his own 1990 retelling of 'the story of British economic "failure" after 1870' McCloskey wove his narrative around a comparison of national product per head in 1900 and 1987 featuring the usual array of advanced industrial economies as well as South Korea, the USSR, Argentina, India and Mexico.[28]

The measures by which these professional economic historians depicted Britain's economic record were undoubtedly a major advance on the kinds of figures with which the first pessimists had buttressed their interpretations. Estimates of the output of the economy in its entirety – including agriculture and services along with manufacturing and mining and encompassing producer and consumer goods industries alike – replaced *ad hoc* statistics pertaining to the production of a few select industries. Calculations of how well the economy as a whole made use of available inputs and techniques added significantly to the picture of British competitiveness that the country's share of this or that overseas market had suggested.[29]

The superior figures with which McCloskey, Floud and Supple worked, however, did not produce an unambiguously flattering portrait of Britain's economic past. McCloskey's original calculations suggested that both real output and productivity growth slowed markedly after 1900. Floud's (1981) figures for the annual growth of total factor productivity between 1873 and 1913 showed that British efficiency improved at only half the German rate (0.4% compared to 0.9%) and only one-third as rapidly as American efficiency (1.2%). The tables Supple assembled indicated that Britain's annual GDP growth between 1950 and 1973 was lower than that of France, Germany, Japan, the Netherlands and the United States and that similar calculations on a per capita basis for 1960–1987 placed Britain ahead of only the United States. According to the numbers McCloskey reproduced in his *If You're So Smart*, Britain's national product per head was 96% of the American figure in 1900 but only 68% of it in 1987, and over the same period France, Germany, and Japan, all of whom had been at income levels well below the British in 1900 (at 57%, 56% and 24% respectively), each attained a higher average national income.[30]

Not surprisingly, the pessimists who in the 1980s pronounced their unfavourable verdicts on Britain's record over the long term readily adopted those measures of descent that their optimistic critics had introduced into the analysis of the country's economic history. While Barnett's audit of Britain's wartime economy was a rich repository of just the sorts of statistics – output figures for selected manufacturing industries – that Aldcroft and Landes had relied on, the measure that gave meaning to his elaborate enterprise was an international comparison of aggregate income: Britain's fall between 1945 and 1985 to 'fourteenth place in the non-communist world in terms of Gross National Product per head'. Elbaum and Lazonick likewise saw the curve of Britain's economic 'decline' inscribed in the indices of overall efficiency and per capita wealth.[31]

CONVERGING ACCOUNTS

The professional economic historians whose works raised serious doubts about a Victorian 'failure' were not oblivious to the fact that their preferred indicators of economic activity did not yield an uncontestable account of British success. Floud conceded in 1994 that the growth of output per capita in Britain between 1880 and 1914 had been 'slower than the growth of the other major industrial countries' and that 'this pattern, of slower growth than that of other countries, has generally persisted to the present day'. Supple acknowledged that

> during the post-war decades the British economy certainly did decline in relative terms: the rates of growth of its total and per capita GDP were persistently lower that those of its rivals; and its rate of productivity growth, although comparing favourably with that of the USA, was resoundingly exceeded by that of France, West Germany, and Japan.

Even McCloskey, always the most animated of the optimists, admitted that 'an historian can tell the recent story of the first industrial nation as a failure, and be right,' at least 'by comparison with a few countries and a few decades'.[32]

How, then, did these specialists in the application of quantitative techniques to the economic past sustain a positive interpretation of Britain's historical performance in the face of such an equivocal numerical record? One response was to diminish the weight of the very same calculations they had pressed into the debate to begin with. Estimates of 'productivity growth using national aggregates of output, labor, and capital' were 'a fragile foundation on which to erect theories of British success or failure', warned McCloskey before going on to argue two paragraphs later that 'the measure of productivity suggests no great failure of Britain on this score'. Floud cautioned his readers that 'before any reliance' could be placed on his figures showing that improvements in British efficiency had proceeded a good deal more slowly than the growth of German and American total factor productivity before 1914 'the fragility of the calculations' underlying them had to 'be stressed', 'errors and imprecision in measurement and in calculation' producing 'very large margins of error'.[33]

Another tack to which the optimists resorted in the face of apparently unfavourable statistical findings was to minimize the size of the disparities between the British figures and those of its competitors. Floud commented about Britain's annual increase in output per person employed in the 1873–1913 period, which at 0.9% was one-half the American rate of 1.8% and two-thirds the German rate of 1.4%, that it was 'slightly below the rate of growth experienced by Germany and the United States'. McCloskey described the 8% gap between Germany's national product per head in 1987 ($9,954) and Britain's ($9,178), when in 1900 Britain's per capita income had been 80% greater, as a 'minor' variation 'accounted for by minor national differences in attention to detail'.[34] In the extreme case, the ambiguities of the measurements could provoke the historian to condemn any attention whatsoever to those numbers suggestive of a suboptimal British performance. To talk of British per capita income falling below that of France, Germany or Japan, McCloskey thundered, was 'at best tasteless in a world of real tragedies – Argentina, for example, once rich, now subsidizing much and producing little; or India, trapped in poverty after much expert advice' and 'at worst . . . immoral self-involvement, nationalist guff accompanied by a military band playing "Land of Hope and Glory"'.[35]

More constructively, the specialist economic historians refurbished their sanguine accounts of Britain's past economic performance by concentrating their attention on those figures that cast this history in the most favourable light. 'The main British story since the late nineteenth century', McCloskey wrote, was 'the more than trebling of British income.' The salient point was that as of 1987 'Britain's income per head' was 'six times that of the Philippines and thirteen times that of India'.[36]

With this reformulation of the optimist's picture of Britain's economic achievements over the long run, the controversy about British 'decline' was substantially recast. When McCloskey argued that 'a 228 percent increase of production between 1900 and 1987 is more important than an 8 percent "failure" in the end to imitate German habits of attention to duty', it was clear that the disagreement between rival interpreters of British economic history was no longer about which measures best captured the nation's economic performance or even about what the best estimates of these numbers looked like.[37] The dispute between optimists and pessimists was now about how to construe the agreed indices. Were Britain's attainments best captured by the rate at which the economy's output, income or efficiency grew between one date and another or by the comparison of these rates with those achieved by other countries? If comparison offered the more insightful angle of judgement, was Britain better evaluated in terms of other industrial nations such as Japan, Germany and France, or should it be set alongside countries such as Mexico and India that had yet to reap the full advantages of western innovations in technique and organization?

The professional economic historians of the 1970s and 1980s made a heavy intellectual investment in refining the measures used to assess how the British economy had functioned over time. The return was a sustained improvement in our understanding of Britain's economic past. These better measures of British economic activity, though, were as amenable to a pessimistic interpretation as to an optimistic construction of Britain's history. Consequently, they came to serve as the common arsenal from which scholars of both persuasions selected their weapons and were no longer themselves the subject of intellectual combat. The heart of the controversy over British 'decline' thus ceased to be the empirical record of the nation's production and distribution since 1870 and became instead the contrasting understandings of economic life that the protagonists brought to the interpretation of this record. The debate, in other words, was now essentially about figures of speech and not figures, about metaphors more than measures.

Metaphors of controversy

Discussion of the rhetorical aspect of the scholarly argument over British 'decline' must begin with the work of Donald N. McCloskey. He was the first scholar to submit the narrative structure of the stories historians told about Britain's economic past to serious intellectual scrutiny, and he did so with his customary forcefulness and wit. A confirmed optimist in his reading of the British record, he concentrated his analysis on the language of the pessimists.

McCloskey observed that the metaphors that scholars critical of Britain's economic past preferred were drawn from the domains of medicine and sport, and here he was undoubtedly right. Where Landes and Aldcroft wrote of leads lost and laggings behind, Wiener identified a British 'economic retardation', Barnett a 'geriatric of nervous disposition' and Elbaum and Lazonick a 'century-long affliction'. Of course, Britain's ill-health was intimately connected with its position in the race. It was precisely because of its technological and organizational infirmities that it had fallen from first place in the economic marathon.[38]

Such figures of speech, McCloskey argued, were terribly inappropriate to Britain's economic history. They confused the self-conscious competition of organized collectivities with the unintended outcomes of individual strivings: Britain's

> forty-five million souls were not trying to score points on Germany or the United States. They were trying to earn a living and gain the pearly gates, on their own, making individual choices daily with no collective goal in mind.

Such ways of speaking also misrepresented economic life as a winner-take-all affair in which the also-rans went home with little or nothing: 'What is most wrong about the metaphor of leadership in a race of industrial might, though, is that it assumes silently that first place among the many nations is vastly to be preferred to second, or twelfth' when 'the prize for second in the race of economic growth was not poverty. The prize was great enrichment.' Most serious of all, the metaphors that the pessimists employed suggested that Britain had suffered real catastrophe during a period when 'nothing awful' happened to the country's economy. The figures of speech that Landes, Wiener and Elbaum and Lazonick took from sport and medicine perversely presented 'the happy outcome of Britain's [three-fold] growth [in national product per head over eighty-seven years] as a tragedy'.[39]

The accounts of Britain's past that found little to complain of in its economic record naturally depended as heavily on metaphor as the judgements that Britain's critics pronounced, and McCloskey admitted as much. 'The optimists like me', he wrote, 'want the story to be one of "normal" growth, in which "maturity" is reached earlier by Britain.'[40] How does such a narrative line compare with the structure of the pessimists' story? How well do its metaphors work?

The figures of speech that the specialist economic historians preferred, like those of their intellectual adversaries, owed a debt to the biological sciences. Hence McCloskey's appropriation of the term 'maturity'. The metaphors to which they gave voice also drew upon the vocabulary of athletics. McCloskey himself described modern economic history as a race in which 'the rich nations converge' while Pollard wrote of a 'catching-up process' whereby 'a formerly leading economy with no particular resource advantages ... was being caught up technically by others similarly endowed'.[41] And just as 'disease' presaged 'defeat' in the pessimists' version of the tale, according to the optimists' narrative 'maturity' marked a final tape beyond which all contestants were of equivalent stature. Thus Supple, writing about the comparatively slow growth of productivity in both Britain and the United States, could suggest that it 'reflected the fact' that the two economies 'had already achieved a measure of economic maturity, so that other countries grew more rapidly in part because they were catching-up with the pioneers'.[42]

The great virtue of this construction of Britain's economic history is that it does justice to the improvements in efficiency and to the gains in wealth that the country achieved from the late nineteenth century. At the same time, however, it misrepresents the nature of economic life. Worse still, it tells a story that isn't Britain's.

In the hands of McCloskey and like-minded analysts, 'maturity' is a state without end and the antithesis of 'decline'. In the biological realm, of course, things are very different. There 'maturity', the fullest development of an organism's faculties, is the prelude to the inevitable diminution of these powers, whether that decrepitude comes incrementally or at a single catastrophic stroke. Understood in this way, 'maturity' and 'decline' form part of a sequence, and the 'maturity' of the British economy after 1840 (as the volume of essays McCloskey edited in 1971 dated it) would in no way foreclose the possibility of its 'decline' after 1870, 1900 or 1945. 'Maturity' also serves in favourable accounts of Britain's economic past as a finishing line beyond which natural growth is severely constrained; thus the inevitability of inferior performances by the richest economies. The sustained expansion of the leading industrial nations after reaching 'maturity', however, and the periodic acceleration of their growth rates suggest that 'maturity' in this sense is a singularly inappropriate way of characterizing economic affairs.[43]

The metaphor of 'convergence' is the optimists' short-hand way of describing economic life on the far side of the finishing line of 'maturity'. Here all the successful industrial economies are on an equal plane as each has ascended to the same plateau. With one follower within the first wave of nations after another catching up with the pioneers, their economic histories come to an end, and overtakings and surpassings among them disappear. Such a story, though, is completely at odds with the tale that the quantitative measures that McCloskey, Floud and Supple assembled all told: that Britain, once well ahead of the United States, Germany, France and Japan with respect to income and efficiency, in time fell below them. It may well be, as those who champion 'convergence' insist, that the numerical disparities are small, but the very fact of these inequalities must drain the metaphor of much of the explanatory power with which the professional economic historians invested it.

Both parties to the quarrel over Britain's economic performance in the past assimilated the facts of the country's economic history to a distinctive narrative line, and in each case the metaphors that governed the story came from the domains of medicine and sport. For the pessimists, images of illness and finishes out of the money did the heavy analytical duty. Among the optimists, the language of health and dead-heats prevailed. Neither reading serves the subject quite well enough. If the rhetoric of 'disease' and 'defeat' mistakenly conjures up the ruin of Rochdale or the sack of Ebbw Vale, terms like 'convergence' and 'catching-up' erroneously exclude the manifest fact that Britain's wealth is not the equal of other nations. Perhaps it is no wonder that the war of words over Britain's 'decline' still continues after three full decades of the most dedicated, innovative and skilful scholarship.

Conclusion

The academic debate over British 'decline' has proceeded with great vigour for three decades now in part because those who criticized the nation's economic performance after 1870 and those who defended it *both* made significant contributions to the understanding of Britain's economic history. The specialist economic historians who viewed the record in a decidedly positive light brought a rigour to the identification of the proper measures of performance and an insistence on aggregate indices of efficiency and income that took the conversation well above the selective, *ad hoc* and sometimes irrelevant yardsticks against which the original pessimists held Britain. Their adversaries in the second generation of nay-sayers rightly maintained that the question of British performance was necessarily about the long term and that no scholarship confined to the 1870–1914 period, no matter how brilliant, could answer it adequately.

That the debate has survived so many determined efforts to settle it also reflects the ambiguities inherent in the statistical record. In practice both schools of thought came to agree that the efficiency with which Britain produced and distributed in agriculture, manufacturing, mining and services together and the overall wealth that these activities generated constituted the best gauges of Britain's accomplishments as an economic unit. The best estimates of these quantities, however, furnished support to both optimistic *and* pessimistic readings of the nation's performance. Since these measures themselves presented no clear-cut resolution of the issues fundamental to the argument, the narrative constructions to which pessimists and optimists alike necessarily resorted loomed very large in the controversy over Britain's 'failure'.

The metaphors at issue, like the measures of descent, indicate that the parties to this dispute unknowingly occupied a good deal of common ground. Just as each camp came to put its faith in overall indices of productivity and wealth, both sides consistently treated economic life as a race and the outcome as a function of the contestants' physical state. In neither case, though, did the preferred figures of speech do full justice to the subject – and the inadequacies of the respective rhetorics helped nourish the opposing arguments. If the economic life of nations is not a contest in which a single winner reaps all the prize money and all the remaining competitors are consigned to misery, neither is it an event with a well-defined finish, the crossing of which, in and of itself, confers sufficient satisfactions thereafter.

The frailties, on the one side, of 'disease' and 'failure', and, on the other, of 'maturity' and 'convergence' as apt story-lines for the narrative of Britain's economic history are instructive precisely because they make clear how much the debate about 'decline' has taught us after all. First, there can be no doubt whatsoever that the British economy has grown quite substantially since the last quarter of the nineteenth century, that living standards in the 1990s are far beyond what the ordinary citizen of 1870, 1900 or even 1930 would have thought possible, and that the average Briton today enjoys a degree of material security and comfort comparable to that of the average American, German, Frenchman and Japanese. Second, it is no less true that over the long term British efficiency and British income have advanced relatively slowly – that is, in comparison with what the other industrial economies have achieved – and that British living standards, though certainly affluent, and, by comparison with those of Mexico or the Philippines, more than affluent, are not quite what they have become elsewhere. The optimists and the pessimists, it must be said, have both got a good deal right.

There is, moreover, considerable scope for scholars of each persuasion to teach us still more about Britain's economic past. The professional economic historians might well put their theoretical understandings and quantitative techniques to the task of explaining the industry-level failures that they have always acknowledged to have been a part of the historical record.[44] The pessimists on the other hand, who since the pioneering work of Aldcroft and Landes have always seen economic performance as inseparable from the beliefs, values and ideals by which the British have ordered their lives, might do well to investigate the cultural sources of the nation's considerable economic growth since 1870.[45] With so much intellectual investment on which to capitalize, it would be a shame indeed if arguments about Britain did not continue to enrich the economic history of nations.

Notes

1 Two disclaimers are imperative at the outset. The first is that I am not a disinterested observer of the intellectual events discussed here. Readers who are interested in my 'pessimistic' construction of British economic history should consult *The Decline of Industrial Britain 1870–1980* (London: Routledge, 1992) or *Managing Industrial Decline: Entrepreneurship in the British Coal Industry Between the Wars* (Columbus: Ohio State University Press, 1992). The second is that the references to this essay do not furnish more than a minimal introduction to the voluminous literature devoted to Britain's economic performance. A more extensive, but by no means complete, listing can be found in the bibliography of my *The Decline of Industrial Britain*.
2 Organization for Economic Co-operation and Development, *National Accounts*, vol. 1 *1960–1991* (Paris: OECD, 1992), reported in Robert Skidelsky, 'Not So Gentrified', *Times Literary Supplement*, 7 May 1993, p. 14.
3 Derek H. Aldcroft, 'The Entrepreneur and the British Economy, 1870–1914', *Economic History Review*, 2nd series, XVII (August 1964), pp. 113 and 114 [and in Derek H. Aldcroft and Harry W. Richardson, *The British Economy 1870–1939* (London: Macmillan, 1969), pp. 141–2 and 143].
4 David S. Landes, 'Technological Change and Development in Western Europe, 1750–1914', in *The Cambridge Economic History of Europe*, vol. VI *The Industrial Revolution and After: Incomes, Population, and Technological Change (I)*, ed. H.J. Habakkuk and M. Postan (Cambridge: Cambridge University Press, 1965), pp. 558 and 564. This essay later appeared as chapters 2–5 and 8 of David S. Landes, *The Unbound Prometheus: Technological Change and Industrial Development in Western Europe from 1750 to the Present* (Cambridge: Cambridge University Press, 1969), and the passages cited here can be found on pp. 330–1 and 337. In point of chronological fact, Landes put forward the case for entrepreneurial 'failure' and British 'decline' before Aldcroft. He first advanced the arguments cited here in a paper on 'Entrepreneurship in Advanced Industrial Countries: The Anglo-German Rivalry' before a conference on entrepreneurship and economic growth in November 1954, and his chapter for the Cambridge volume was completed in 1961–2. That Aldcroft was familiar with them when he produced his own version of the indictment is certain. See Aldcroft, 'The Entrepreneur,' p. 116, note #7 [Aldcroft and Richardson, *British Economy*, p. 142, note #7).
5 Charles Wilson, 'Economy and Society in Late Victorian Britain', *Economic History Review*, 2nd series, XVIII (August 1965), pp. 195, 189 (quoting G.M. Young, *Portrait of an Age*), and 198.
6 Lars G. Sandberg, 'American Rings and English Mules: The Role of Economic Rationality', *Quarterly Journal of Economics* LXXXIII (February 1969), pp. 26 and 42–3.
7 Wilson, 'Economy', p. 194 (emphasis in the original).
8 Donald N. McCloskey, 'Did Victorian Britain Fail?' *Economic History Review*, 2nd series, XXIII (December 1970), p. 459 [and in Donald N. McCloskey, *Enterprise and Trade in Victorian Britain: Essays in Historical Economics* (Boston: George Allen and Unwin, 1981), p. 106).

9 R.C. Floud, 'Britain, 1860–1914: A Survey', in *The Economic History of Britain Since 1700*, vol. II *1860 to the 1970s*, ed. Roderick Floud and Donald McCloskey (New York: Cambridge University Press, 1981), p. 25.
10 Sidney Pollard, *Britain's Prime and Britain's Decline: The British Economy 1870–1914* (New York: Edward Arnold, 1989), pp. 271 and 265.
11 W.D. Rubinstein, *Capitalism, Culture, and Decline in Britain 1750–1990* (New York: Routledge, 1993), p. 24.
12 Martin J. Wiener, *English Culture and the Decline of the Industrial Spirit 1850–1980* (New York: Cambridge University Press, 1981), p. 158.
13 Correlli Barnett, *The Audit of War: The Illusion and Reality of Britain as a Great Nation* (London: Macmillan, 1986), pp. 8 and ix.
14 Bernard Elbaum and William Lazonick, 'An Institutional Perspective on British Decline', in *The Decline of the British Economy*, ed. Bernard Elbaum and William Lazonick (Oxford: Clarendon Press, 1986), p. 1.
15 Donald N. McCloskey, 'Editor's Introduction', in *Essays on a Mature Economy: Britain after 1840*, ed. Donald N. McCloskey (Princeton, NJ: Princeton University Press, 1971), pp. 1 and 7.
16 The principal contributions to the debate about the Victorian 'climacteric' included E.H. Phelps Brown and S.J. Handfield-Jones, 'The Climacteric of the 1890s: A Study in the Expanding Economy', *Oxford Economic Papers* IV (1952), 266–307; D.J. Coppock, 'The Climacteric of the 1890s: A Critical Note', *The Manchester School of Economic and Social Studies* XXIV (January 1956), 1–31; and A.E. Musson, 'British Industrial Growth 1873–1896: A Balanced View', *Economic History Review*, 2nd series, XVII (December 1964), 397–403. For the ways in which this literature defined the intellectual context in which Aldcroft, Landes and Wilson worked see Aldcroft, 'The Entrepreneur', pp. 113–14 (Aldcroft and Richardson, *British Economy*, pp. 141–2), Landes, 'Technological Change', p. 463 (*Unbound Prometheus*, pp. 235–6) and Wilson, 'Economy', p. 184.
17 Thus the title of his 1965 article in the *Economic History Review*.
18 Sandberg, 'American Rings', p. 27.
19 McCloskey, ed. *Essays*.
20 Seven years earlier Pollard had published *The Wasting of the British Economy* (London: Croom Helm, 1982), a highly critical account of British economic performance, and, especially, government economic policy after the Second World War. He was adamant in *Britain's Prime*, however, that 'the faults of the decline after 1945' could not 'be shuffled off to earlier generations' (p. 271).
21 Aldcroft and Landes also compiled myriad indices of 'backwardness', such as how much coal was cut by machine, the proportion of coke produced in by-product recovery ovens, and the percentage of iron intended for steel-making that was sent directly to the converters in liquid form. Like these measures of performance, these figures related to specific branches of manufacturing and mining and were compared with the relevant figures for other countries. Since the effects of Britain's outdated practices ought to have been captured by the indices of 'decline', it is on the latter that I concentrate here.
22 Aldcroft, 'The Entrepreneur', p. 116 (Aldcroft and Richardson, *British Economy*, p. 145) and Landes, 'Technological Change', p. 496 (*Unbound Prometheus*, p. 269).
23 Aldcroft, 'The Entrepreneur', p. 118 (Aldcroft and Richardson, *British Economy*, p. 147) and Landes, 'Technological Change', p. 501 (*Unbound Prometheus*, p. 273).
24 Landes, 'Technological Change', pp. 554–5 (*Unbound Prometheus*, pp. 328–9) and Aldcroft, 'The Entrepreneur', p. 124 (Aldcroft and Richardson, *British Economy*, p. 154).

25 Wilson, 'Economy', pp. 185 (emphasis in the original) and 190.
26 McCloskey, 'Did Victorian Britain', pp. 457–8, tables 2 and 3 (*Enterprise and Trade*, pp. 104–5, tables 5.2 and 5.3).
27 With respect to the measures of performance, Rubinstein occupies a rather anomalous position in the optimists' camp. The first chapter of his *Capitalism, Culture, and Decline* provides as fine a collation of comparative production indices for the major industries (pp. 8–9, 13 and 15, tables 1.1–1.3) as a pessimist of the Aldcroft or Landes stamp could hope to find. For Rubinstein, though, they depict Britain's rational adaptation to the distribution of its economic advantages and are not in any way indicative of a 'decline'. To support his claim that Britain's comparative advantage lay in finance and commerce he adduces just the kind of *ad hoc* evidence that Aldcroft and Landes had employed: the size of the deposits of the largest British, American and Japanese commercial banks (p. 38) and the volume of passenger traffic through the airports of Tokyo, London, Frankfurt, Chicago and Paris (p. 39). Similarly, to support his claim that Britain performed as well economically as any other industrial nation he compares home ownership in the United States and Britain and the distribution of colour televisions in Britain and France (pp. 41–3).
28 Floud, 'Britain', pp. 5–9, including tables 1.1–1.3; Floud, 'Britain, 1860–1914: A Survey', in *The Economic History of Britain Since 1700*, ed. Roderick Floud and Donald McCloskey, 2nd edition, vol. II *1860–1939* (New York: Cambridge University Press, 1994), pp. 14–16, including tables 1.4 and 1.5; Barry Supple, 'British Economic Decline Since 1945', in *The Economic History of Britain Since 1700*, ed. Floud and McCloskey, 2nd edition, vol. III *1939–1992*, pp. 320–6, including tables 11.1, 11.3, 11.4 and 11.6; and Donald N. McCloskey, *If You're So Smart: The Narrative of Economic Expertise* (Chicago: University of Chicago Press, 1990), pp. 40–9, including table 1.
29 The new economic historians also brought their more sophisticated quantitative methods to bear on the performances of particular trades. In addition to Sandberg's work on cotton textiles, McCloskey defended the records of coal and steel and Floud that of machine tools. Comparable work by Peter H. Lindert and Keith Trace on chemicals and Robert C. Allen on iron and steel arrived at less reassuring conclusions, and intense debates about these and other individual industries have continued to constitute an important aspect of the controversy over Britain's 'decline'. Unfortunately, a proper discussion of these exchanges cannot be included here. For the papers by McCloskey, Floud and Lindert and Trace noted above see McCloskey, ed., *Essays* and see Allen's 'International Competition in Iron and Steel, 1850–1913', *Journal of Economic History* XXXIX (December 1979), 911–37.
30 McCloskey, 'Did Victorian Britain', pp. 457–8, tables 2 and 3 (*Enterprise and Trade*, pp. 104–5, tables 5.2 and 5.3); Floud, 'Britain', 1st edition (1981), p. 22, table 1.9; Supple, 'Decline', p. 321, tables 11.2 and 11.3; and McCloskey, *If You're So Smart*, p. 47, table 1.
31 Barnett, *Audit*, pp. 7–8; and Elbaum and Lazonick, 'An Institutional Perspective', pp. 9–10.
32 Floud, 'Britain', 2nd edition (1994), p. 14; Supple, 'Decline', p. 322; and McCloskey, *If You're So Smart*, p. 44.
33 McCloskey, 'Did Victorian Britain', p. 459 (*Enterprise and Trade*, pp. 105–6) and Floud, 'Britain', 1st edition (1981), p. 23.
34 Floud, 'Britain', 1st edition (1981), p. 9 and McCloskey, *If You're So Smart*, p. 46.
35 McCloskey, *If You're So Smart*, p. 48.
36 *Ibid.*, pp. 46 and 48.
37 *Ibid.*, p. 46.

38 Characteristic expressions of the pessimists' metaphors, including those cited here, can be found in Aldcroft, 'The Entrepreneur', pp. 115–18 and 121 (Aldcroft and Richardson, *British Economy*, pp. 144–7 and 151); Landes, 'Technological Change', pp. 496, 516–17, 553, 558 and 581 (*Unbound Prometheus*, pp. 269, 289, 326, 331–2 and 355); Wiener, *English Culture*, pp. 10 and 167 ('Appendix: British Retardation – The Limits of Economic Explanation'); Barnett, *Audit*, p. 55; and Elbaum and Lazonick, 'An Institutional Perspective', p. 1. McCloskey's dissection of these figures of speech appears in his *If You're So Smart*, pp. 40–9.

39 The quotations reproduced in this paragraph are from McCloskey, *If You're So Smart*, p. 44 ('forty-five million'), p. 43 ('what is most wrong'), p. 44 ('the prize for second'), p. 46 ('nothing awful') and p. 48 ('happy outcome').

40 *Ibid.*, p. 45.

41 *Ibid.*, p. 46; and Sidney Pollard, 'Entrepreneurship, 1870–1914', in *The Economic History of Britain Since 1700*, ed. Floud and McCloskey, 2nd edition, vol. II 1860–1939, p. 66 and Pollard, *Britain's Prime*, p. 270.

42 Supple, 'Decline', p. 324.

43 Roderick Floud, a member in excellent standing of the optimistic school of thought, made the very same point: 'any such theory of "catching-up" implies a discontinuity in technological progress, such that at some moment a limit was reached at which Britain stopped while others caught up; but there is very little direct evidence for such a theory.' See Floud, 'Britain', 1st edition (1981), p. 24.

44 See, for example, McCloskey, 'Editor's Introduction', pp. 6–7 on the chemicals industry; Pollard, 'Entrepreneurship,' pp. 81–2 on machine tools, agricultural machinery and electrical engineering, p. 85 on worsted and pp. 86–7 on coal-tar dyes and alkali production; and Supple, 'Decline', pp. 329 and 336 on manufacturing in general.

45 The classic statement of the 'cultural' explanation of 'decline', of course, is Wiener, *English Culture*.

2

1066 AND A WAVE OF GADGETS

The achievements of British growth

Deirdre N. McCloskey

The American question and the unpredictability of creative achievement

In his strange little dialogue *Ion*, Plato presents a dilemma: either the ability to sing Homer and comment elegantly is a routine art, a *techne*, which can then be written down and taught to others; or else it is not, in which case its origin is mysterious. He makes a similar claim here and elsewhere about all human skills, from music to entrepreneurship. Either the skills can be made routine or they cannot (e.g. *Gorgias* 449d). Almost anyone can be taught to sing, if 'singing' is taken as following notes on a page. Up, down, down, up, up. But between the routinely skilful singer struggling in the church choir and Luciano Pavarotti is a creative gap.

The man Ion is a masterful rhapsode, a singer and expositor of the Homeric epics. But he cannot explain his technique, and is bored by other poets. Socrates concludes that 'not by *techne* do the poets and their rhapsodes sing, but by power divine, since if it were by *techne* that they knew how to treat one subject finely, they would know how to deal with all the others too' (534c). That is, if Ion's mastery came from a routine skill he could apply it indifferently to other subjects, as one can type on all keyboards if on one. Driving a car is routine, and so can be applied mechanically to all cars. But the skill of Sterling Moss racing at Monte Carlo is creative, not routine. It cannot be routinely transmitted from one person to another.

The rhapsode singing Homer is not exercising an 'art' (this is not the European word after the Romantics, Art with a capital A, but plain Greek *techne*, the craft of performing routine readings of Homer or routine medical cures with known, write-downable rules). On the contrary, like the poet the rhapsode is possessed by God, transmitting divine madness like one ring in a chain of rings dangling from a magnet – that is, he is if he is not merely a trickster, a flatterer of men, an entertainer, a sophist. Knowledge in Plato's account is a craft that can be written down and taught to others, a justified true belief like the technique for making shoes or for making truth tables or for making predictions from large-scale econometric models.

Plato was not pleased by creativity. The trouble with creativity is that it does not follow rules that a philosopher can come to know. If a philosopher or an economist or an engineer cannot know the rules then he cannot control the achievements. Plato's utopia was rule governed.

The unpredictability of achievement has been irritating also to many intellectuals after Plato. Francis Bacon, who in aid of certitude put Nature and the enemies of the King upon the rack, sought 'not pretty and probable conjectures, but certain and demonstrable knowledge' (*New Organon*, Preface, 329). He sought the justified belief that has no need of tacit knowledge or creativity. Like Plato he detested the idols of the marketplace, the unpredictable talk in which 'words plainly force and overrule the understanding' (xliii, 337). 'You attempt to refute me,' says Socrates in the *Gorgias*, 'in a rhetorical fashion, as they understand refuting in the law courts. ... But this sort of refutation is quite useless for getting at the truth' (471e), since it is merely pretty and probable conjecture exercised in the agora among men (cf. *Gorgias* 471e, 473e–474a; *Phaedrus*, 260a, 261c–d, 262c, 267a–b, 272d). Bacon envisioned the new sciences as avoiding the frailty of human argument, producing certitude mechanically: 'the mind itself (must) from the very outset not (be) left to take its own course, but guided at every step, and the business done as if by machinery' (Preface, 327). It has ever been the programme of philosophy, whether natural or metaphysical, political or moral, to have the business done as if by machinery. Knowledge is said by Plato and his heirs to be mechanical, coming from the justifications of experimental method or clear and distinct ideas.

But the programme of reducing creativity to a *techne* faces a decisive difficulty, of an economic character. The difficulty is that *profitable* creativity, the creativity that results in substantial, non-routine achievements, cannot possibly be mechanical. It cannot possibly be because if it were then everyone would buy the machine and use it. The new technique would become then routine and unprofitable, contrary to the premise.

Understand that 'profitability' is a metaphor. The gains to creativity need not be literally financial. The problem with reducing creativity to *techne* will be found in routines for science and for art as much as in routines for becoming a millionaire. But the financial case provides a check on reasoning about creativity and achievement. If the creativity of a William Lever or a Henry Ford cannot be mechanized, to produce such achievements whenever desired, it must *a fortiori* be true also of Picasso and Dante.

The main argument against a routinized theory of creativity can be summarized in what may be called The American Question: 'If you're so smart why ain't you rich?' The question cuts deeper than most philosophers care to admit. The test of riches is a fair one if the theory claims to deliver the riches, in gold or in glory. The Question embarrasses anyone claiming profitable expertise who cannot show a profit, the historian second-guessing generals or the critic propounding a formula for art. He who is so smart claims a Faustian knowledge,

> Whose deepness doth entice such forward wits
> to practice more than heavenly power permits.

The contradiction in predicting creativity is best seen in divination. Is prediction a *techne*? If the future were routinely predictable by a seer, who for a modest fee would reveal his prediction to you and me, we could prepare, profitably. The predictions would be valuable, at least until the rest of the crowd learned it. Socrates attacked the other sophists for charging for their advice, to which the other sophists retorted that at least their advice was worth something (Isocrates, Soph., cited in Jaeger 1944, III, p. 57). It was said that the philosopher Thales of Miletus made a fortune buying up the olive crop in his district (Cicero, *Div.*, I, xlix, 111), 'in order to show that even a philosopher if he sees fit is able to make money'.

And yet most of these philosophers and seers, like modern professors of economics, were not rich. An economist who claims to know what is going to happen to the price of corn is claiming to know how to make money. Many models printed for free in the journals of agricultural economics imply foreknowledge of the price of corn. But then one might ask the American Question. With a little borrowing on the equity of his home or his reputation for sobriety the agricultural economist can make enormous sums. If an agricultural economist could predict the price of corn better than the futures market he would be rich. Yet he does not put his money where his mouth is. He is not rich. It follows that he is not so smart. The same holds for all diviners, macroeconomists, astrologers, urban economists and technical elves. Auden sings, 'No, Virgil, no: Not even the first of Romans can learn / His Roman history in the future tense, / Not even to serve your political turn; / Hindsight as foresight makes no sense.'

The postmodern economist is modest about profitworthy detail, the detail from which she could buy low and sell high. She must be modest especially about the proud claim of economics in the 1960s, the claim to fine-tune the economy by making detailed adjustments to money and taxes in order to offset a depression just around the corner. As economists realize now after much tragedy sprung from hubris, if an economist could see around the corner she would be rich. Fine-tuning violates the ancient and justified jibe at predictors: why ain't you rich? The Roman poet Ennius was only one among many to sneer at predictors, 'who for themselves the path do not know, yet for others show the way' (Cicero, *Div.*, I, lviii, 132). A fine-tuner would see dozens of paths for personal enrichment. The economists go on relating impossibly detailed scenarios into the microphones of television reporters, but in their hearts they know they are wrong.

The American Question puts fundamental limits on what we can say about ourselves. It puts a limit on mechanical models of human creativity. In 1943 Picasso noticed that a bicycle seat put together with handle bars made a *Bull's Head* (Galerie Louise Leiris, Paris). If we were so smart we would have spotted the bull's head long before, and Picasso's achievement would have been a mere reproduction. And, incidentally, Picasso would not have been rich.

The American Question does not make mechanical models useless for interesting history or routine prediction: the sun coming up tomorrow or the size of the sixth form predicted from the numbers in the fifth. It merely makes them useless for gaining an edge about the future. 'Prescience' is an oxymoron, like cheap fortunes: pre-science, knowing before one knows. Prescience is required for central planning of scientific as much as economic creativity. Karl Popper and Alasdair MacIntyre among others have pointed out that knowing the future of science requires knowing the science of the future. It is not to be done. MacIntyre notes that the unpredictability of mathematical innovation is a rigorous case, resting on theorems concerning the incompleteness of arithmetic and the incalculability of certain expressions, proven by Godel, Church and Turing in the 1930s. And 'if the future of mathematics is unpredictable, so is a great deal else' (1981, p. 90). If someone claims to know the method that yields good science, why isn't he scientifically rich?

Socrates uses the example of prescience in the Ion. Allan Bloom once remarked of the passage:

> If divining is to be considered an art, it is strange in that it must profess to know the intentions of the gods; as an art, it would, in a sense, seem to presuppose that the free, elusive gods are shackled down by the bonds of intelligible necessity. Divining partakes of the rational dignity of the arts while supposing a world ruled by divine beings who are beyond the grasp of the arts. (1970, p. 57)

As the sceptic about prediction would say, the claim of divining to be an art, Greek *techne*, mere bookable craft, is absurd. It claims to fill with routine the creative gap.

An economist examining the business world is like a critic examining the art world. Economists and other human scientists can reflect intelligently on present conditions and can tell useful stories about the past. These produce wisdom, which permits broad, conditional 'predictions'. Some are obvious; some require an economist. But none is a machine for achieving fame or riches. None is a creative achievement, unless it, too, is lit by the unpredictable.

A WAVE OF GADGETS

The argument concerns the margin, where supernormal profits and reputations for genius are being made. It says that the routine observer's knowledge is not the same as the creative doer's, the critic is no improvement as artist over the artist, the model of the future is no substitute for the entrepreneur's god-possessed hunch. The critics become ridiculous only when they confuse speaking well about the past with doing well in the future. Critics of art and literature stopped being ridiculous this way a long time ago. It would be a fine thing if critics of society would join them in their modest and sober sophistication.

And so a theory of creativity and achievement has a dilemma at its core: either creativity is routine (in which case it is not creativity, but ordinary *techne*); or else it is not routine (in which case there had better not be a theory about it). Theory X would assume that free, elusive creativity is shackled down by the bonds of intelligible necessity. The theory of creativity and achievement, in other words, is bound up with the theory of liberty. The particular way it is bound up, I would claim, is that creativity and achievement can only take place in free parts of a society. As David Hume said, 'It is impossible for the arts and sciences to arise, at first, among any people, unless that people enjoy the blessings of a free government' (1741, p. 82). He emphasized the 'at first': copying the routine is something any tyranny can do, but the creative moment, especially, he said, in commerce, depends on freedom. To the extent that creativity is reduced to *techne* the possibility of genuine achievement is eliminated, since *techne* is routine. And in the free parts the achievement is necessarily unpredictable.

The assertion runs counter to the notions of Plato and Bacon and other central planners of the intellect, providing us with machines for achievement. In modern times it runs counter to Weber's notion that creativity will be bureaucratized. Schumpeter, for example, argued in 1942 that innovation in advanced capitalism would take place henceforth in great industrial laboratories, by routinized, authoritarian, technical creativity. The Manhattan Project (eventually leading to the making of the first A bomb) was supposed on all sides to be an example: give us the bureaucrats and we will finish the job. Again the modern notion is mistaken. Weber's prediction that modern business will come to be run like an army shows a clerkly lack of experience in both businesses and armies. It was in the free and unrationalized parts of the Manhattan Project that its engineering creativity worked. The rationalized parts provided necessary but routine sustenance. When the bureaucrats constrained the freedom of the scientists they slowed the project – as in the requirement that each scientist lock up his results each night in a personal safe (they would regularly forget their combinations, and call on Richard Feynman to crack the safes each morning). Likewise, on the British side, the Enigma project, in which Alan Turing and company outwitted the German codemakers, depended on freedom, or so Turing passionately believed.

The bureaucracies, to be sure, provide the system of incentives within which the freely creative operate. The bureaucrat is therefore in the position of a banker facing entrepreneurs. He can refuse the loan or agree to it. He is a professional audience for the persuasive powers of the entrepreneurs. Think of a university administrator listening to the proposals to change the curriculum. The role of professional audience is not to be disdained. The society will not achieve much in which the entrepreneurs are not given loans when their creations offer promise, or given applause or papal blessings, to name other coin. Incentives can be offered. But the creativity itself cannot be produced by formula, or else it would already have been. (It can be killed, of course, by any number of formulas, such as that applied to Russia 1917–1991.)

A Whiggish view of Britain's first age of economic creativity, to 1860

The most important case of modern creativity and achievement is the Industrial Revolution. Yet British creativity in business is of surprisingly early date. Give me a lever and a place to stand on, said boasting Archimedes, and I shall move the world. What is odd about his world is that for all its creativity in some directions it did not apply the lever, or anything much else, to practical use. Practical use was a matter for slaves. Macaulay, historian of freedom and eloquent among the early defenders of capitalism, noted that Archimedes 'was half ashamed of those inventions which were the wonder of hostile nations, and always spoke of them slightingly as mere amusements, trifles in which a mathematician might be suffered to relax his mind after intense application to the higher parts of his science' (Macaulay 1830, p. 450).

Applied technology, as Joel Mokyr has argued in a recent book, *The Lever of Riches*, was a Northern European achievement. The Industrial Revolution, in Mokyr's view, is not properly thought of as a late and sudden shift to capitalism. It was the culmination of a millennium of technological creativity. In the 1930s a British schoolboy, when asked on an examination to explain the Industrial Revolution, penned an immortal line: 'About 1760 a wave of gadgets swept over England.' Mokyr amends the child's wisdom: About 900–1995 AD a wave of gadgets swept over Europe (Mokyr 1990). The 'Dark Ages' contributed more to our physical well-being than did the spirit-gladdening ages of Pericles or Augustus. From classical times we got toy steam engines and erroneous principles of motion. From the ninth and tenth centuries alone the cold plains of the North supplied the horse collar, the stirrup and the mouldboard plough. An explosion of ingenuity down to 1500 yielded in addition the blast furnace, cake of soap, cam, canal lock, carrack ship, cast iron pot, chimney, coal-fuelled fire, cog boat, compass, crank, crossstaff, eyeglass, flywheel, glass window, grindstone, hops in beer, marine chart, nailed horseshoe, overshoot waterwheel, printing press, ribbed ship, shingle, ski, spinning wheel, suction pump, spring watch, treadle loom, water-driven bellows, weight-driven clock, wee drop of whiskey, wheelbarrow, whippletree (see 'The Wonderful One-Hoss Shay'), and the windmill. Down to 1750 the pace slackened, without stopping. Then came 'The Years of Miracles', as Mokyr calls them, from 1750 to 1900. The Industrial Revolution has raised the bread, ships and innocent amusement available to the ordinary person by a factor of twelve. I repeat: conservatively, a factor of twelve, now promising to give the entire world the living standard of Camberley. It is the characteristic modern achievement.

How much was it a product of routine and how much of creativity? Creativity leads to profit in some coin, if only pure delight. The economist Israel Kirzner has argued recently that profit is a reward for what he calls 'alertness'. Sheer — or as we say 'dumb' — luck is one extreme. Hard work is the other. Alertness falls in between, being neither luck nor routine work. Pure profit, says Kirzner, earned by pure entrepreneurs (and pure artists), is justified by alertness.

Mokyr's story of European ingenuity can be told in Kirzner's metaphors, to the advantage of both. As both emphasize, the systematic search for inventions can be expected in the end to earn only as much as its cost. The routine inventor is an honest workman, but is worthy therefore only of his hire. The cost of routine improvements in steam engines eats up the profits. It had better, or else the improvements are not routine. Routine inventions, as Mokyr says, are not free lunches. 'The cold and calculating minds of Research-and-Development engineers in white lab coats worn over three-piece suits' made some of the inventions. But only some, and these not the most important, nor earning high profits.

The classical economist down to the present says there is no free lunch. You do not get something for nothing. Make more guns and you must make less butter. Scarcity reigns. But the Industrial Revolution and its long preparation do not appear to have been a matter of scarcity and tradeoffs. Something happened beyond the grim sacrifice of one generation for the comforts of the next. There was, says Mokyr, 'an increase in output that is not commensurate with the increase in effort and cost necessary to bring it about'. The fact has been known in economics since the 1950s, when Moses Abramowitz and Robert Solow first drew attention to the so-called 'Residual'. The Residual is the enrichment left over after routine investment has explained as much as it can. It is embarrassingly large and all attempts to explain it by hard work of a classical kind have failed.

If hard work was not the cause, is the explanation to be found at the other extreme of Kirzner's spectrum, sheer, dumb luck? Mokyr turns over the notion that the Industrial Revolution happened by luck, and rejects it. After all, it happened in more than one place ripe for it (in Belgium and New England as in Britain, for instance) and spread selectively (to Northern but not Southern Italy; to Japan and latterly Korea but not China). It is patterned, as luck is not.

Well, then, is it Kirzner's metaphor of 'alertness' that explains Mokyr's 'lever of riches'? Yes. Mokyr makes a distinction between microinventions (such as the telephone and the light bulb, both searched for methodically), which responded to the routine forces of research and development, and macroinventions (such as the printing press and the gravity-driven clock), which did not. He stresses throughout that both play a part in the story. Yet he is more intrigued by the macroinventions, which seem less methodical and, one might say, less economic, more creative. Gutenberg just did it, says Mokyr, and created a galaxy (block printing even for books was commonplace in the late fifteenth century, and so Mokyr may perhaps have chosen a poor example; but the distinction remains). Mokyr's story of macroinventions can be aligned with economic metaphors of 'alertness', and connected thereby to unpredictable profit and thence to creativity.

But there is something missing in the metaphor and the story, needed to complete the theory. From an economic point of view, alertness by itself is highly academic, in both the good and the bad sense. It is both intellectual and ineffectual, the occupation of the spectator, as Addison put it, who is 'very well versed in the theory of a husband or a father, and can discern the errors of the economy, business, and diversion of others better than those engaged in them'.

If his observation is to be effectual the spectator has to persuade a banker. Even if he is himself the banker he has to persuade himself, in the councils of his own mind. What is missing, then, from the theory of technological change is power. Between the conception and the creation, between the invention and the innovation, falls the shadow. Power runs between the two. An idea without a bankroll is merely an idea. In order for an invention to become an innovation the inventor must persuade someone with a bank roll. We are back to professional audiences listening to the orations of the entrepreneurs.

This is as true of literary or scientific opportunity as it is of technological invention. Until he won the Goncourt Prize in 1919, Proust was not much considered. The Prize persuaded the French public to take him seriously. Until Saul Bellow put his imprimatur on the books, William Kennedy (author of *Ironweed* and other Albany novels) worked as a reporter on a bad newspaper. Intellectual bankers need to be persuaded as much as financial ones.

Mokyr understands this, and calls it 'openness to new information'. The word is better 'persuasion' than sheer 'information'. He quotes a contrast between the delightful stage of alertness and the less delightful stage of persuasion, 'a struggle against stupidity and envy, apathy and evil, secret opposition and open conflict of interests, the horrible period of struggle with man, a martyrdom even if success ensues'. Any academic or businessperson can supply instances. What matters, to put Mokyr's theme in rhetorical form, are the conditions of persuasion.

Europe's fragmented polity made for pluralistic audiences, by contrast with intelligent but stagnant China. 'Nothing is more favourable to the rise of politeness and learning', wrote Hume, 'than a number of neighbouring and independent states, connected by commerce and policy' (1741, p. 85). An inventor persecuted by the Inquisition in Naples could move to Holland. 'It seems that as a general rule', writes Mokyr, 'the weaker the government, the better it is for innovation.' As Nathan Rosenberg and L.E. Birdzell (1986) have put the point, 'The first requisite for the release of these potentialities was the expansion of the sphere within which trade could be conducted with some degree of freedom from the arbitrary exercise of external power.' The requisite achieved by 1700 was freedom, and in particular the freedom to persuade competing audiences.

Early in his book Mokyr asserts oddly that there is no connection between capitalism and technology: 'Technological progress predated capitalism and credit by many centuries, and may well outlive capitalism by at least as long.' One doubts it. Capitalism was not, contrary to the Marxist story, a modern invention. As the medievalist David Herlihy put it in 1971, 'research has all but wiped from the ledgers the supposed gulf, once thought fundamental, between a medieval manorial economy and the capitalism of the modern period' (p. 155). Any idea requires capitalism and credit in order to become an innovation, regardless of whether the surrounding society is fully capitalistic. The Yorkshireman who invested in a windmill c. 1185 was putting his money where his mouth was, or else putting someone else's money there. In either case he had to persuade.

What makes alertness work, then, and gets it power, is persuasion. At the root of technological achievement is a rhetorical environment that makes it possible for creative people to test their unpredictable notions. The Industrial Revolution, in other words, had a rhetorical origin. The climate of persuasion was favourable for creativity. It is no accident, I am claiming, that the nations where speech was free to a fault were the first in economic achievement: Holland, Scotland, England, Belgium and the United States.

The story is Adam Smith's Bargain: leave me alone and I'll make you rich. The claim is that freedom leads to achievement. The claim, I repeat, is an old and battered one, sneered at by clerks in all ages, who know that it is not freedom but a particular dogma which leads to achievement in God's eyes. Without being comparably dogmatic I suggest mildly that Whiggism deserves a fresh hearing, the more so in a post-Marxian age.

The Whig view of British creative 'failure', 1860 to the present

The economy of Britain in the first eighty years of industrialization, 1780–1860, was so smart that it was rich. In the teeth of a sharply rising population and a world war income per head over the eighty years doubled. Macaulay wrote in 1830:

> The present moment is one of great distress. But how small will that distress appear when we think over the history of the last forty years; a war, compared with which all other wars sink into insignificance; taxation, such as the most heavily taxed people of former times could not have conceived; a debt larger than all the public debts that ever existed in the world added together; the food of the people studiously rendered dear; the currency debased, and imprudently restored. Yet is the country poorer than in 1790? We formerly believe that, in spite of all the misgovernment of her rulers, she has been almost constantly becoming richer and richer. (1830, pp. 184–5)

Marx and Engels wrote in 1848 that 'The bourgeoisie, during its rule of scarce two hundred years, has created more massive and colossal productive forces than have all preceding generations together.' With this one can agree. There was more to be done in 1848 or 1860, but what had been achieved was astounding.

The ability of intellectuals to look a gift horse in the mouth should never be underestimated. The creative gift of the Industrial Revolution is beyond compare the greatest achievement of civilization. And yet the clerks have always had their doubts. They wish to fit the achievements of nations to the life of man, finding a cycle of ages from dust to dust. It is ever popular to announce that The End Is Near, giving one a reputation for hardheadedness. The reason again is that achievement is unpredictable. The resources and ingenuities we already know are limited, as anyone can see. It takes an optimistic faith to suppose that creativity will provide, around the corner. Again Macaulay:

> We cannot absolutely prove that those are in error who tell us that society has reached a turning point, that we have seen our best days. But so said all who came before us, and with just as much apparent reason. (1830, p. 186)

We cannot absolutely prove it because if we were so smart we would already know how to make the days better, now. The study of historical examples cannot provide predictions, merely wisdom.

Consider, for example, the achievements of the British economy over the *second* century of the Industrial Revolution. It is widely believed that in Britain the century has been one of 'failure'. Intellectuals are accustomed to second-guessing the achievements of the market. Their contempt for economic achievements shows in their readiness to suppose that they could have done better. The debate about British performance has flipped and flopped since the 1920s between prosecutions and defences of the late Victorians. The sons of Victorian fathers, prominent among them that great second-guesser John Maynard Keynes, attributed Britain's difficulties between the wars to Victorians long dead. Around 1940 the charge was stated at length by historians such as Duncan Burn. During the early 1960s the case for the prosecution, thrice told, was brought to a peak of eloquence by historians such as David Landes. In the late 1960s and 1970s, unexpectedly, the Victorians acquired defenders, mainly Americans trained in technical economics. Around 1980 the prosecution was renewed by another group of historians and historical economists. And by the late 1980s the defence also had been renewed. The cycle of revision makes the head ache, but no more so than twenty other long-running controversies in economics.

The British experience of being first in manufacturing and then disgracefully 'failing' is still supposed to contain a moral for us all. Britain was the first industrial nation, and the first to become mature – some would say, with charming ageism, senile. Britain's past looks to many like the world's future. We are all British in the end. And if capitalism works, as others would claim, it should certainly have worked in Britain, most of all in the grand old days of *laissez-faire*, in that late Victorian age.

The story of achievement frittered away is laid out in a few pages of Landes's classic work of 1965, containing a conference paper of 1954, reprinted and extended as a book in 1969, *The Unbound Prometheus: Technological Change and Industrial Development in Western Europe from 1750 to the Present*. The main question of the middle third of Landes's book is, 'why did industrial *leadership* pass in the closing decades of the nineteenth century from Britain to Germany?' (Landes, 1969, p. 326, italics added). His answer in brief is:

> Thus the Britain of the late nineteenth century basked complacently in the sunset of economic hegemony. . . . (N)ow it was the turn of the third generation, the children of affluence, tired of the tedium of trade and flushed with the bucolic aspirations of the country gentleman. . . . (T)hey worked at play and played at work. (p. 336)

What is most wrong about the metaphor of leadership in a race of industrial might is that it assumes silently that first place among the many nations is vastly to be preferred to second, or twelfth. Leadership is number-one-ship. In the motto of the great American football coach, Vince Lombardi: 'Winning isn't the most important thing; it's the only thing.'

Landes reports correctly that 'Within fifteen years (of cheering the Prussian victory over perfidious France in 1870) . . . the British awoke to the fact that the Industrial Revolution and different rates of population growth had raised Germany to Continental hegemony and left France far behind' (1969,

p. 327). He is correct that in fact the British in the 1880s did fret about German 'hegemony' and did speak of the necessity to 'awaken'. The British at the time certainly did believe the Lombardi motto, *numero uno* or nothing.

It is the usual panic of the intellectuals, the sort we are seeing now in the United States *vis-à-vis* Japan and Europe. The journalists and professors are enchanted by the image of foreign trade as a football game. Landes yields to the magic, asserting unconsciously the salience of coming first *and only first*. For example: 'To be sure, it is easy to demonstrate the exaggeration of these alarms. Germany's gains still left her far *behind* Britain as a commercial power' (p. 328, italics added). Landes is not thinking critically about his historical sources or his economic story. The metaphors of disease, defeat and decline are too harshly fixated on Number One to be right for an economic tale. The Lombardi motto governs narrowly defined games well enough. Only one team wins the Super Bowl. The fixation on Number One, though, forgets that in economic affairs being Number Two, or even Number Twelve, is very good indeed.

The sporting metaphor, in other words, is not a sensible way of measuring the achievement of the British economy since the late nineteenth century. Its 45 million souls were not trying to score points on Germany or the United States. They were trying to earn a living and gain the pearly gates, on their own, making individual choices daily with no collective goal in mind. In the century after 1860 the residence of the souls in Britain – or, better, in a world economy integrated from the mid-nineteenth century on – gave them steadily expanding choice; and they had been relatively rich at the outset. The prize for second in the race of economic growth was not poverty. The prize was great enrichment, if rather less enrichment than certain other groups of people abroad, mainly poorer people. Since 1860, in other words, Britain has grown well, from a high base.

By contrast, the diseases of which the pessimists speak so colourfully are romantically fatal; the sporting or military defeats are horribly total; the declines from former greatness irrevocably huge. An historian can tell the recent story of the first industrial nation as a failure, and be right by comparison with a few countries and a few decades. The historian would sell books to Americans in the last years of the twentieth century, because Americans – or at least the Americans who write the newspaper articles and frame the trade policies – are anxious about loss of 'leadership'.

On a wider, longer view, however, the metaphor of failure in a race is strikingly inapt. Before the British the Dutch were the 'failure'. The Dutch Republic has been 'declining' practically since its birth. With what result? Disaster? Poverty? A 'collapse' of the economy? Not at all. The Netherlands has ended small and weak, stripped of its empire, no longer a strutting power in world politics, a tiny linguistic island in a corner of Europe – yet fabulously rich, with among the highest incomes in the world (now as in the eighteenth century), a domestic product per head quadrupling since

1900, astoundingly successful by any standard but Lombardi's. Again the perspicacious Macaulay in 1830:

> If we were to prophesy that in the year 1930 a population of fifty million (he was very nearly right), better fed, clad, and lodged than the English of our time, will cover these islands, that Sussex and Huntingdonshire will be wealthier than the wealthiest parts of the West Riding of Yorkshire now are . . . that machines constructed on principles yet undiscovered will be in every house . . . many people would think us insane. (p. 185)

Though historically mistaken the pessimistic story is the dominant one. Failure to keep up in technological change, it is said, explains why British growth dropped after 1875, in comparison with its mid-century pace and in comparison with that of the new industrializing countries. The failure in turn is said to have caused British shares of world markets to fall. Martin Wiener's pessimistic storytelling, for instance, has Britain 'surrendering a capacity for innovation and assertion' by 1901 (1981, p. 158). Such a remark jars in the alternative and optimistic story, which tells of a necessarily less bulky Britain engaging nonetheless in such innovation and assertion as radar, the Battle of Britain, jet engines and the structure of deoxyribonucleic acid.

The historians are second-guessing the inventors and entrepreneurs. An historian of Victorian England pretends to be able to see opportunities missed by businesspeople at the time. Usually the historian has not done as much looking into the question of whether by-product coking of coal (say) or the Solvay process of soda-making would be profitable as the most negligent banker would have done at the time. The historian exaggerates the advantage of hindsight: that by-product coking was at length adopted does not mean that it was adopted too late in Britain, if adopted earlier in Germany. He utilizes a mechanical model of human creativity, in which it is child's play to see how to create better.

British observers in the early nineteenth century, like Americans in the Jazz Age, were startled at the ease with which the country had taken industrial leadership. Britain was the first, but a few of its intellectuals were nervously aware of the strangeness of a small island running the world. In 1840, early in British success, J.D. Hume warned a select committee of Parliament that tariffs on imports of wheat would encourage other countries to move away from agriculture and towards industry themselves, breaking Britain's monopoly of world manufacturing: 'we place ourselves at the risk of being surpassed by the manufactures of other countries; and . . . I can hardly doubt that (when that day arrives) the prosperity of this country will recede faster than it has gone forward.'

This was nonsense in 1840 and continues to be nonsense today, clothed in the sporting rhetoric of 'competitiveness'. Britain was made better off by the industrialization of the rest of the world, in the same way that you would be made better off by moving to a neighbourhood of more skilled and healthy people. British growth continued from 1840 to the present, making Britons steadily better off. Likewise, Americans are made better off when Japan 'defeats' them at car-making, because then they will do something they are comparatively good at – banking, say, or growing soybeans – and let the Japanese do the car-making or the consumer electronics.

The stories, then, are wrong. They are routinely applied to Britain and now America, but they are mistaken. As much as American intellectuals delight in telling and retelling them in the sports bar, urging us to buckle up our football pads for *Head to Head: The Coming Economic Battle among Japan, Europe and America* (L. Thurow, 1992) or to finally get down to *Minding America's Business: The Decline and Rise of the American Economy* (R.B. Reich, 1993), the story is wrong about America. And it was just as wrong about Britain a century ago. The story of *The Rise and Fall of the Great Powers* (P. Kennedy, 1988) is a fairytale.

It is true that Britain and America have grown slower than some other countries. Why was that? Because Britain and America started richer. The story of industrial growth in the past century has been a story of convergence to British and American standards of excellence. Germans in 1900 earned about half of what Britons earned; now they are about the same. If sporting metaphors must be used, it was like aerobic dancing, in which everyone wins. The falling British share of world markets was no index of 'failure', any more than a father would view his falling share of the poundage in the house relative to his growing children as a 'failure'. It was an index of maturity.

The trouble with the pessimistic choice of story in the literature of British and American 'failure' is that it describes this happy achievement as a tragedy. Such talk is at best tasteless in a world of real tragedies – Argentina, once rich, now subsidizing much and producing little; or India, trapped in poverty after much expert economic advice. The economists and historians appear to have mixed up the question of why Britain's income per head is now six times that of the Philippines and thirteen times that of India – many hundreds of percent points of difference which powerful forces in sociology, politics and culture must of course contribute to explaining – with the more delicate and much less important questions of why British income in 1987 was 3 per cent less than the French or 5 per cent more than the Belgian.

So the telling of a story of America following Britain into 'decline' is dangerous nonsense. It is nonsense because it is merely a relative decline, caused by the wholly desirable enrichment of the rest of the world. It is dangerous because it leads us to blame foreigners for our real failings, in secondary education, say, or in the maintenance of bridges.

Nothing awful happens to Britain in this story and no neurotic blame or xenophobic hysteria is in order. Macaulay's common sense and historical perspective in 1830 should be revived:

A WAVE OF GADGETS

The political importance of a state may decline, as the balance of power is disturbed by the introduction of new forces. Thus the influence of Holland and of Spain is much diminished. But are Holland and Spain poorer than formerly? We doubt it. Other countries have outrun them. But we suspect that they have been positively, though not relatively, advancing. We suspect that Holland is richer than when she sent her navies up the Thames, that Spain is richer than when a French king was brought captive to the footstool of Charles the Fifth. (pp. 183–4)

The main British story since the late nineteenth century is the more than trebling of British income as others achieved British standards of living or somewhat beyond. A 228 per cent increase of production between 1900 and 1987 is more important than an 8 per cent 'failure' in the end to imitate German habits of attention to duty. Looked at from India, Britain is one of the developed nations. The tragedy of the century past is not the relatively minor jostling among the thoroughbreds in the lead pack of industrial nations. It is the appalling distance between the leaders at the front and the donkeys at the rear.

The story can be told statistically, from the tables of the leading student of world growth and trade, Angus Maddison. He assembled recently the statistics of national output for 31 countries from 1900 to 1987. Expressed in the purchasing power of 1980, some of the countries are as shown in Table 2.1. Note, in contrast to the journalism of economic 'failure' in the mature industrial countries, that:

- Americans are still richer than anyone else, after years of 'failure'. In 1987 the Americans earned $13,550 per head (in 1980 prices), about 40 per cent higher than, say, the Japanese or the (West) Germans.
- Britain is still rich by international standards. After a century of 'failure' the average Briton earns a trifle less than the average Swede and a trifle more than the average Belgian. If you don't believe it, stay at a Belgian hotel. But the British average is over three times that of Mexico and fourteen times that of India. If you don't believe it, step outside your hotel in Calcutta.

To use the image of the race course the whole field, followers as well as leaders, advanced notably – usually by factors of three or more since 1900 in real output per head. The main story is this general advance. The tripling and more of income per head relieved much misery and has given life-affording scope to many people otherwise submerged: think of your great grandparents.

In the face of a world-girdling achievement of modern economic growth the fixation on a trivial 'lag' of Britain and now America behind some of

Table 2.1 The economic achievement of nations: rich and poor in 1900 and 1987 (in dollars of 1980 purchasing power)

Country	National product per head		Factor of increase
	1900	1987	
Rich countries			
United Kingdom	2,798	9,178	3.2
Belgium	2,126	8,769	4.1
France	1,600	9,475	5.9
Germany	1,558	9,964	6.4
United States	2,911	13,550	4.6
The newly rich			
Japan	677	9,756	14.4
The enriching			
South Korea	549	4,143	7.5
USSR	797	5,948	7.5
The newly poor			
Argentina	1,284	3,302	2.6
The poor			
India	378	662	1.8
Mexico	649	227	4.1

Source: Angus Maddison, *The World Economy in the Twentieth Century* (Paris: Development Centre of the Organization for Economic Co-operation and Development, 1989), p. 19.

the other leaders is strange. It arises from the intellectual conviction that 'economic creativity' is an oxymoron, that any fool could do better. It arises, too, from an aristocratic fixation on competition, *à la* Lombardi, so scornful of bourgeois co-operation in business. Many in Britain bemoan the loss of Empire and delight in describing a powerful industrial nation of 55 million people as 'a small island'. Intellectuals mope around the senior common room regretting a lost vocation for instructing the natives. Many American leaders of opinion have adopted the British despair and indulge in sage talk that 'we must do better'. Soon enough it will be stiff upper lips, old chaps. In spoofing this lugubrious Anglo-Saxon attitude no one has improved upon Sellars and Yeatman, in their classic of sixty years ago, *1066 and All That*. The précis of memorable English achievements in creativity from blue Celts and Boadicea to modern times ends abruptly on p. 115, after the Great War – because then 'America became Top Nation and history came to a.'

References

Bacon, Francis. 1620. *The New Organon*. In S. Warhaft, ed., *Francis Bacon: A Selection of His Works*. Indianapolis: Bobbs-Merrill, 1965.

Bloom, Allan. 1970. 'An Interpretation of Plato's Ion.' *Interpretation* 1 (Summer): 43–62. Reprinted in Thomas Pangle, ed., *Roots of Political Philosophy: Ten Forgotten Socratic Dialogues*, 371–95. Ithaca: Cornell University Press, 1987.

Coleman, Donald and MacLeod, Christine. 1986. 'Attitudes to New Techniques: British Businessmen, 1800–1950', *Economic History Review* 2nd ser. 39: 588–611.

Crafts, N.F.R. 1979. 'Victorian Britain Did Fail', *Economic History Review* 2nd ser. 32: 533–537.

Herlihy, David. 1971. 'The Economy of Traditional Europe', *Journal of Economic History* 31 (March): 153–64.

Hume, David. 1741. 'Of the Rise and Progress of the Arts and Sciences.' In Hume, *Essays*. London: Routledge, n.d.

Jaeger, Werner. 1944 (1971). *Paedeia: The Ideals of Greek Culture*. Vol. III. trans. G. Highet. New York: Oxford University Press.

Kennedy, Paul. 1988. *The Rise and Fall of the Great Powers*. New York: Vintage Books.

Kennedy, William P. 1987. *Industrial Structure, Capital Markets and the Origins of British Economic Decline*. Cambridge: Cambridge University Press.

Kirzner, Israel. 1985. *Discovery and the Capitalist Process*. Chicago: Chicago University Press.

Landes, David. 1969. *The Unbound Prometheus: Technological Change and Industrial Development in Western Europe from 1750 to the Present*. Cambridge: Cambridge University Press.

Macaulay, Thomas Babington. 1830. 'Southey's Colloquies.' Pp. 132–87 in Vol. II of *Critical, Historical and Miscellaneous Essays*. Boston: Houghton Mifflin, 1882 (1860 ed.).

McCloskey, D.N. 1970. 'Did Victorian Britain Fail?' *Economic History Review* 2nd ser. 23: 446–59.

McCloskey, D.N. 1973. *Economic Maturity and Entrepreneurial Decline: British Iron and Steel, 1870–1913*. Cambridge, Mass.: Harvard University Press.

McCloskey, D.N. and Sandberg, Lars C. 1971. 'From Damnation to Redemption: Judgments on the Victorian Entrepreneur', *Explorations in Economic History* 9: 89–108.

McCloskey, D.N., ed. 1971. *Essays on a Mature Economy: Britain after 1840*. London and Princeton, NJ: Methuen and Princeton University Press.

MacIntyre, Alasdair. 1981. *After Virtue*. Notre Dame, Ind.: University of Notre Dame Press.

Mokyr, Joel. 1990. *The Lever of Riches: Technological Creativity and Economic Progress*. New York and Oxford: Oxford University Press.

Nicholas, Stephen. 1982. 'Total Factor Productivity Growth and the Revision of Post-1870 British Economic History', *Economic History Review* 25: 83–98.

Nicholas, Stephen. 1985. 'British Economic Performance and Total Factor Productivity Growth, 1870–1940', *Economic History Review* 38: 576–82.

Plato, *Gorgias*, trans. W.R.M. Lamb. Cambridge, Mass.: Harvard University Press, 1925.

Plato, *Ion*, ed. Andrew M. Miller. Bryn Mawr, PA: Bryn Mawr College, 1984.

Plato, *Phaedrus*, trans. H.N. Fowler. Cambridge: Harvard University Press, 1914.

Reich, Robert B. 1993. *Minding America's Business: The Decline and Rise of the American Economy*. New York: Vintage Books.

Ricardo, David. 1817. *The Principles of Political Economy and Taxation*. London: Everyman, 1911, 1973.

Rosenberg, Nathan and Birdzell, L.E. Jr. 1986. *How the West Grew Rich: The Economic Transformation of the Industrial World*. New York: Basic Books.

Thurow, Lester C. 1992. *Head to Head: The Coming Economic Battle Among Japan, Europe and America*. New York: Morrow.
Wiener, Martin. 1981. *English Culture and British Industrial Decline 1850–1980*. Cambridge: Cambridge University Press.
Xenophon. *Memorabilia and Oeconomicus*. Trans. E.C. Marchant. Loeb Series. London and Cambridge: Heinemann and Harvard, 1926.

Part II

ECONOMIC GROWTH AND PERFORMANCE

3

INDUSTRIAL PERFORMANCE, THE INFRASTRUCTURE AND GOVERNMENT POLICY

An international comparison of British performance and policy 1800–1987

Robert Millward

Introduction

The focus of debate on British economic decline has usually been the manufacturing sector. Yet recent research has shown that differences in national productivity levels, that is, in national income per head across countries of the western world, cannot easily be explained by trends in productivity in the manufacturing sector. They have to be sought in other parts of the economy. This chapter reports on research on the links between the infrastructure and industry in the nineteenth and twentieth centuries, to shed light on that issue and on government policy.

The focus is long-term factors in economic growth. Two aspects of British industrial history are already well integrated in the literature on decline. One is that Britain was not only the first industrializing nation but also was relatively well endowed with labour. The second is that British industrialization was export orientated, a feature linked in part to her earlier maritime ventures and imperial possessions. These two features go a long way to explaining several features of late nineteenth- and twentieth-century Britain: why, that is, Britain was vulnerable to the growth of world industrial production from the late nineteenth century; why twentieth-century economic policy had a decidedly imperial bias; why Britain came to be so strong in financial services (cf. Rubinstein, 1988; Cain and Hopkins, 1993).

Other features have not yet been adequately explained. There is no doubt that British industrial policy in the twentieth century has been highly *dirigiste*. This is what Rubinstein (1994, p. 36) has recognised and Wiener (1985) has not. From the financial relief afforded to cotton and steel in the 1920s, the legislation for coal, electricity and urban transport, not to mention the BBC, in the 1920s and 1930s, through the wholesale nationalization of transport and fuel in the 1940s, the battery of investment incentives for manufacturing in the 1950s and thereafter, the planning framework for industry in the 1960s, price controls and the promotion of market leaders in the 1970s, there has been no shrinkage from intervention in industry. These are not policies which reflect an anti-industrial spirit. However, whilst many economic historians would acknowledge this, there are several features of economic, and especially industrial, policy which have not yet been integrated with the discussion of Britain's relative industrial decline. First is that the twentieth-century response to economic problems had a decidedly collectivist dimension. Rubinstein (1994, pp. 52–6) may be right that the culture was no more anti-capitalist than that of Germany or the USA but the outcome in Britain was certainly so. Recall that by the 1950s, under Conservative ministers, more than half of capital formation was being undertaken by government. Secondly, industrial intervention in the twentieth century was very strong in the infrastructure industries and it focused very much on industrial ownership rather than arm's length regulation.

In this chapter I shall argue that in order to understand these dimensions of industrial policy, a third feature of Britain's inheritance has to be brought on stage. This is the fact that Britain shifted out of agriculture much more rapidly than other countries. The urban population grew at unprecedented rates and created massive urbanization problems which coloured governmental responses to a wide range of economic issues. This feature, when linked to recent research on the long-term productivity characteristics of British manufacturing, helps to clarify the role of the infrastructure in the economy and to explain much of industrial policy in the twentieth century. For most of the current century, Britain has had a mixed economy and, from the 1950s, a buoyant financial sector. This was the reality of Britain's economic structure yet it was not espoused or glorified by either of the main political parties who spent most of their time on capital versus labour fights.

The next section sets out the recent findings on the long-term productivity of British industry and how that has pointed to the importance of sectors other than manufacturing. Then the chapter addresses the link between Britain's industrialization, urbanization and the role of the infrastructure. The third central feature of Britain's inheritance – the overseas dimension – is not the focus of this chapter though it is integral to the conclusions drawn at the end.

Comparative manufacturing productivity: stability not decline

The traditional story of British industrialization can, through recent research findings, be reinforced and amplified to suggest that manufacturing has not played the overwhelming role it has often been given in accounts of British decline — in, for example, Elbaum and Lazonick (1986) — and that the major differences in productivity growth across the countries of the western world over the nineteenth and twentieth centuries are located outside the manufacturing sector. The traditional story here is that the industrialization of Britain, c. 1760–1840, involved methods of production which were relatively more labour intensive than those found in later industrializers. By the late nineteenth century Britain had, thereby, sunk a considerable 'capital' in a labour intensive technology and a relatively skilled one at that. Such a story can be found in Habbakuk (1962) or McCloskey (1971) or indeed Elbaum and Lazonick (1986) though without necessarily drawing their policy conclusions. The fact that Britain's technology was relatively labour intensive reflected, especially *vis-à-vis* the USA, the relative scarcity of land and capital and relative abundance of skilled labour. The fact that, by the late nineteenth century, the technology was 'sunken' was a result of Britain being the first to industrialize. Although technological advance, from the middle of the century, proved faster in mass production, capital intensive production methods this does not mean that such methods were economically better for Britain — or for that matter France. Craft production methods in cotton, coal, motor vehicles, shipbuilding, were simply cheaper for Britain.

Such a characterization of British industrialization can be reinforced with the aid of Broadberry's recent research (1993, 1994a,b; see also Maddison, 1991) on comparative industrial productivity. National income per head was, of course, higher in Britain than elsewhere in the early nineteenth century — possibly of the order of 30% higher than the USA in 1820, and much higher than Germany. What is now clear is that, in *manufacturing*, output per head was significantly higher in the USA even at this early date. This means that the American superiority preceded much of the development of managerial capitalism which Chandler (1990), Lazonick (1991) and others have invoked as the key to the success of the USA. Moreover, the comparative position in labour productivity across the manufacturing sectors of Britain, the USA and, indeed, Germany, once it industrialized, *did not significantly change over the 100 or so years from 1870*. What did change were the non-manufacturing parts of the economy.

To illustrate these points, Table 3.1 records various dimensions of productivity. The number of observations is small and for reasons of space I have been selective, but the data are quite consistent with the detailed figures of Broadberry (1993) and with his conclusions about long-term trends.

The pattern in manufacturing is most striking. Output per head in the USA was double that of the UK in 1870 and Broadberry has shown (1994b) that the American lead existed in the early part of the century. This comparative productivity performance is remarkably stable over the two centuries. In the 1980s it was still the case that the USA figure was double that in

Table 3.1 Productivity in the United Kingdom, the USA and Germany (1870–1987 UK=100)

| | Manufacturing | | | | | | National output* | |
| | USA | | | Germany | | | USA | Germany |
	(1)	(2)	(3)	(1)	(2)	(3)	(4)	(4)
1870**	203	94	205	100	60	116	95	48
1899**	139	188	167	99	98	100	98	51
1937**	208	151	188	100	73	110	143	173
1975**	207	142	189	133	107	130	152	103
1987	188	110	183	108	77	117	129	104

Source: Broadberry, 1993, Tables 2, 4 and 5.
Notes:
(1) Output per employee
(2) Capital per employee
(3) Total factor productivity
(4) GDP per employee
* Using Paasche-type purchasing power parities.
** The manufacturing data for 1870 refer to 1869 for the USA and 1875 for Germany. The national output data for 1899 refer to 1890, for 1937 to 1938 and the 1975 data refer to 1973.

the UK. There is therefore no catch-up here, no convergence. In Germany there is not quite the same stability partly because of the two world wars. In the 1960s and 1970s Germany shot ahead and the small number of observations is slightly misleading here. Nevertheless, the long-term trend does seem to be one where labour productivity in manufacturing in Germany was about the same as in Britain in the 1870s, the 1930s and the 1980s. This stability extends also to overall productivity, that is total factor productivity in manufacturing, with the USA slightly less than double the UK and Germany about 20% higher.

This stability of comparative productivity in manufacturing has been experienced against a backcloth of considerable changes in comparative capital intensities. In the early nineteenth century, the capital–labour ratio was much higher in Britain than in Germany as one might expect. It was also, however, higher than USA. By the late nineteenth century the figure for the USA was nearly double that in Britain though the differences in production methods were by no means straightforward. Current research suggests that, from the beginning, the USA was a great user of natural resources – raw materials, land – and later of specialized resource-using machinery. Initially it was only in the parts of manufacturing using very skilled labour that substitution by capital was profitable. The American advantage here also included a relatively homogeneous demand in a big internal market. Hence mass production techniques emerged with great scope for increases in labour productivity. It is in the twentieth century that Britain has come to adopt more capital intensive techniques with, as Table 3.1 shows, a secular trend to approximating the measured American capital intensity by the 1980s.

It is clear then that the large growth in national income per head in the nineteenth century in the USA and Germany, and in particular, the process of catching up to Britain, cannot be explained by changes in comparative productivity in *manufacturing*. Rather it is the non-manufacturing sectors which account for the USA overtaking UK national income per head levels by the turn of the century. As a first approximation one can point to the development of transportation and the opening of the prairies. In the case of Germany the effects of structural change through the decline in agriculture's share is likely to be part of the story. Even so it is not until the 1970s that Germany reaches UK income levels. Both world wars of course played a major part, with the USA gaining considerable relative advantage in these periods (cf. Broadberry, 1988).

The infrastructure and urbanization

The labour intensity of Britain's industrialization was a central feature of the economic inheritance bequeathed to the late nineteenth and twentieth centuries. The implications of another central feature have not been traced through in the same way. This is the scale and speed of the reduction in agriculture's share of economic activity and the associated problems of urbanization.

Britain's experience does seem to be distinctive. Industrialization up to 1840 saw a massive reduction in agriculture's role in the economy. Given that Britain had higher income levels than other countries in the early eighteenth century, it is debatable whether they rose much during the first phase of factory industry. There is, however, no doubt about the sectoral shift. By 1840 only one-quarter of Britain's labour force was in the primary sector and less than 30% of the adult labour force was in agriculture. These proportions were well below those in other European countries, let alone the USA, and even when these other countries reached the income levels achieved in Britain by 1840, they had much bigger shares of labour in the primary sector (50% in Germany, 49% in France in 1870) and of male adult labour in agriculture (51% in Belgium in 1850, 58% in Austria in 1880; Crafts, 1985, pp. 57–9).

The associated impact on urbanization is more complicated. England and Wales saw their maximum rate of city population growth in the 1820s. This was earlier than any other country for which good records exist and took place in a small country so that the overall level of urbanization of 46% in 1840 and 65% in 1870 contrasts sharply with Germany (30% in 1870, 56% in 1900) and France (31% in 1870 and 44% in 1910). This high density living created many well-known problems related to the infrastructure. Even the railways, it should be recalled, in vivid contrast to the USA, had to fit into a well-developed existing transport system and opened up hardly any new communities or economic activities. The impact of urban population growth on the economy was sometimes direct in that pressures were created for improvements in local infrastructure industries: water supply, tramways, gas and later electricity supply. The other effects were indirect but called for a significant improvement and expansion of the housing stock, public health facilities and policing. A classic indicator of the congestion and health of these urban areas is that the secular decline in mortality in Europe over the eighteenth and nineteenth centuries was halted in England earlier than elsewhere, that is in the period 1830 to 1875 'and seems to have coincided . . . (in all countries) . . . with the years of greatest social hardship caused by industrialisation' (Vallin, 1991, p. 45).

Now Williamson (1990, pp. 2–4) has tended to play down the size of Britain's urban problem by pointing out that several other European countries achieved their maximum city growth not very long after Britain (France and Germany in the period 1830–60, for example) and that Britain's rate of growth of 2.5% in the 1820s looks modest next to 4.2% for the Third World in the 1960s. For our purposes, however, there are three matters which make Britain's experience important and distinctive. First is that the political culture sympathetic to, and capable of, the delivery of a collective response to these urban problems did not exist in the early nineteenth century. Legislation to facilitate local and central collective action in public health, transport, policing, water supply, gas and electricity, did not materialize until the 1850–80 period, in particular until the arrival of the mandatory clauses of the 1875 Public Health Act. Secondly, we should recall that income levels had probably not risen much, if at all, in the industrialization phase up to 1840. As a result of both these factors, investment in urban infrastructure was low. As Williamson himself records (1990, ch. 10), whereas all fixed capital grew at 0.85% per annum in the period 1800–60, the local infrastructure capital stock was growing at only 0.24%. The legacy for the late nineteenth century was massive, especially for the town councils providing policing, public health, roads and poor relief. I have estimated the impact of population change by cross-section analyses of 25 towns, mainly in the industrial Midlands and the North of England for the period 1870–1914 (Millward and Sheard, 1995). When an increase in a city population was accompanied by an expansion of city boundaries and housing stock, town council expenditure increased roughly in line. A 10% rise in population would be accompanied by a 10% rise in recurrent expenditure on labour, maintenance, other operating costs and loan charges. When population rose in a city without any increase in land space – and this was often the case – expenditure shot up; a 10% rise in population saw a 30% increase in expenditure.

The consequences of Britain's distinctive urbanization and its links with the previous section's discussion of manufacturing may be explored by looking at sectoral shares in the economy over the long term. I use Feinstein's work on capital formation (Feinstein, 1972; Feinstein and Pollard, 1988) since it is the most reliable for the long period under review. Figure 3.1, derived from the data in Table A.1 of the appendix (see p. 60–1), brings out firstly the relatively modest and yet stable role of the manufacturing sector. After an initial rise in the first phase of factory industrialization, investment in manufacturing accounted for a fairly stable 20% of UK investment – world war periods aside. Thus manufacturing is not a dominant part of the economy in this respect. At the same time, and contrary to some of the stories of British decline, it has not fallen over the long term. Indeed 'industry', more widely defined to include commerce (but not transport, electricity, telecommunications, etc. which are included in infrastructure) has seen a long-term secular rise in its share of capital formation, with commerce noticeably accounting for the post-1945 increase. Agriculture, of course, shows a secular decline and it is agriculture which accounts for the declining share of the tradable goods sector down to the 1930s. It is the rise in commerce which reverses that trend. Hence, as Rubinstein (1994, p. 33) has emphasized with other data, private sector services have replaced agriculture, with manufacturing relatively stable.

An important link in our story is provided by the fact that the counterpart to the decline of agriculture was the rise in the share of the infrastructure during the nineteenth century, continuing to 60% by the 1930s. In the next section I shall explore how that related to the productivity patterns recorded earlier and how it affected government economic policy. In the meantime it may be noticed that the most important feature of the infrastructure for our purposes is not the railway, even for the nineteenth century, since its

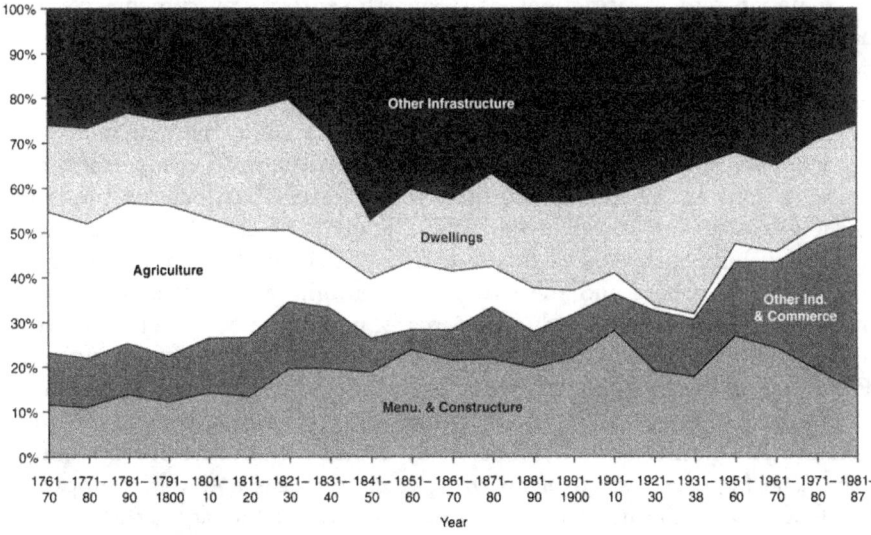

Figure 3.1 Distribution of investment in the UK 1761–1987.

expansion in the middle of the century seems to have been mainly at the expense of other parts of the infrastructure, especially dwellings. Rather it is the rise in investment in urban areas in public health, water supply, transport and electricity in the late nineteenth century, the huge rise in dwellings in the inter-war period and, though this is not apparent from Figure 3.1, the rising importance of the public sector in the infrastructure from the late nineteenth century through to the 1970s.

Infrastructure performance and government policy

Britain's craft-based production methods, its urbanization problems, its overseas trading dimension confronted policy-makers with both economic and social problems. In a narrow economic sense, the industrial inheritance generated three problems. The massive decline in Britain's share of world exports in the twentieth century can be traced in part to the overseas focus of early industrialization which made Britain vulnerable to the rise of new industrializing countries. At the same time, the craft-based nature of production meant, as Broadberry has emphasized (1994a), that it could not take advantage of technological advance occurring in mass production capital intensive methods. Thirdly, the entrenched labour intensive methods of production which had proved so successful over the nineteenth century rendered labour much less mobile than in the USA. These three economic issues are enough to account for Britain's relative decline and one associated with a substantial regional problem. They amount to a massive problem of adjustment which would have challenged any country, any culture, any educational system.

To understand the reactions of twentieth-century governments we also have to take into account the role of the infrastructure. Apart perhaps from housing, infrastructure activities generate economic problems that are not easily resolved under unfettered private ownership. External effects pervade water supply, public health, policing, transport, whilst natural monopoly elements are usually present in electricity and gas supply, roads, trams and railways. During the first phase of factory industrialization, the provision of these services had largely been left to the private sector. In tracing subsequent developments, it is useful to distinguish the infrastructure industries (essentially transport and fuel) from what might be labelled local social overhead (health, housing, education, roads, policing, poor relief). The work of Foreman-Peck and myself (1994) on the infrastructure industries suggests, at the risk of some simplicity, that, following the initial era of free competition, there were two cycles of government intervention at the end of which Britain had an almost wholly collectively owned set of infrastructure industries. The large expansion of railways, telegraph, gas and water supply in the first half of the nineteenth century was carried forward by a flurry of joint stock companies but the natural monopoly elements in these sectors were enough to eradicate significant local competition 'in the field' by the

1860s and thereby to generate widespread complaints from business and residential users. The first cycle of government intervention started in the middle of the century and saw regulation of the private companies but the regulatory regime was increasingly regarded as ineffective, and in the case of local utilities, was part of the drive to municipalization of major sectors of tramways, electricity and gas supplies and of practically all of water supply by the First World War. A second cycle can be identified which starts in the early years of the twentieth century and sees technical developments, especially in electricity, which render regional or even national modes of economic organization more efficient than local ones. Again arm's length regulation characterizes the initial government response in the inter-war period but again this is deemed to have failed and is followed by wholesale nationalization of transport and fuel in the 1940s. Recent research suggests that the decision not to nationalize cotton, motor vehicles and most other manufacturing industries reflected the pragmatic rather than strongly ideological basis of the nationalizations (Millward and Singleton, 1995, ch. 14). As long as those sectors producing traded goods could meet the post-war export targets, they were left alone.

The economic story for social overheads has yet to be told. Table 3.2 shows that investment in local infrastructure accounted for 36% of UK investment in the 1870s rising to 44% by the early 1900s. Even when dwellings are excluded, investment in the local infrastructure accounts for one-quarter of UK total capital formation in the Edwardian period. Local government played a major role in this expansion such that by the early 1900s its investment was not much less than that of the whole of manufacturing industry. This created severe fiscal tensions since there were few government grants to alleviate town councils with pressing urban programmes. The local tax – rates – was stretched to the limit and led many councils in the North and the Midlands to use income from property holdings and profits from gas and other utilities to subsidize the rates. By the First World War such practices were becoming discredited and the inter-war period saw a bigger central government involvement in all local infrastructure activities. The housing stock mushroomed and by the 1930s investment in dwellings was nearly double that in manufacturing.

The net effect of these government policies for the infrastructure is illustrated in Table 3.3 showing the balance of the economy between the private and public sectors. As late as the 1880s about 90% of capital formation was in the private sector. The credibility of capitalism was effectively undermined in the first half of the twentieth century. By the 1930s less than 70% of investment was in the private sector and by the 1950s the figure actually fell below one-half, a clear manifestation of the drift of government policy in the twentieth century.

In the light of all this, what do we know about the performance of the infrastructure? Recall that increases in US national income per head, relative

Table 3.2 Local government and UK investment, 1870–1910 (annual average gross domestic fixed capital formation)

(in £m at 1900 prices)	(1)	(2)	(3)	(4)	(5)
1871–5	7.4	24.1	8.2	71.7	111.4
1876–80	15.3	28.6	6.4	71.8	122.4
1881–5	9.0	23.3	0.8	82.4	115.4
1886–90	11.4	21.2	6.5	69.0	108.1
1891–5	19.3	23.9	10.3	75.2	128.7
1896–1900	27.6	38.1	13.2	104.8	183.8
1901–5	41.2	40.6	15.2	125.6	222.3
1906–10	25.2	30.0	15.9	105.8	176.9

Source: Feinstein, 1972, Appendix Tables 39 and 40; Feinstein and Pollard, 1988, Appendix Tables II and IX.

Notes:
(1) Local government; (2) Dwellings; (3) Other local infrastructure; (4) Rest of the economy (covers manufacturing, mining, quarrying, agriculture, railways, shipping, distribution and other services); (5) Total.

Local infrastructure is defined as gas, water and electricity supplies, transport and communications (excluding railways and shipping) and all public and social services (and hence includes some central government investment, such as that by the Post Office in telecommunications, but this was very small). The figures for local government were based on those at current prices in Feinstein (1972) and converted to constant 1900 prices by assuming the local authority share of local infrastructure spending (excluding housing) at constant prices was the same as the share at current prices. There is an element of double counting from the small amounts spent by local authorities on housing which appear in both column (1) and column (2); the offset is a small underestimate of 'other local infrastructure' in the third column which is calculated residually.

Table 3.3 Distribution of investment in the UK by sector, 1856–1987 (% distribution of gross domestic fixed capital formation)

(At current prices)	(1)	(2)	(3)	(4)	(5)
1856	93.7	5.4	0	1.0	100
1865	93.8	6.6	0	0.5	100
1873	92.4	7.2	0	0.4	100
1883	89.8	9.7	0	0.4	100
1893	83.4	15.6	0	1.0	100
1903	81.7	17.3	0	1.0	100
1913	84.4	13.0	0	2.6	100
1920	78.6	18.7	0	2.7	100
1924	74.1	21.9	0	4.0	100
1937	69.7	24.7	1.6	4.0	100
1951	47.8	24.3	18.9	9.0	100
1964	56.0	19.0	20.2	4.8	100
1973	70.8	9.7	15.3	4.2	100
1987	84.3	5.1	6.1	4.5	100

Notes:
(1) Private sector; (2) Local government; (3) Public corporations; (4) Central government; (5) Total.
Source: Appendix Table A.2, pp. 61–2.

to the UK, in the nineteenth century seem to be explained largely by what was happening outside the manufacturing sector. The convergence of British income per head towards US levels can be dated from the 1950s though elements of such a movement are detectable in the inter-war period. Here again the Table 3.1 data imply that this is largely associated with productivity changes outside manufacturing. There is, as yet, no comprehensive study that has pinned down the details of this and there are several sectors involved besides the infrastructure, commerce in particular.

Table 3.4 is a first attempt at assembling the relevant data from sectoral studies. Some of the nineteenth-century figures are derived from Kendrick's 1961 estimates of American total factor productivity growth and from the Matthews, Feinstein and Odling-Smee study of British economic growth (1982). The latter suggests that in the sixty years before the First World War, British productivity growth is higher in manufacturing than commerce and higher than in all identified sub-divisions of the infrastructure (except gas, electricity and water which in any case had a small weight in this period). The results then are consistent with the pattern spelled out earlier in the chapter in so far as productivity growth in manufacturing over the whole period 1856 to 1913, as a first approximation, is the same in both the USA and the UK, though the American growth is higher towards the end. The explanation of the rise of USA national income per head relative to the UK is to be found in the lower growth of UK productivity in commerce and the infrastructure as compared to these sectors in the USA. Relevant studies of individual parts of the UK infrastructure are sparse. Foreman-Peck (1987) has compared the nineteenth-century UK railway system with that of the USA (which he implies was more tightly regulated) and with the more planned systems of continental Europe. After allowing for the mileage of track and density of traffic, he concludes that construction costs were significantly higher in the UK than in these other countries. In the case of local utilities the private sector is dominant up to the 1870s. Detailed studies of the gas industry suggest that the private companies had higher costs than the municipal enterprises, though this was in part due to the coal prices, wage rates and interest charges they faced and in part to the municipals running more modern plant (Millward and Ward, 1987). After controlling for the differences in factor prices, the differences in costs were not statistically significant though these results relate to the end of the century and may be obscuring high cost private companies taken over by local governments earlier on.

In the twentieth century, but particularly since 1945, the relative performance of manufacturing and the infrastructure is reversed. Productivity growth in UK manufacturing over the whole of the period 1950–85 is similar to that in the USA. The UK infrastructure sector shows, however, a relatively better performance. Already in the inter-war period, there is the evidence from the experience of the Central Electricity Board. The

Table 3.4 Productivity growth in the infrastructure and the economy, 1856–1985 (annual average percentage growth in total factor productivity)

	All economy	Manufacturing	Gas, electricity, water	Transport and communications
1856–1913				
UK	0.64	0.9	0.6	0.5
1873–1913				
UK	0.45	0.6	1.6	0.7
USA	1.12	1.59[1]	2.97–4.06[2]	2.51–2.80[3]
1924–37				
UK	0.70	1.9	1.8	2.4
USA	1.16	3.73[4]	2.45–3.47[2]	1.82–2.17[5]
1951–64				
UK	2.0	2.0	3.3	2.4
USA[6]	1.3[7]	2.0	3.7	1.0–3.7
1964–73				
UK	2.4	3.1	4.3	3.7
USA[8]	0.4[7]	1.8	2.4	1.6–3.0
1973–85				
UK	0.9	1.3	1.8	1.4–2.4
USA	0.1[7]	1.4	1.2	0.1–2.3

Sources: The UK data for 1856–1973 are taken from Matthews, Feinstein and Odling-Smee, 1982. The 1973–85 UK figures were calculated from the data for each sector on GDP at 1980 factor cost, the share of income from employment in GDP, gross capital stock at 1980 replacement cost (all in CSO, *National Income and Expenditure* 1979 and 1986) and estimates of manhours, derived (cf. Millward, 1990) from Employment Gazette, Dept of Employment 1987 (Historical Supplement). The US data for 1873–1937 are derived from the total factor productivity indices in Kendrick (1961) and the 1951–85 data are taken from Griliches (1988) where 'utilities' are assumed to cover gas, electricity and water. Kendrick (1987) is an alternative source for 1951–85 and his figures are higher but the relative position of manufacturing and the other industries is the same.

Notes
1 1869–1909.
2 The first figure is manufactured gas (1869–1914 and 1919–37) and the second figure is electric utilities (1899–1913 and 1919–37).
3 The first figure relates to telephone and telegraph 1879–1909 and the second figure to railroads, using the average figure for 1865–78 as the starting point.
4 1919–37.
5 1919–37. The first figure relates to telephones and telegraphs and the second to railroads.
6 1949–66.
7 Private industry, i.e. all sectors except government.
8 1966–73.

planning and construction of the national grid and the elimination of inefficient plants (including several municipals) closed the productivity gap with the USA in this sector (Foreman-Peck, 1994, p. 40). More generally, in the post Second World War period productivity growth in the UK infrastructure exceeds that in UK manufacturing. By using Griliches' data (1988) on the USA, it is also shown in Table 3.4 that the British performance in the infrastructure exceeds that in the comparable transport and fuel sectors of the USA. For gas, electricity and water, British productivity growth is higher over the period 1964–85, more than offsetting the slight difference with the USA in the first sub-period. For transport and communications, the data are sometimes only available as two separate figures. The lower one is transport and carries a much bigger weight than the higher one for telecommunications. On that basis, it is clear again that the British sector performs better than the American. This is significant since, myths to the contrary, the UK had a nationalized sector which was, in this sense, outperforming both private British manufacturing industry and the more loosely regulated transport and fuel sectors of the USA.

Conclusion

It is misleading to gauge the fortunes of the British economy over the last two centuries by what happened in the manufacturing sector. This is not only because manufacturing accounted on average for only about one-fifth of capital formation but also because movements in national income per head relative to the USA and Germany are largely a function of productivity change outside the manufacturing sector. Relative productivity levels in manufacturing do not seem to have changed much on a long-term perspective, with Germany about 15–20% higher and the USA double the British levels. The sources of the productivity change outside manufacturing, especially in commerce and the infrastructure require much more research. Outputs in these sectors are not easy to measure. It would appear that productivity growth rates in transport, communications, commerce and public services in nineteenth-century Britain were all below that in manufacturing and even further behind similar infrastructure sectors in the USA. In the twentieth century, and especially post-1945, the reverse seems to be the case and is again consistent with the movements in national income per head in the UK and USA. That is, productivity growth in transport and communications, the utilities sector and public services all exceed that in manufacturing industry and I have quoted direct evidence from the USA to show that productivity growth in their transport and utilities sectors was less than in Britain. These patterns will perhaps surprise some people since the nineteenth century was the era, in Britain, of relatively unfettered competition in the infrastructure sector whilst the twentieth century saw substantial regulation and direct state ownership.

In this chapter I have also linked these developments to government policy and the role of the infrastructure in the economy. The main driving force of British industrial policy in the late nineteenth and twentieth centuries was the collapse of exports and the organizational problems of the infrastructure, both issues traceable to distinctive features of British industrialization. In effect, they significantly undermined the credibility of capitalism during the first half of the twentieth century. A key indicator is that by the early 1950s, under a Conservative government, one half of capital formation was undertaken by the public sector. There was no 'cordon sanitaire' around industry, to use Martin Wiener's words, no lack of industrial spirit (1985). Rather if we judge from actions and outcomes it was capitalism which lacked credibility. At the same time the overseas dimension of the economy remained important economically and politically, as Cain and Hopkins (1993) have shown, and the financial service sector flourished.

The outcome was an economic policy which, in its stance towards the structural features of the economy that we have been examining, had three intriguing features. First, Britain had a mixed economy (not unlike France but different from the USA) and one which was supported wholeheartedly by neither political party whose rhetoric was mainly about capital versus labour. Yet the mixed economy dominated from about the late 1920s until now and saw the likes of Harold Macmillan supporting the nationalization of milk supply and Tony Blair seemingly willing to leave the provision of water supply to the private companies. Secondly, industrial policy was highly interventionist from the 1930s onwards, initially coal and the infrastructure but then later manufacturing. All the variants were tried from investment incentives to nationalization to regional subsidies and all seemed to satisfy no one. Thirdly, the service sector was thriving, especially financial services, electricity and telecommunications. Profit rates were high in these sectors, so were salaries, and employment expanded in the south-east. Yet this also flourished without many admirers or public defenders.

Appendix

Table A.1 Investment in the UK by industry group, 1761–1987[1] (annual average gross domestic fixed capital formation at current prices in £ million)

	Manufactg and construct.	Other ind., agr. and commerce[2]	Dwellings	Gas, electricity & water	Transport, communications[3]	Public and social services	Total
1761–70	0.50	1.82	0.81	0	0.8	0.3	4.25
1771–80	0.62	2.29	1.21	0	1.11	0.36	5.59
1781–90	1.00	2.92	1.42	0	1.19	0.42	6.95
1791–1800	1.39	4.90	2.14	0	2.25	0.58	11.26
1801–10	2.28	7.87	4.62	0	3.68	1.14	20.13
1811–20	3.32	9.40	6.73	0.28	4.03	1.37	25.13
1821–30	5.5	8.5	8.2	0.3	3.7	1.5	27.6
1831–40	7.3	9.7	9.3	0.6	8.1	1.9	36.9
1841–50	9.0	10.1	6.3	1.2	19.3	2.2	46.1
1851–60	13.0	10.8	8.8	2.7	16.7	2.6	55.7
1861–70	17.2	15.9	13.0	3.6	26.0	4.0	79.7
1871–80	28.1	26.2	25.8	4.4	33.7	8.8	122.6
1881–90	19.9	17.9	19.4	3.6	32.1	7.3	100.2

INDUSTRY AND THE INFRASTRUCTURE

Table A.1 continued

	Manufactg and construct.	Other ind., agr. and commerce[2]	Dwellings	Gas, electricity & water	Transport, communications[2]	Public and social services	Total
1891–1900	31.1	20.6	27.5	7.9	39.6	12.2	138.9
1901–10	52.3	24.0	32.2	11.5	50.9	14.8	185.7
1911–20	115.7	37.8	13.2	9.5	67.8	10.9	254.9
1921–30	74.5	66.4	112.8	40.7	97.1	19.5	409.0
1931–8	79.5	66.4	154.1	55.8	68.1	35.8	459.7
1951–60	802	610	603	331	394	217	2,957
1961–70	1,604	1,454	1,250	770	648	805	6,531
1971–80	4,464	7,448[3]	4,512	1,243	2,439	2,994	23,100
1981–7	7,910	21,656[3]	11,429	2,961	4,433	7,049	55,438

Sources
C.H. Feinstein, *National Income, Expenditure and Output in the United Kingdom 1865–1965*, Cambridge University Press, 1972, Appendix Tables 39, 41 and 61.
C.H. Feinstein and S. Pollard, *Studies in Capital Formation in the United Kingdom 1750–1920*, Oxford University Press, 1988, Appendix Tables II and IX.
Central Statistical Office, *National Income and Expenditure*, HMSO, 1971 (Table 55), 1979 (Table 10.6).
Central Statistical Office, *United Kingdom National Accounts*, HMSO, 1990 (Tables 13.6 and 13.8).

Notes
(1) The data for 1761–1850 exclude all Ireland and are taken from Feinstein and Pollard (1988). The 1851–1920 data come from the same source and include all Ireland. From 1921 S. Ireland is excluded. The data for 1921–60 are from Feinstein (1972), for 1961–70 from Central Statistical Office (1971), for 1971–80 from CSO (1979, 1990) and for 1981–7 from CSO (1990). From 1951 the transfer costs of land and buildings are no longer included in the individual industry entries but are all attributed to the entry for 'other industry and commerce' which is calculated residually for this table for these years.
(2) Other industry and commerce consists of mining, quarrying, agriculture, distribution, financial services, tourism and other parts of commerce. Road haulage is also included in the entries for the years 1921–50 and all UK transfer costs of land and buildings from 1951.
(3) Includes the leasing value of assets owned by the financial service sector and leased out to other sectors. This totalled £2,411 million in 1979 and £4,876 million in 1987 (see p. 146 of CSO, 1990).

Table A.2 Investment in the UK economy by sector and industry group (gross domestic fixed capital formation at current prices in £ million); Selected years, 1856–1987[1]

(A) *By sector*[2]

	Private sector	Local government	Public corporations	Central government	Total
1856	52.3	3	0	0.5	55.8
1865	85.5	6	0	0.5	91.1
1873	115.7	9	0	0.5	125.2
1883	101.4	11	0	0.5	112.9
1893	90.6	17	0	1	108.6
1903	170.0	36	0	2	208.0

Table A.2 continued

	Private sector	Local government	Public corporations	Central government	Total
1913	162.2	25	0	5	192.2
1920a[1]	na	na	0	na	577.6
1920b[1]	379	90	0	13	482
1924	277	82	0	15	374
1937	400	142	9	23	574
1951	901	460	358	170	1,889[1]
1964	3,280	1,112	1,187	281	5,860[1]
1979	26,139	3,588	5,641	1,557	36,925[1]
1987	62,146	3,779	4,525	3,345	73,795[1]

(B) *By industry group*

	Manufactg and construct.	Other ind., agr. and commerce[2]	Dwellings	Gas, electricity & water	Transport, communications[3]	Public and social services	Total
1856	14.6	12.5	7.1	2.7	16.2	2.7	55.8
1865	17.9	18.4	10.8	4.0	36.2	3.8	91.1
1873	22.4	30.5	23.1	3.5	37.7	8.0	125.2
1883	18.3	18.8	21.2	4.1	43.5	7.0	112.9
1893	21.5	18.3	21.2	5.9	30.7	11.1	108.6
1903	55.5	27.8	38.6	16.2	53.5	16.4	208.0
1913	48.9	40.5	15.7	8.8	64.6	13.7	192.2
1920a[1]	251.3	123.7	24.8	24.5	130.7	22.6	577.6
1920b[1]	152	115	62	24	115	14	482
1924	62	71	94	38	93	16	374
1937	126	78	168	60	95	47	574
1951	552	328	376	122	212	150	1,889
1964	1,346	1,219	1,210	758	707	561	5,860
1979	7,101	7,649	11,387[4]	1,696	3,525	4,151	36,925
1987	10,581	15,509	25,687[4]	3,343	5,830	8,786	73,795[4]

Sources
C.H. Feinstein, *National Income, Expenditure and Output in the United Kingdom 1865–1965*, Cambridge University Press, 1972, Appendix Tables 39, 41 and 61.
C.H. Feinstein and S. Pollard, *Studies in Capital Formation in the United Kingdom 1750–1920*, Oxford University Press, 1988, Appendix Tables II and IX.
Central Statistical Office, *United Kingdom National Accounts*, HMSO, 1986, 1990.

Notes
(1) The data for 1856 to 1920a are taken from Feinstein and Pollard (1988) and include S. Ireland. The 1920b-1964 data are from Feinstein (1972) and the 1979–87 data from Central Statistical Office (1990) and exclude S. Ireland. From 1951 the transfer costs of land and buildings are not included in the individual industry entries in Part B of the table but are included in the totals for each year; in the source for Part A of the table they appear to be included in the private sector figures.
(2) There is no breakdown of public and private sectors in Feinstein and Pollard (1988). The data in Feinstein (1972) for government and public corporations are regarded as very reliable and so the private sector entries for 1856–1920a were calculated as the difference between those figures and the total investment figures in Feinstein and Pollard (1988).

Table A.2 continued

(3) Other industry and commerce consists of mining, quarrying, agriculture, distribution, financial services, tourism and other parts of commerce. Road haulage is also included in the entries for the years 1924b to 1964.
(4) Includes the leasing value of assets owned by the financial service sector and leased out to other sectors. This totalled £2,411 million in 1979 and £4,876 million in 1987 (see CSO, 1990, p. 146).

Acknowledgement

Thanks to Roisin Higgins for research assistance.

References

Broadberry, S.N. (1988), 'The Impact of Two World Wars on the Long-Run Performance of the British Economy', *Oxford Review of Economic Policy*, Vol. 4, No. 1, Spring, pp. 25–37.
Broadberry, S.N. (1993), 'Manufacturing and the convergence hypothesis: what the long run data show', *Journal of Economic History*, Vol. 53, No. 4, pp. 772–95.
Broadberry, S.N. (1994a), 'Technological Leadership and Productivity Leadership in Manufacturing since the Industrial Revolution: Implications from the Convergence Debate', *Economic Journal*, Vol. 104, No. 423, pp. 291–302.
Broadberry, S.N. (1994b), 'Comparative Productivity in British and American Manufacturing during the Nineteenth Century', *Explorations in Economic History*, Vol. 31, No. 4, pp. 52–118.
Cain, P.J. and Hopkins, A.G. (1993), *British Imperialism: Crisis and Deconstruction 1914–1990*, London: Longman.
Central Statistical Office (1971, 1983), *National Income and Expenditure*, HMSO.
Central Statistical Office (1986, 1990), *United Kingdom National Accounts*, HMSO.
Chandler, A.D. Jr (1990), *Scale and Scope: The Dynamics of Industrial Capitalism*, London, Belknap Press of Harvard University Press.
Crafts, N.F.R. (1985), *British Economic Growth during the Industrial Revolution*, Oxford: Clarendon Press.
Department of Employment (1973, 1985), *New Earnings Surveys*, April, HMSO.
Department of Employment (1973, 1987), *Employment Gazette*, August and December 1973, February 1987, HMSO.
Elbaum, B. and Lazonick, W. (eds) (1986), *The Decline of the British Economy*, Oxford: Clarendon Press.
Feinstein, C.H. (1972), *National Income, Expenditure and Output in the United Kingdom 1865–1965*, Cambridge: Cambridge University Press.
Feinstein, C.H. and Pollard, S. (1988), *Studies in Capital Formation in the United Kingdom 1750–1920*, Oxford: Oxford University Press.
Foreman-Peck, J. (1987), 'Natural Monopoly and Railway Policy in the Nineteenth Century', *Oxford Economic Papers*, Vol. 39, pp. 699–718.
Foreman-Peck, J., (1994), 'Industry and Industrial Organisation in the Inter-war Years', in R. Floud and D. McCloskey (eds), *The Economic History of Britain since 1700: Volume 2 : 1860–1939*, Cambridge, 1994, pp. 386–414.
Foreman-Peck, J. and Millward, R. (1994), *Public and Private Ownership of British Industry 1820–1990*, Oxford: Oxford University Press.

Gamble, A. (1990), 'Britain's Decline: Some Theoretical Issues', in M. Mann (ed.), *The Rise and Decline of the Nation State*, Oxford: Blackwell.

Griliches, Z. (1988), 'Productivity Puzzles and R&D: Another Non-Explanation', *Journal of Economic Perspectives*, Vol. 2, pp. 9–21.

Habbakuk, H. John (1962), *American and British Technology in the Nineteenth Century: The Search for Labour-saving Inventions*, Cambridge: Cambridge University Press.

Kendrick, J.W. (1961), *Productivity Trends in the United States*, Princeton: National Bureau of Economic Research.

Kendrick, J.W. (1987), 'Service Sector Productivity', *Business Economics*, Vol. 22, No. 2, April, pp. 18–24.

Kennedy, W. (1987) 'Service Sector Productivity', *Business Economics*, Vol. 22, No. 2, April, pp. 18–24.

Lazonick, W. (1991), *Business Organisation and the Myth of the Market Economy*, Cambridge: Cambridge University Press.

McCloskey, D.N. (1971), 'International Differences in Productivity? Coal and Steel in America and Britain before World War I', in *Essays on a Mature Economy: Britain after 1840*, London: Methuen.

Maddison, A. (1991), *Dynamic Forces in Capitalist Development: A Long-Run Comparative View*, Oxford: Oxford University Press.

Matthews, R.C.O., Feinstein, C.H. and Odling-Smee, J.C. (1982), *British Economic Growth 1856–1973*, Oxford: Clarendon Press.

Millward, R. (1990), 'Productivity in the UK Services Sector: Historical Trends 1856–1985 and Comparisons with USA 1950–85', *Oxford Bulletin of Economics and Statistics*, Vol. 52, No. 4, pp. 423–436.

Millward, R. and Sheard, S. (1995), 'The Urban Fiscal Problem 1870–1914: Government Expenditure and Finances in England and Wales', *Economic History Review*, Vol. 48, No. 3, August, pp. 501–35.

Millward, R. and Singleton, J. (eds) (1995), *The Political Economy of Nationalisation in Britain 1920–50*, Cambridge: Cambridge University Press.

Millward, R. and Ward, R. (1987), 'The Costs of Public and Private Gas Enterprises in Late Nineteenth Century Britain', *Oxford Economic Papers*, Vol. 39, pp. 719–37.

Rubinstein, W.D. (1994), *Capitalism, Culture and Decline in Britain 1750–1990*, London: Routledge.

Rubinstein, W.D. (1988), 'Social Class, Social Attitudes and British Business Life', *Oxford Review of Economic Policy*, Vol. 4, No. 1, Spring, pp. 51–8.

Szreter, S. (1988), 'The Importance of Social Intervention in Britain's Mortality Decline, c. 1850–1914: A Reinterpretation of the Role of Public Health', *Social History of Medicine*, Vol. I, No. 1, pp. 1–37.

Vallin, J. (1991), 'Mortality in Europe from 1720 to 1914: Long Term Trends and Changes in Patterns by Age and Sex', in R. Schofield, D. Reher and A. Bideau (eds), *The Decline of Mortality in Europe*, Oxford: Clarendon Press.

Wiener, M.J. (1985), *English Culture and the Decline of the Industrial Spirit 1850–1980*, Harmondsworth: Penguin.

Williamson, J.G. (1990), *Coping with City Growth During the British Industrial Revolution*, Cambridge: Cambridge University Press.

Wohl, A.S. (1983), *Endangered Lives: Public Health in Victorian Britain*, London: Methuen.

4

COMPETITIVENESS AND GROWTH

New perspectives on the late Victorian and Edwardian economy

David Greasley and Les Oxley

Introduction

A quarter century ago D. McCloskey observed that few beliefs are so well established in the credo of British economic history as the belief that the late Victorians failed (McCloskey 1970, p. 446). Subsequent debate has weakened the fundamentalism, but the search for a widely accepted characterization of Britain's economic performance during the late Victorian and Edwardian era has not yielded consensus. Indeed, entrenched images are hard to dislodge, and historical accounts of the late nineteenth century British economy remain dominated by discussions of failure (Floud 1994, p.1). Within these debates, optimistic interpretations of late Victorian performance have gained credence as the criteria for making judgements have been specified more carefully (Pollard 1989). This chapter seeks to strengthen further the basis for assessing performance by utilizing recent developments in econometric time series analysis to investigate the allegation that the late Victorians failed.

Modern time series methods may shed useful light on the central quantitative issues of whether or not the British economy experienced decline in the late nineteenth century relative either to past performance or to competing economies. The possibility of a British growth slowdown has been debated extensively since the pioneering work on the climacteric (Phelps Brown and Handfield Jones 1952). Uncertainty remains, partly because alternative estimates of GDP and the associated productivity measures show wide disparity for the pre-1914 period (Feinstein 1972; Greasley 1986). There are also doubts surrounding the validity of the statistical methods which have been used to describe the available data, and it is here that modern time series methods have a role to play. The issue of

Britain's comparative decline raises more complex questions. At a simple level, it cannot be contested that other industrial economies have grown more quickly since 1870. The important question of whether faster growth elsewhere was due to Britain's decline or to international economic convergence, associated, for example, with the spread of industrialization, can also be approached via modern time series analysis.

The next section introduces the time series methods used here to explore Britain's late Victorian and Edwardian economic performance. These methods are utilized initially to investigate the existence of slowdowns in the growth of British GDP, GDP per capita, GDP per worker, GDP per total factor input, and industrial production. To anticipate the results, we find no evidence of a climacteric prior to 1914, but the First World War does appear to break Britain's long-term growth trend, a discontinuity that we link to a sharp deterioration in industrial competitiveness in the immediate post-war years. Thereafter we consider how time series methods can be used to investigate the existence of international economic convergence or divergence, and examine British GDP per capita in comparison to that of France and the USA. Rather than pointing to Britain's decline, the results favour the existence of international convergence, although the pace appears protracted in the case of Britain and the United States.

Time series tests of economic performance

The modelling of economic time series has been powerfully influenced by the idea that the levels of most macroeconomic variables are non-stationary, suggesting random shocks permanently influence future output and employment levels (Nelson and Plosser 1982). In contrast, economic historians' investigations of Britain's late nineteenth-century performance have typically assumed that levels of GDP are stationary around the long-term trend, and that economic fluctuations are transitory in effect (Solomou 1994; Feinstein, Matthews and Odling-Smee 1983). Should the assumption of trend stationarity be invalid, the growth rate measures which underpin the discussion of both the climacteric and the late nineteenth-century business cycle would be rendered suspect (Greasley and Oxley 1995). Further, while modern time series methods typically find the levels of macroeconomic variable to be non-stationary, growth rates often appear stationary, and this perspective may shed useful light on the alleged slowdown in the trend growth of the late Victorian and Edwardian economy (Greasley 1992).

Output time series, denoted by y_t, which are non-stationary in levels have the property that random fluctuations influence future values of output, such that:

$$y_t = \mu + \alpha y_{t-1} + \varepsilon_t \tag{1}$$

Here non-stationarity implies that $\alpha = 1$; hence the current level of output y_t depends on the past value y_{t-1} and a random component ε_t, and output accumulates over time as a random process. Typically, time series analysis investigates whether or not differencing the data induces stationarity. In the case where the data are expressed in logarithmic form, and the first differences, $y_t - y_{t-1}$, are stationary, output will exhibit a constant rate of growth. Tests for stationarity thus offer a simple route to investigating possible slowdowns in late nineteenth-century economic and productivity growth which does not rest on growth rates estimated by assuming trend stationarity. Further, such tests do not involve pre-specifying possible turning points in trend growth, or identifying cyclical peaks to ensure comparable endpoints.

Tests for stationarity focus on the value of α in equation (1) (Dickey and Fuller 1981). Non-stationarity implies $\alpha = 1$, whereas for the trend stationary alternative, where the effects of output shocks are transient, $\alpha < 1$. The usual $t-$ ratios for testing the statistical significance of α are not distributed as Student's t, but as the Dickey-Fuller τ. Attempts to ascertain the stationary properties of pre-1914 British GDP series thus far have not yielded clear results, partly because of inconsistencies between the output, expenditure and income-side measures. The income and expenditure-side estimates appear to be non-stationary, and the output-side estimates stationary (Greasley and Oxley 1995). Further conflicting evidence arises with the average estimates, which combine income, expenditure and output data. For example, Feinstein's compromise series appears stationary whereas Solomou and Weale's balanced estimates appear non-stationary (Solomou and Weale 1991).

Time series tests utilizing pre-1914 GDP estimates do not yield a simple solution to whether or not the late Victorian or Edwardian British economy witnessed a growth slowdown. The income-side estimates, probably the most robust of the GDP series, do point to a constant growth rate, since in first difference form these data appear stationary (Greasley 1992). Alternatively, Feinstein's compromise series, the most widely deployed British GDP series, seemingly conforms to the trend stationary model, giving some validity to economic historians' traditional trend-cycle decomposition of late nineteenth-century economic growth. Further, utilizing a trend stationary perspective does not identify a singular representation of trend growth. On the basis of endpoint calculations there appears to be a marked slowdown in GDP growth of approximately 33 per cent around 1899 (Feinstein, Matthews and Odling-Smee 1983). Alternatively, from a similar trend stationary perspective, but on the basis of filtering techniques, the slowdown in GDP growth appears minimal, although each of these trend stationary approaches identifies an 1899 turning point (Crafts, Leybourne and Mills 1989).

To make progress in characterizing late nineteenth-century British economic performance requires a more satisfactory basis for establishing whether GDP levels are stationary or non-stationary. A finding of non-stationary levels would lead to simple tests for growth rate stationarity. However, if GDP levels are trend stationary, criteria would need to be defined to allow the timing and force of possible trend breaks to be investigated. The principal approach here involves extending the sample period over which the stationarity tests are conducted to 1856–1938. To anticipate, British GDP and GDP per capita, irrespective of the series used, appear trend stationary over this period, with breaks in trend growth apparent around the years of the First World War. Additionally, for the 1856–1913 period, we investigate the stationary properties of two productivity measures, GDP per worker and GDP per total factor input. The results for these productivity indicators, which point to constant pre-1914 growth rates, are invariant to the choice of GDP estimates, and shed light on important dimensions of late Victorian and Edwardian economic performance.

A central consideration in the conduct of stationarity tests concerns the possibility of structural breaks in the time series, the chance of which rises with the extension of sample size. Recent research highlights that non-stationarity may be erroneously accepted if there are discontinuities in the time series (Perron 1989, Rappoport and Reichlin 1989). The issue of structural breaks has resonance for the debates surrounding the existence of a British climacteric. If the British economy did experience a late nineteenth-century climacteric, stationarity tests would be biased towards finding non-stationarity and a constant rate of growth. Fortunately there are extensions to stationarity tests which allow the incorporation of possible structural breaks. Indeed such tests permit the timing of any discontinuities in economic growth to be investigated, and provide a valuable tool for examining the existence of the climacteric.

Extensions to stationarity tests incorporating structural breaks utilize dummy variable to assess the significance of possible discontinuities (Greasley and Oxley 1996c, 1998a). There are two commonly deployed strategies. One adopts prior historiographical information to identify likely breakpoints, and proceeds to test the significance of these (Perron 1989). Alternatively, searching procedures which investigate for possible breaks at every year in the sample period may be used (Christiano 1992, Zivot and Andrews 1992). If, following Perron, the breakpoints are pre-specified, equations A, B, and C form the basis of the stationarity tests. As with equation (1), non-stationarity implies $\alpha=1$, but the alternative hypothesis is now trend stationarity segmented by breaks:

$$y_t = \mu + \theta Du + \beta t + dD(TB) + \alpha y_{t-1} + \sum_{i=1}^{n} \delta \Delta y_{t-i} + \varepsilon_t \tag{A}$$

$$y_t = \mu + \beta t + \gamma DT^* + \alpha y_{t-1} + \sum_{i=1}^{n} \delta \Delta y_{t-i} + \varepsilon_t \tag{B}$$

$$y_t = \mu + \theta Du + \beta t + \gamma DT + dD(TB) + \alpha y_{t-1} + \sum_{i=1}^{n}\delta\Delta y_{t-i} + \varepsilon_t \quad (C)$$

where y is output; t a time trend;
$D(TB) = 1$ if $t = TB$, 0 otherwise;
$Du = 1$ if $t > TB$, 0 otherwise;
$DT^* = t - TB$, and $DT = t$ if $t > TB$ and 0 otherwise,
and TB refers to the time of the break.

Models A, B and C use the specified dummy variables to allow different forms of discontinuity to be incorporated into the tests. Model A incorporates the effects of a crash in which output falls (or rises if the effect is positive) in the year after the break and growth resumes at the previous rate from the lower (higher if the effect is positive) output level; model B a trend change in which the rate of growth accelerates (or decelerates) from the year after the break; and model C a joint crash and trend change which combines the two effects, when testing the non-stationary null hypothesis, $\alpha = 1$. Under the segmented trend alternative hypothesis, $\alpha < 1$, and significance is tested against the Perron critical values, which have larger absolute size than the Dickey-Fuller τ (Perron 1989).

Applying Perron's testing strategy requires the prior specification of breakpoint years. Zivot and Andrews favour an alternative approach based upon the recursive searching for discontinuities at every year within the sample period. They deploy dummies similar to Perron's to incorporate crash and trend breaks, but dispense with the single year dummy, $D(TB)$. Under the searching approach, critical values for testing the significance of α with breaks at any year are much greater in absolute value than Perron's, raising a stronger barrier to the rejection of non-stationarity and the identification of discontinuities. The approach here stresses the value of using prior historical information for specifying breakpoints. However, the recursive searching strategy does provide a useful check on the veracity of discontinuities established by a Perron-type approach.

Time series tests, once extended to incorporate possible structural breaks in the data, provide the evidence on the stationary properties of the pre-1914 GDP and productivity series necessary for a more robust characterization of British economic performance. These methods will also identify any breaks in trend growth, and thereby provide evidence on any British decline relative to past performance. Further, time series tests can be readily extended to investigate British performance compared to that of competing economies. Here the central issue is whether faster growth elsewhere stemmed from frailties in the British economy or from a process of convergence associated with the international spread of industrialization. Typically, the convergence hypothesis has been approached via cross-sectional tests which correlate initial income levels with growth rates, but there are some doubts about the robustness of these tests and time series alternatives have been developed (Bernard and Durlauf 1995).

Whether economies are converging or diverging can be assessed by considering the stationary properties of comparative GDP per capita series. Here we investigate British GDP per capita in relation to that both of the USA and France. Non-stationarity in the bivariate series implies that output fluctuations are not transmitted between each country, and that the two economies are diverging. Since non-stationarity means that shifts in comparative GDP per capita have permanent effect, it precludes convergence. Conversely, stationary comparative GDP per capita indicates catching-up or long-run convergence since the two economies will move together. The distinction between catching-up and long-run convergence relates to the process by which catching-up may lead to long-run convergence and long-term income equality.

To summarize, time series tests for convergence involve a two stage process. First, the stationarity tests show a tendency for either catching-up or divergence. Secondly, where the tests show stationary comparative GDP per capita and hence favour catching-up, the possibility of long-run convergence can be assessed by investigating the existence of a deterministic trend in the stationary series. The existence of a trend implies that the catching-up process remains incomplete and that long-run convergence has not been attained. To anticipate, the results from the bivariate comparisons of British GDP per capita in relation to both France and the USA, rather than suggesting British decline, favour the existence of convergence processes, though long-run convergence has not yet been attained.

Late Victorian and Edwardian performance in historical perspective

Assessments of late nineteenth century British economic performance typically focus on the related issues of GDP and productivity growth. The two indicators are closely intertwined, and accounts which emphasize slower economic growth generally highlight the retardation of productivity growth as the proximate cause, since labour and capital stock growth show less variability (Matthews *et al.* 1982). This perspective allows some progress to be made in gauging the record of pre-1914 GDP growth against previous experience despite the inconsistencies between the time series properties of the alternative estimates. Levels of GDP per worker, and GDP per total factor input (the weighted average of labour and the capital stock) appear non-stationary for the 1856–1913 period, irrespective of the GDP estimates utilized. The results in Table 4.1 adopt Feinstein's compromise GDP index as the numerator in the productivity series.

While the levels of both productivity indicators are non-stationary, their first differences, which approximate the growth rate since these data are

Table 4.1 Tests for the stationarity of British productivity, 1856–1913

	k	ADF
GDP per worker	1	−1.520
GDP per total input	0	−2.196

Note: ADF is the augmented Dickey-Fuller statistic, where the lowest degree of augmentation, k, yielding serially uncorrelated errors, is chosen. This practice is followed throughout. The data are in levels and from Feinstein (1972) and Greasley (1992).

expressed in logarithmic form, are stationary. On these results, the pre-1914 British economy did not experience a productivity climacteric. By implication, since slower productivity growth has been considered the most likely cause of slower GDP growth, British economic growth did not experience pre-1914 retardation. However, this interpretation depends on the robustness of stationarity tests, which may be fragile in the presence of structural discontinuities associated, for example, with a climacteric. Zivot and Andrews' searching procedures provide the simplest approach to investigating possible discontinuities within the period 1856–1913, since there is no reason to associate an endogenous growth slowdown with the events in any particular year. In effect searching methods look for significant trend breaks, crashes and combined crash and trend changes at each year within the sample period.

The results in Table 4.2 suggest the incorporation of structural breaks in the stationarity tests does not overturn the null hypothesis of non-stationarity. For GDP per worker the searching highlights 1885 as the year in which a trend break yields the largest absolute '*t*' statistic for model B, but the break is not significant at the 5 per cent level according to Zivot and Andrews' critical values. Nor are any significant crashes or combined crash and trend breaks revealed for GDP per worker. The extended tests also do not overturn the finding that pre-1914 levels of GDP per total factor input are non-stationary. Here the maximum absolute '*t*' value for a model B

Table 4.2 Tests for the stationarity of productivity 1856–1913

	k	crash	trend	crash and trend
GDP per worker	0	−3.826	−4.196	−4.254
		1872	1885	1883
GDP per total input	1	−4.385	−4.254	−4.221
		1902	1898	1897

Note: Only the maximum ADF statistic for each model, and the year it occurs, is reported.
Source: Zivot and Andrews (1992).

trend break occurs in 1898, but a trend break there, or crash and joint crash and trend breaks at any point in the sample do not overturn the non-stationarity in the levels data. The findings of constant British productivity growth over the 1856–1913 period appear robust, and cast doubt on the existence of a late Victorian or Edwardian climacteric.

More direct evidence on the possibility of a GDP growth slowdown can be gained by extending the sample period over which the stationarity tests are conducted. In Table 4.3 results are reported for two GDP indexes, industrial production, and GDP per capita for the period to 1938. In all cases the levels of the series appear non-stationary, and the growth rates constant. However, the possibility that structural breaks may disguise the true segmented trend stationary representation looms larger in the extended sample period since the British economy experienced a number of early twentieth century macroeconomic shocks, which may have dislocated growth trends (Greasley and Oxley 1996a, 1997). It might also be possible to identify a pre-1914 climacteric within a longer-term perspective.

A Perron-type approach to testing for the stationarity of output-based variables appears preferable for the period to 1938 since the historiography highlights a range of macroeconomic shocks which may have segmented trend growth. The First World War itself, by disrupting world trade, factor markets and technological progress, may have created discontinuity in industrial and economic growth (Ashworth 1960, Milward 1970). Post-war supply shocks around 1919–20 associated with reduced hours and lower productivity possibly further reduced British output and competitiveness (Dowie 1975, Broadberry 1990). Thereafter aggregate demand might have been adversely affected by the return to the gold standard in 1925 and the collapse of the USA's economy after 1929 (Keynes 1925, Eichengreen 1992). Elsewhere we have considered the impact each of these events had on the stationary properties of British industrial production over the period 1879–1938 (Greasley and Oxley 1996b). Industrial production appears to follow a segmented trend stationary process over these years with breaks around 1914 and 1920. In contrast the return to the gold standard in 1925, and the USA's crash after 1929, appear to have only transitory effect on Britain's industrial growth.

Table 4.3 Stationary tests for GDP, GDP per capita and industrial output, 1856–1938

	k	ADF
GDP (Feinstein)	1	−2.538
GDP (Greasley)	1	−2.470
GDP per capita (Feinstein)	6	−1.520
Industrial output	0	−3.358

These results for industrial production reinforce those for productivity by casting doubt on the existence of a pre-1914 climacteric. Industrial growth trends appear stable to the First World War, but the time series tests identify significant output crashes around 1914 and 1920, though trend growth also accelerates after 1920. Even so, a gap between actual industrial output, and that which would have been realized if pre-1914 trends had been maintained, persists until 1937. On these results it was the impact of the First World War, rather than late Victorian frailties, that caused a break in long-established industrial growth trends. It might be argued that the war exposed weaknesses in the late-Victorian and Edwardian industrial economy leading to the collapse of industrial production by the early 1920s. However, the output losses and the protracted post-war recovery appear more likely to stem from a loss of aggregate competitiveness arising in the war years rather than from earlier structural or technological weaknesses. Examination of the real exchange rate for the pound sterling illustrates this perspective.

On the basis of the conventionally deployed GNP deflators, British competitiveness shows little variation, at least with respect to the United States, over the half century from 1879; see Figure 4.1. British prices tend to rise faster than those of the United States to 1899, then fall relatively to 1913, shifts which are reflected in the real exchange rate given the nominal rate was fixed by the gold standard. By 1925 the real exchange rate was around 10 per cent above the 1913 level, but remained below the 1900 rate. These data do not suggest the British economy was experiencing a major competitiveness problem either before or after the First World War. The faster rise in British prices to 1899 was accompanied by some loss of world market share, whereas British exports grew strongly after 1900 in

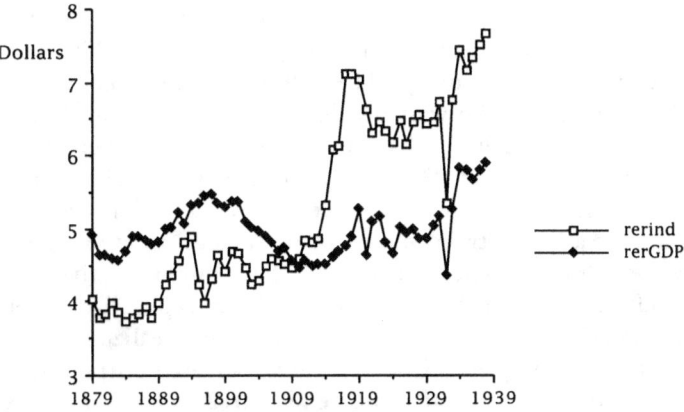

Figure 4.1 Sterling's real exchange rate.
Sources: Nominal exchange rates and national product deflators: Friedman and Schwartz (1982); industrial export prices: Lipsey (1960) and Feinstein (1972).

conjunction with improved competitiveness. From the pre-1914 experience a 10 per cent revaluation of sterling against the dollar by the 1920s ought not to have caused industrial collapse. What seems possible, however, is that the national product deflators grossly understate the loss of British industrial competitiveness around the years of the First World War (Wolcott 1993). Utilising industrial export prices, see Figure 4.1, the real exchange rate facing British industrialists was at least one-third above the 1913 level in the 1920s.

The implications of these real exchange rate movements for the debates surrounding late Victorian and Edwardian performance seem clear enough. The deterioration in British competitiveness against the dominant industrial economy of the twentieth century, the United States, chiefly occurred after 1914. Indeed the sterling–dollar real exchange rate utilizing industrial export prices may be represented as a segmented trend stationary process with the discontinuity arising during the First World War (Greasley and Oxley 1996b). The statistical results for competitiveness mirror those for industrial production, and cast further doubt on the existence of a pre-1914 climacteric. The suddenness and magnitude of the war-related loss of industrial competitiveness appear sufficient to explain post-war industrial collapse. Further, it does seem that the finding that the First World War caused the major discontinuity in British industrial growth carries over to GDP and GDP per capita.

The simplest approach to verifying that the First World War created the major discontinuity in British GDP growth during the 1856–1938 period utilizes the Zivot and Andrews' search procedure (1992), which tests for breaks in every year. The results in Table 4.4 also consider GDP per capita and industrial production. For GDP, incorporating breaks removes the apparent non-stationarity in the levels data irrespective of the index used. Models A and C, the crash, and combined crash and trend variants of the tests, give the highest absolute 't' value, and highlight the years of the First World War as the major discontinuity. The results for GDP per capita reinforce the evidence in favour of a wartime discontinuity. The most plausible interpretation of the statistics is that both GDP and GDP per capita crashed around the years of the First World War, but they then show little sign of faster growth from the lower post-war level before 1938. The absolute 't' values for the joint crash and trend model in both cases, though significant, are below those for the crash only model, highlighting that the principal wartime effect was a fall in GDP and GDP per capita. Reversion to pre-1914 GDP and GDP per capita trend growth was not realized during the interwar years. Nor was the magnitude of the war-related output crash trivial. GDP throughout the interwar years remained 24 per cent below levels that would have been realized if pre-war trends had been maintained.

The Zivot and Andrews type findings for industrial production over the 1856–1938 period correspond closely to the Perron-type results for the

Table 4.4 Tests for stationarity 1856–1938 (Zivot and Andrews' approach)

	k	Crash	Trend	Crash and trend
GDP (Feinstein)	2	−9.179*	−4.624*	−8.174*
		1918	1906	1918
GDP (Greasley)	2	−8.993*	−4.470*	−7.889*
		1918	1906	1918
GDP per capita	2	−8.076*	−5.014*	−7.516*
		1918	1901	1918
Industrial production	1	−4.888*	−3.807	−5.440*
		1915	1871	1915

* Denotes significant at the 5 per cent level based upon the critical values of Zivot and Andrews (1992).

shorter sample period. The First World War marks the break in the long-established industrial growth trend irrespective of the statistical approach deployed. In contrast to GDP and GDP per capita, industrial growth shows significant acceleration after the wartime crash. The joint crash and trend model C yields a higher absolute 't' value than the crash only model A, a finding which reinforces the Perron-type results showing faster post-1920 industrial growth. In a limited sense industry appears to do better than the wider economy between the world wars since by 1937 industrial output reaches levels that would also have been attained if the pre-1914 trend had continued. On a similar perspective, GDP never regains before 1938 the losses associated with the First World War crash. The lack of post-war trend reversion for GDP and GDP per capita explains why the model B trend change results appear to show significant pre-1913 slowdowns. If the significant wartime crash in GDP levels is excluded from the representation of trend growth, pre-1913 trends inevitably appear faster in the absence of post-war trend reversion. The model B trend change only results should not be taken as evidence in favour of a late Victorian or Edwardian climacteric.

The British economy viewed in comparison to previous performance did not experience late nineteenth-century decline. Rates of GDP, productivity and industrial output growth show no signs of pre-1913 slowdown, according to the time series test results reported here. In contrast, the years of the First World War witness major discontinuities both in Britain's competitiveness, and in economic and industrial growth. The statistical results point to a war-related output collapse creating a gap between actual industrial output, and that which would have been attained had the pre-war growth trend been sustained, persisting throughout the interwar years. Even more detrimental were the downward shifts in GDP and GDP per capita around the First World War, since these were never made good before the onset of the Second World War. The perspective on GDP trends emerging from the application of time series methods thus appears rather different from traditional accounts. Typically, British GDP growth trends have been portrayed as 'U' shaped with rates falling from 2.2 per cent per annum between 1856 and 1873 to 1.8 per cent per annum between 1873 and 1913, and then rising to 2.2 per cent per annum between 1924 and 1937 (Matthews *et al.* 1982). The results here place the late Victorian and Edwardian economy in better light, but offer a more pessimistic view of the interwar economy. GDP growth rates appear constant at 1.93 per cent per annum throughout the 1856–1938 period, but the similar post-1918 growth rate was from a 24 per cent lower base.

British economic performance in international perspective

By 1914 Britain had lost the pre-eminent position in the world economy established by the middle decades of the nineteenth century on the basis of its early industrial start. The spread of industrialization to western Europe, the United States and parts of Asia reduced Britain's share of world industrial production. In the cases of cotton, iron and coal, the 50–60 per cent shares of world output attained in the 1850s were reduced to 15–25 per cent shares by 1913 (Crouzet 1982). Britain's position in world trade held up more strongly, and income per capita remained well above the European average. Indeed, Britain was the largest exporter of manufactures, with a 30 per cent share of the world total in 1913, which may be compared to a 41 per cent share in 1880 (Saul 1965). Income per capita was 30–40 per cent above French and German levels in 1913, and the British lead over European incomes more generally exhibits no deterioration to 1913 (Bairoch 1982).

Assessing Britain's performance in international perspective raises complex issues, partly because the alternative indicators of production, competitiveness and prosperity show different pre-1914 patterns. More importantly, the spread of industrialization naturally created an element of catching-up by later starters. The central issue is whether Britain's loss of pre-eminence resulted from the operation of convergence forces within the world economy or from Britain's decline. These alternatives are investigated here by utilizing stationarity testing as a time series-based test of convergence. Here convergence implies that shifts in GDP per capita in one economy should be transmitted internationally (Oxley and Greasley 1995a and Greasley and Oxley 1998b, 1998c). By considering shifts in Britain's GDP per capita relative to that of France and the United States, these time series tests allow some progress to be made in establishing whether convergence forces can account for the loss of British pre-eminence.

If the relative GDP per capita time series, for example for Britain compared to France, is non-stationary, income per capita in the two economies will not converge. Non-stationarity implies that any divergence between GDP per capita in the two economies will infinitely persist. Alternatively, stationarity implies GDP per capita convergence via, for example, the effective transmission of productivity raising technological shocks. Time series tests for convergence thus use the stationary properties of relative GDP per capita time series to establish whether pairs or groups of economies are moving together or diverging. As well as distinguishing convergence and non-convergence, these tests also differentiate between the process of convergence, that is, catching-up, and long-run convergence which equates to per capita income equality.

Accordingly, Bernard and Durlauf (1996) formally offer two definitions of convergence, where τ_t denotes all information available at time t.

Definition 1. Convergence as catching-up. Countries i and j converge between dates t and T if the (log) per capita output, y, disparity at t is expected to decrease in value. If $y_{i,t} > y_{j,t}$,

$$E\left(y_{i,t+T} - y_{j,t+T} \mid \tau_t\right) < y_{i,t} - y_{j,t}$$

Definition 2. Convergence as equality of long-term forecasts at a fixed time. Countries i and j converge if the long-term forecasts of (log) per capita output, y, are equal at a fixed time t,

$$\lim_{k \to \infty} E\left(y_{i,t+k} - y_{j,t+k} \mid \tau_t\right) = 0$$

The two definitions have clear implications for the time series properties of comparative GDP per capita, and therefore lead to simple time series-based tests for convergence. As defined, tests of catching-up and long-run convergence hinge on the time series properties of $y_i - y_j$. The natural route for such tests involves the extension of Dickey-Fuller-type tests to the bivariate difference in log GDP per capita between pairs of countries, i and j:

$$y_{it} - y_{jt} = \mu + \alpha(y_{i,t-1} - y_{j,t-1}) + \beta t + \sum_{k=1}^{n} \delta \Delta(y_{i,t-k} - y_{j,t-k}) + \varepsilon_t \quad (2)$$

where y indicates the logarithm of GDP per capita. If the difference between the series is non-stationary, $\alpha = 1$, and GDP per capita in the two economies will diverge. Stationarity implies $\alpha < 1$, indicating either catching-up, if $\beta \neq 0$, or long-run convergence if $\beta = 0$.

The pioneering time series research on convergence utilizes GDP per capita estimates for fifteen countries over the 1900–87 period, and generally finds against the existence of convergence (Bernard and Durlauf 1995). Data for the European economies in the sample in comparison to France are illustrated as Figures 4.2 and 4.3. Among these European economies, on the basis of the pairwise time series tests defined by equation (2), only

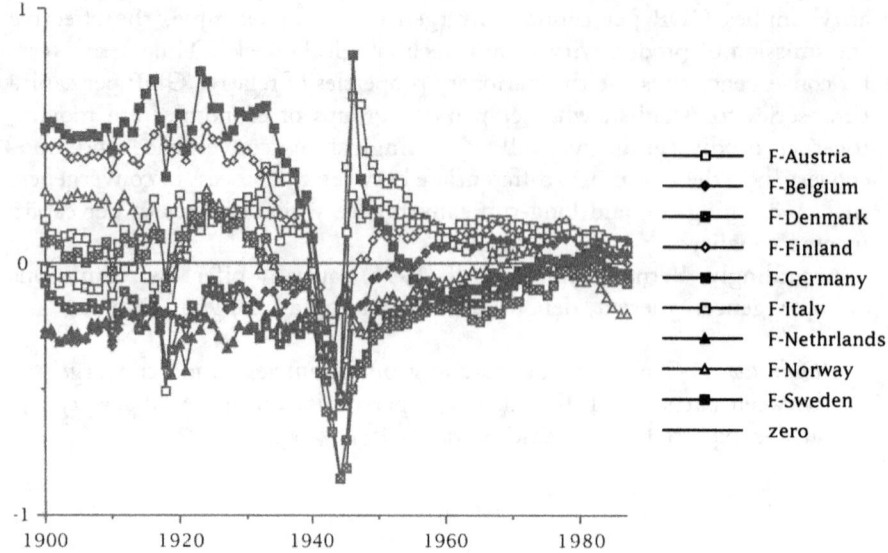

Figure 4.2 GDP per capita (relative to France).
Source: The data are from Bernard and Durlauf (1995).
Note: F denotes France, and zero corresponds to equal GDP per capita.

Austria, Italy and the Netherlands experience either catching-up or long-run convergence with France (Oxley and Greasley 1995b). Further, in comparison with the United States, only the results for Norway show catching-up. In general these pairwise findings support Bernard and Durlauf's multivariate results (1995), and appear to run counter to the idea of twentieth-century convergence within the world economy.

The results from the time series-based convergence tests have direct relevance to understanding British economic performance. Britain's GDP per capita appears non-stationary relative to that of France and the United States between 1900 and 1987. These findings suggest a pessimistic interpretation of Britain's economic performance in that the non-stationarity implies that the United States GDP per capita lead may persist, and that faster twentieth-century French GDP per capita growth does not stem from a process of convergence. However, there are important reservations surroundings the robustness of the time series findings which highlight non-stationarity and non-convergence. One of these concerns the sample period over which the tests are conducted, and another, the possibility that structural breaks in the data may disguise stationarity and convergence.

The two world wars and the intervening collapse of the international economy militated against convergence. The turbulence of the early twentieth-century decades may partly explain why results for a sample period

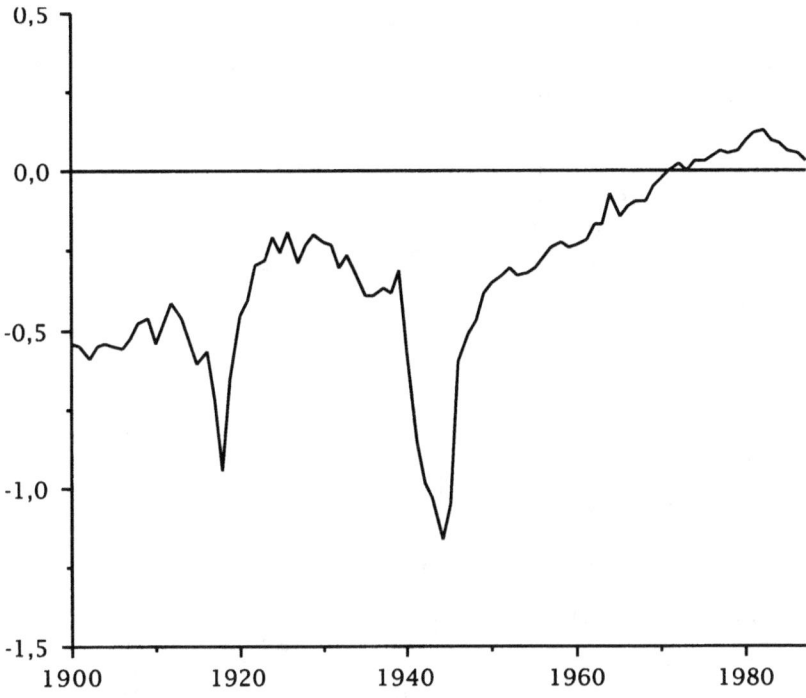

Figure 4.3 GDP per capita (France–Britain).

with a 1900 startpoint favour divergence. Convergence forces are likely to have been stronger between 1870 and 1914, given the extent of factor and commodity flows during these years (Williamson 1995). Extending the sample period over which the time series tests are conducted back to 1870 appears especially appropriate, given the chief interest here surrounds late Victorian and Edwardian economic performance. Equally relevant, since stationarity tests are fragile in the presence of structural discontinuities, is the possibility that the two world wars cause structural breaks in the convergence process. Time series convergence tests may be extended to incorporate possible discontinuities in the process by utilizing either Zivot and Andrews or Perron-type procedures.

The results in Table 4.5 consider the convergence of Britain's GDP per capita with that of the USA and France for various periods since 1870. None of these results favour the existence of convergence since non-stationarity cannot be rejected in any of the pairwise comparisons. Zivot and Andrews-type searching procedures provide the simplest approach to ascertaining whether or not the finding of non-convergence stems from the neglect of discontinuities. Macroeconomic shocks, for example those associated with the

Table 4.5 Stationarity tests for comparative GDP per capita

		k	ADF
Britain–France	1871–1913	0	–3.496
	1871–1938	0	–2.734
	1871–1987	1	–3.078
Britain–USA	1870–1913	0	–2.760
	1870–1938	0	–1.991
	1870–1992	0	–2.613

Table 4.6 Stationarity tests for comparative GDP per capita (Zivot and Andrews' methods)

		k	crash	trend	crash and trend
Britain–France	1871–1913	1	–4.359	–5.146*	–5.125*
			1906	1901	1901
	1871–1938	1	–5.120*	–3.276	–5.080*
			1918	1897	1921
	1871–1987	1	–3.683	–3.949	–5.236*
			1954	1942	1939
Britain–USA	1870–1913	3	–3.552	–2.614	–3.609
			1892	1896	1892
	1870–1938	3	–4.475	–4.364	–4.678
			1930	1926	1922
	1870–1992	3	–4.303	–4.828*	–5.342*
			1966	1950	1941

* Denotes significant at the 5 per cent level.

world wars, would need to have a different impact in each economy to segment the process of convergence, which makes the prior identification of possible breakpoints problematical. The Zivot and Andrews-type results in Table 4.6 do overturn the finding of non-convergence in GDP per capita, in both the USA and France pairwise comparisons with Britain.

Britain's performance compared to France shows dissimilarities from that relative to the United States where the process of convergence appears protracted. In each of the three sample periods, 1871–1913, 1871–1938 and 1871–1987, the British–French GDP per capita relativity appears stationary. These results consistently favour the catching-up version of the convergence hypothesis since the comparative stationary series do contain significant time trends. The timing and nature of the discontinuities in the convergence process are different for each of the sample periods. The 1871–1913 results indicate a faster rate of French catching-up after 1901, since the trend change only model B gives the highest absolute '*t*' value in this year. In the longer sample periods the effects of the two world wars are the principal sources of discontinuity in the convergence process. For the 1871–1938 period the crash only model A yields the highest absolute 't' value in 1918, whereas the impact of the Second World War appears rather different in that the joint crash and trend model C with a 1939 breakpoint dominates over the 1871–1987 period, highlighting the greater strength of the post-Second World War convergence process. Generally, however, the results suggest that the British and French economies have been on converging paths throughout the twentieth century. Elsewhere, once the effects of discontinuities are incorporated, we show that the French economy has been converging with most of the continental European economies, shown in Figure 4.2, during the twentieth century, and so, by implication, has the British economy (Oxley and Greasley 1995b).

Britain's performance relative to the USA exhibits a different pattern. The USA's GDP per capita first exceeded the British level in 1879, and subsequent to the stronger British performance in the 1890s, surged ahead to global leadership during the early decades of the twentieth century (Greasley and Oxley 1998a). In the periods 1870–1913 and 1870–1938, the incorporation of possible discontinuities does not overturn the non-stationarity in comparative British–USA GDP per capita. The absence of pre-Second World War convergence points to the likelihood of singular early twentieth-century advantages for the USA, notably those associated with mass markets, abundant natural resources and tariff barriers, giving rise to distinctive organizational and technological innovation. To the extent that the origins of the USA's ascendency pre-dates the First World War, the basis for her twentieth-century pre-eminence does not appear to stem simply from disruption to the European economy and the convergence process resulting from the world wars. Over the 1870–1992 period convergence between the British and the US economies can be observed in the time series properties of relative GDP per capita, with a tendency towards British catching-up apparent in the post-Second World War years.

Concluding remarks

New developments in econometric time series analysis offer the opportunity for a fresh look at the economic performance of late Victorian and Edwardian Britain, both in relation to the earlier record and to experience elsewhere. The time series results reported here run counter to the idea of British decline. British GDP and productivity growth appear, on the basis of the stationarity test results, constant over the period 1856–1913. In longer-term perspective it was the effects of the First World War that disrupted long-established British growth trends. A wartime macroeconomic shock, rather than late Victorian structural, organisational, entrepreneurial or technological weaknesses, segmented long-term British economic growth. In contrast to traditional views, the statistical results here place the late

Victorian and Edwardian economy in better light, but offer a more pessimistic impression of the interwar economy. The origins of the depressed interwar economy appear to stem from a general and sudden collapse of competitiveness following the First World War. British GDP growth, according to the time series test results, was constant at 1.93 per cent per annum over the 1856–1938 period. However, the long-term growth trend was dislocated by the effects of the First World War. Levels of British GDP throughout the interwar years remained 24 per cent below those that would have been realized had the pre-1913 growth path not been segmented by the effects of the war.

Assessing British economic performance in international perspective raises more complex issues, but these too have been investigated using modern time series methods. The crux of the comparative decline debate centres on whether faster growth elsewhere was due to British failure or to a catching-up process associated with the spread of industrialization through the world economy. Time series-based tests shed light on this issue by using the stationarity properties of comparative GDP per capita series to ascertain whether economies are converging or diverging. The results here point to the convergence of British GDP per capita with that of France and the USA. The process of Britain's convergence with the USA does appear protracted. Nevertheless, the distinctive advantages favouring the USA's economy during the early decades of the twentieth century are eroded in the years after the Second World War. In contrast, convergence forces within the European economy are apparent throughout the years since 1870. Faster growth in France, and other European economies, in the twentieth century, on the basis of the time series test results reported here, arose from a process of convergence rather than from Britain's decline.

References

Ashworth, W. (1960), *An Economic History of England 1870–1939*, London: Methuen.

Bairoch, P. (1982), 'International Industrialization Levels from 1750–1980', *Journal of European Economic History*, 11, pp. 269–334.

Bernard, A.B. and Durlauf, S.N. (1995), 'Convergence in International Output', *Journal of Applied Econometrics*, 10, pp. 97–108.

Bernard, A.B. and Durlauf, S.N. (1996), 'Interpreting Tests of the Convergence Hypothesis', *Journal of Econometrics*, 71, pp. 161–74.

Broadberry, S.N. (1990), 'The Emergence of Mass Unemployment: Explaining Macroeconomic Trends in Britain during the Trans-World War 1 Period', *Economic History Review*, 2nd ser., 43, pp. 271–82.

Christiano, L.J. (1992), 'Searching for a Break in GNP', *Journal of Business and Economic Statistics*, 10, pp. 237–50.

Crafts, N.C.R., Leybourne, S.J. and Mills, T.C. (1989), 'The Climacteric in Late Victorian Britain and France: A Reappraisal of the Evidence', *Journal of Applied Econometrics*, 4, pp. 103–17.

Crouzet, F. (1982), *The Victorian Economy*, London: Methuen.

Dickey, D.A. and Fuller, W.A. (1981), 'Likelihood Ratio Tests for Autoregressive Time Series with a Unit Root', *Econometrica*, 49, pp. 1057–72.
Dowie, J.R. (1975),'1919–20 is in Need of Attention', *Economic History Review*, 2nd ser., 28, pp. 429–50.
Eichengreen, B. (1992), 'The Origins and Nature of the Great Slump Revisited', *Economic History Review*, 2nd ser., 45, pp. 213–39.
Feinstein, C.H. (1972), *National Income, Expenditure and Output of the United Kingdom, 1855–1965*, Cambridge: Cambridge University Press.
Feinstein, C.H., Matthews, R.C.O. and Odling-Smee, J.C. (1983), 'The Timing of the Climacteric and its Sectoral Incidence in the U.K. 1873–1913', in C.P. Kindleberger and G. di Tella (eds), *Economics in the Long View*, London: Clarendon Press.
Floud, R. (1994), 'Britain 1860–1914: A Survey', in R. Floud and D. McCloskey (eds), *The Economic History of Britain since 1700*, 2nd edn, vol. 2, *1860–1939*, Cambridge: Cambridge University Press.
Friedman, M. and Schwartz, A. (1982), *Monetary Trends in the United States and the United Kingdom, 1870–1970*, Chicago: Chicago University Press.
Greasley, D. (1986), 'British Economic Growth: The Paradox of the 1880s and the Timing of the Climacteric', *Explorations in Economic History*, 23, pp. 416–44.
Greasley, D. (1992), 'The Stationarity of British Economic and Productivity Growth', *Journal of Applied Econometrics*, 7, pp. 203–9.
Greasley, D. and Oxley, L. (1995), 'Balanced Versus Compromise Estimates of UK GDP, 1870–1913', *Explorations in Economic History*, 32, pp. 262–72.
Greasley, D. and Oxley, L. (1996a), 'Technological Epochs and British Industrial Production, 1700–1992', *Scottish Journal of Political Economy*, 43, pp. 258–74.
Greasley, D. and Oxley, L. (1996b), 'Discontinuities in Competitiveness: The Impact of the First World War on British Industry', *Economic History Review*, 2nd. ser., 49, pp. 83–101.
Greasley, D. and Oxley, L. (1996c), 'Explaining the United States Industrial Growth, 1860–1991: Endogenous Versus Exogenous Models', *Bulletin of Economic Research*, 48, pp. 65–82.
Greasley, D. and Oxley, L. (1997), 'Unit Roots and British Industrial Growth, 1923–92', *Manchester School*, 65, pp. 192–212.
Greasley, D. and Oxley, L. (1998a), 'Comparing British and American Economic and Industrial Performance 1860–1993: A Time Series Perspective', *Explorations in Economic History*, 35, pp. 171–95.
Greasley, D. and Oxley, L. (1998b), 'A Tale of Two Dominions: Comparing the Macreconomic Records of Australia and Canada since 1870', *Economic History Review*, 51, pp. 294–318.
Greasley, D. and Oxley, L. (1998c), 'Time Series Based Tests of the Convergence Hypothesis: Some Positive Results', *Economics Letters*, 56, pp. 143–7.
Keynes, J.M. (1925), *The Economic Consequences of Mr. Churchill*, London: L. and V. Woolf.
Lipsey, G.R. (1960), 'The Relation between Unemployment and the Rate of Change of Money Wage Rates in the United Kingdom, 1862–1957: A Further Analysis, *Economica*, 27, pp. 1–31.
McCloskey, D. (1970), 'Did Victorian Britain Fail?', *Economic History Review*, 2nd. ser., 23, pp. 446–59.
Matthews, R.C.O., Feinstein, C.H. and Odling-Smee, J.C. (1982), *British Economic Growth, 1856–1973*, Oxford: Clarendon Press.
Milward, A.S. (1970), *The Economic Effects of the World Wars on Britain*, London: Macmillan.
Nelson, C.R. and Plosser, C.I. (1982), 'Trends and Random Walks in Economic Time Series', *Journal of Monetary Economics*, 10, pp. 139–62.

Oxley, L. and Greasley, D. (1995a), 'A Time Series Perspective on Convergence: Australia, UK, and USA since 1870', *Economic Record*, 71, pp. 250–70.

Oxley, L. and Greasley, D. (1995b), 'Convergence in International Output: Some Alternative Results', working paper, University of Edinburgh.

Perron, P. (1989), 'The Great Crash, the Oil Price Shock, and the Unit Root Hypothesis', *Econometrica*, 99, pp. 1361–401.

Phelps Brown, E.H. and Handfield Jones, S.J. (1952), 'The Climacteric of the 1890s: A Study in the Expanding Economy', *Oxford Economic Papers*, 4, pp. 266–307.

Pollard, S. (1989), *Britain's Prime and Britain's Decline, 1870–1914*, London: Edward Arnold.

Rappoport, P. and Reichlin, L. (1989), 'Segmented Trends and Non-Stationary Time Series', *Economic Journal*, 99, Supplement, pp. 168–77.

Saul, S.B. (1965), 'The Export Economy 1870–1914', *Yorkshire Bulletin of Economic Research*, 17, pp. 5–18.

Solomou, S. (1994), 'Economic Fluctuations, 1870–1913', in R. Floud and D. McCloskey (eds), *The Economic History of Britain since 1700*, 2nd edn, vol. 2, 1860–1939, Cambridge: Cambridge University Press.

Solomou, S. and Weale, M. (1991), 'Balanced and Compromise Estimates of UK GDP 1870–1913', *Explorations in Economic History*, 28, pp. 54–63.

Williamson, J.G. (1995), 'The Evolution of Global Labor Markets since 1830: Background Evidence and Hypotheses', *Explorations in Economic History*, 32, pp. 141–96.

Wolcott, S. (1993), 'Keynes versus Churchill: Revaluation and British Unemployment in the 1920s', *Journal of Economic History*, 53, pp. 601–22.

Zivot, E. and Andrews, D.W.K. (1992), 'Further Evidence on the Great Crash, the Oil Price Shock, and the Unit Root Hypothesis', *Journal of Economic and Business Statistics*, 10, pp. 251–87.

5

FLAGGING OR FAILING? BRITISH ECONOMIC PERFORMANCE, 1880–1914

B.W.E. Alford

I

The hypothesis that the roots of Britain's relative economic decline in the twentieth century are to be found in the period between 1880 and 1914 involves a number of conceptual and analytical problems. To begin with it implies a later and pronounced experience of decline; in turn, this raises questions of how and when it became a fully developed process. There is, it is true, a substantial body of literature which examines this issue in terms of Britain's comparative international economic development over the past century, with particular focus on the period since 1945. But in this debate the proponents of decline have been vigorously challenged by those who claim that, within a particular group of countries that possess the necessary 'social capabilities', economic development is a process of 'catch-up and convergence', and that over the longer term Britain is as well placed in the economic firmament as those countries with which it is frequently unfavourably compared.[1] In the present context it is not possible to engage in this broader discussion. Accordingly, this chapter will concentrate on the more limited question of whether, between 1880 and 1914, it can be argued that Britain was failing to hold its own in the world economy; whether, in that period at least, it experienced the beginnings of economic decline.

No assessment of economic performance can be value free. Growth accounting, in particular, is frequently cast in an air of historical neutrality, but any interpretation of the data – beyond statistical description in terms of scale or degree – involves value judgements. For example, the rate of growth of GDP may increase during a given period yet in what sense this constitutes a welfare gain depends on explicit or implied judgements on the equity of the distribution of the increase. The impression of neutrality is frequently reinforced by the fact that such data are presented as averages for the whole economy. But this is a form of abstraction: gain or loss, rise or decline, can only be judged from a particular standpoint and, most realistically, this has to be in terms of carefully defined groups in society. Hence, one group's decline may be the means of another's rise. The problem is how the balance is to be struck. And, of course, many aspects of welfare, both positive and negative, are unquantifiable, so that measurable economic performance is thus a somewhat narrow concept.

The quantitative assessment of performance resolves into a distinction between absolute and relative achievement. So far as absolute measures of economic performance are concerned, the picture is clear. On all the usual indicators the trend of income has been consistently upwards since well before 1880. Indeed, this has been a common feature among the so-called advanced economies. At the same time, there have been fluctuations around the trend including some periods of marked absolute decline, as in the early 1930s for example. And whilst all groups in society have gained in these terms, at least until the very recent period, the pattern has been somewhat uneven.

Relative performance is quite another matter. It is easy to demonstrate, by means of a variety of economic indicators, that the relative positions of nations and of distinguishable groups within nations have changed significantly over the past century. As with the concept of relative deprivation as a measure of poverty, however, the question is in what sense does failure to keep up amount to decline. The problem can be illustrated in family terms. Thus we can imagine a middle-class family in the late nineteenth century which subsequently experienced a gradual change in its social position, so that by the late twentieth century the occupations of its members placed the family firmly in the working class, as defined. Yet, at the same time, it can be assumed (not unrealistically) that during the period real wages increased to an extent that the working class descendants enjoy a higher measurable income than their late Victorian middle-class forebears. For all that, it can be suggested that it is a fair observation that the family has experienced not only social decline but, also, economic decline. The experience of nations may be similarly judged.

II

The main statistical indicators of Britain's comparative economic performance between 1820 and 1913 are provided by Tables 5.1 to 5.4.

These data come with the usual warning that they are subject to significant margins of error. In particular, there are substantial index number problems involved in combining separate series for individual industries and sectors into composite series, whilst comparative calculations present thorny problems of how to convert prices and output data for individual countries into common units of measurement.[2] In the latter respect, for example, pre-1914 indices of output rely heavily on measures of physical

Table 5.1 United Kingdom: average annual rates of growth of GDP, 1820–1913 (at constant prices)

	I	II
1820–1870	2.0	na
1856–1913	na	1.9
1882–1913	1.8	1.8
1856–1873	na	2.2
1873–1882	1.9	1.8
1882–1899	2.2	2.2
1899–1913	1.3	1.4

Sources: I A. Maddison, *Dynamic Forces in Capitalist Development* (Oxford: 1991), Tables A5, A6, pp. 207, 210–11; II B.R. Mitchell, *British Historical Statistics* (Cambridge: 1988), p. 836.

Table 5.2 Comparative rates of growth of GDP, 1870–1913 (% per year: annual averages)

	Real GDP	Real GDP per head
UK	1.9	1.0
USA	3.9	1.8
France	1.5	1.3
Germany	2.8	1.6
Italy	1.9	1.3
Japan	2.3	1.4

Source: Maddison, *op. cit.*, pp. 49–50.

Table 5.3 Average annual growth rates of GDP per worker-year in the United Kingdom compared with six other industrial countries

	1873–99	1899–1913
United Kingdom	1.2	0.5
USA	1.9	1.3
Sweden	1.5	2.1
France	1.3	1.6
Germany	1.5	1.5
Italy	0.3	2.5
Japan	1.1	1.8

Source: R.C.O. Matthews, C.H. Feinstein and J.C. Odling-Smee, *British Economic Growth 1856–1973* (Oxford: 1982), p. 31. In relation to the sources listed there some revisions have subsequently been made, but they do not seriously affect the overall picture. See C.H. Feinstein, 'What Really Happened to Real Wages? Trends in Wages, Prices and Productivity in the United Kingdom, 1880–1913', *Econ. Hist. Rev.*, 43 (1990), 329–55.

Table 5.4 Levels of GDP per head of population, 1870 and 1913 (USA=100)

	1870	1913
Austria	76	66
Belgium	107	78
Canada	66	79
Denmark	78	71
Finland	45	37
France	76	65
Germany	78	72
Italy	60	47
Japan	30	25
Netherlands	107	74
Norway	53	43
Sweden	68	58
Switzerland	88	79
UK	133	95
USA	100	100

Source: A. Maddison, *Monitoring the World Economy 1820–1992*, (Paris: 1995) pp. 23–4.

output as against the value of output. This method thus makes no allowance for differences in quality within the same nominal categories of goods and for changes in quality over time.

In broad terms, three features stand out in the above tables. The UK was comparatively slow-growing over a long period; there was a distinct downturn in performance at the turn of the century, as measured by the growth of GDP and GDP per worker-year; UK GDP per head remained close to that of the USA, the highest in the world in 1914. This last feature, however, reflects the longer growth experience of the UK in comparison with other countries.

A more differentiated analysis of Britain's comparative performance has been attempted by Broadberry who concentrates on measuring productivity change in manufacturing.[3] The thrust of Broadberry's analysis is the consistency, or stationarity, of differences in manufacturing productivity between the UK, the USA and Germany from the late nineteenth century up to the present day; and this carries the strong implication that the explanation of any differences in overall economic performance between these economies has to be sought in the non-manufacturing sectors. Space does not allow a critical appraisal of this broad claim but it is necessary to examine the data in a little detail as they relate to the period under consideration.[4]

For a start, these calculations are subject to the kinds of problems already outlined, and the reliance on physical output measures is particularly hazardous.[5] For example, Broadberry himself refers to significant differences in the quality of capital goods, when he analyses comparative technical change in Britain and the USA; but he does not explicitly make the connection between this and the fact that capital goods are a significant part of manufacturing output. The index-number problems, in relation to the weighting of industries in the composite index of output, have already been noted, but in this case of major concern is the fact that the chosen base year is either 1935 or 1937. For a variety of reasons these were hardly typical years for Britain, Germany or the USA. Consequently, it could be that productivity per person employed in the UK was significantly above trend in that year because of the high levels of unemployment in the staple industries, with low productivity units having gone out of production. Adjusting for this difference could make the productivity figures for manufacturing (Table 5.5) more consistent with the estimates of GDP per worker for the whole economy, which present a distinctly different picture (Table 5.6). It is thus necessary to examine in detail the situation in the other comparator economies before any firm reliance can be placed on these base years.

What is significant for our purpose is that, whilst the series exhibit a high degree of stationarity over the long term, there have been substantial swings in comparative productivity for sustained periods within it, as Broadberry points out.[6] It follows that it is unwise to interpret productivity measures in isolation from the level of activity in the economy, as the experience of Britain in the 1980s exemplifies. In that period, productivity in manufacturing rose sharply but output actually fell because of a sharp fall in the level of employment. The point to be made is that such swings of productivity levels indicate the need to pay close attention to the trends in output growth as against fluctuations in output from year to year. In this respect the experiences of the UK and the USA in the inter-war period, for example, were very different. It further follows that the explanation of the recorded differences between GDP per worker for the whole economy over the long period (in the USA, the UK and Germany) and GDP per worker in manufacturing industry, may not have to be sought in the non-manufacturing sectors to the extent that Broadberry suggests (see Table 5.6).

Table 5.5 Manufacturing output per person employed (United Kingdom=100)

	US/UK	*Germany/UK*
1889	195.4	94.7
1899	194.8	99.0
1907	192.0(201.9)	106.4
1913	212.9	119.0

Source: S.N. Broadberry, *op. cit.*
Note: The figure in brackets is based on actual census of production data for that year. The main series are based on extrapolations from 1935 or 1937 production census data.

Table 5.6 Alternative estimates of GDP per person employed (United Kingdom=100)

	I		II	
Year	US/UK	Germany/UK	US/UK	Germany/UK
1870	95.1	47.8	105.9	48.8
1890	98.1	52.3	109.2	53.4
1913	127.9	62.9	142.4	64.1

Source: Broadberry, op. cit., p. 777.
Notes
I = Paasch-type purchasing power parity rates of exchange (PPP)
II = Fisher-type PPPs.

Taken at their face value, these measures of productivity in manufacturing, in common with those cited earlier, show such 'substantial swings' with a marked break around the turn of the century. German productivity rose quite sharply from 99 per cent to 119 per cent of the UK level between 1899 and 1913. The increase in the US position is substantially less but still significant. Moreover, the benchmark comparison for the UK and the USA for 1907, based on actual production censuses for that year, shows a significant difference from the figure in the series which is based on backward extrapolation from 1937 data. This discrepancy must be taken as an indication of a wide margin of error in the data. To what extent the broader pattern of the series is misleading, it is impossible to say; but for this period at least it is in line with the other major economic indicators that have been cited.

III

It is clear that Britain's comparative position in the international economy was not maintained between the late nineteenth century and the First World War. The question is whether this change added up to a failure of economic performance. The strongest case mounted to exonerate Britain from such a charge has been based on a neo-classical model of entrepreneurship and technical change. The literature is well known and, therefore, our comments will concentrate on the salient points.[7] The thrust of the argument is that the performance of the economy was consistent with rational decisions by entrepreneurs, given resource endowments and relative factor prices. The proof relies on a comparative analysis of Britain and the USA, with the implication that the latter set the standard. If labour *relative* to capital was cheaper in the UK than in the USA, it was rational for the British to choose more labour intensive techniques compared with their US counterparts. Within these constraints, it is claimed, Britain was technologically efficient though necessarily with lower productivity than the USA.

The weakness of this analysis, as many commentators have pointed out, is that it is a slave to the unrealistic assumptions of neo-classical economics. In particular it assumes perfect substitution between factors of production and constant returns to scale. Even so, it might be argued, when due allowance is made for these criticisms, this analysis still offers a reasonably accurate picture of reality. There are, however, two fundamental objections to this proposition. First, the economy of the period was far from operating at full employment. A pronounced feature of the labour market was a significant degree of under-employment. For whatever reasons (and we shall return to this point) the Victorian and Edwardian economies were not pushing at the limits of their resources, and to this extent there was a margin of forgone economic growth. Secondly, and more importantly, the analysis of relative factor prices is over-simplified. Even under neo-classical assumptions, comparative choice of technique (capital intensive or labour intensive) is not something that can be identified by reference to relative factor prices taken in isolation. The rational choice of technique will depend on the *degree* of the relative differences in factor prices, given the relative physical productivities of alternative techniques. Thus Arthur Lewis was able to show that by applying plausible assumptions as to relative factor prices in Britain and the USA to the basic neo-classical model, it would have been rational for Britain to have adopted capital intensive techniques, since the gain in physical productivity when multiplied by the relatively higher capital cost would still have resulted in lower average *unit* costs than the average unit costs, for the same level of output, of the labour intensive techniques actually employed. The assumptions as to relative factor prices can be adjusted to show at what point this result would cease to hold, and this requires a level of wages significantly below what is historically plausible. In short, the critical factor is by *how much* is labour relatively cheaper than capital.[8] So, why did Britain persist with comparatively labour intensive techniques?

The neo-classical model carries the implicit assumption that technology was homogeneous between Britain and the USA. But this assumption does not hold. The choice of technology was not just the outcome of relative factor prices, translated into unit costs of output on the basis of a standard mechanical specification. The application of a technology cannot be thus self-contained; it is part of a production and distribution process. The fact is that British firms were unable to operate a given technique with the same degree of efficiency as their American counterparts. One obvious element in this difference was the nature of labour organization. The US labour market was more competitive and much less subject to craft practices and manning restrictions than that in Britain. In broader terms, there were significant differences in the quality of human capital.[9] The British labour force probably contained a significantly higher proportion of skilled shopfloor workers than that of the USA. By contrast, at middle and higher levels of management and technical personnel, the reverse was the case.

Thus it is only when such elements are added into the equation that Britain's choice of techniques can be defined as rational. But it was rationality bounded by the heterogeneity of applied technology with the consequence of lower levels of productivity than were achievable in terms of best practice.

A variant model which might appear to get round some of these difficulties defines relative costs in terms of machine and human capital. Technical progress becomes endogenous and follows a path determined by a learning process that seeks to maintain a competitive position for an economy based on its factor endowments. Thus, on the assumption that skilled labour (human capital) was cheap relative to machine capital in Britain as compared with the USA, this resulted in the adoption in Britain of comparatively intensive human capital techniques. If at some point this process leads to US machine capital intensive technology becoming superior at all factor prices, then British firms will not be able to compete with US technology and will have to search for new techniques that can be applied within their resource and factor endowments.

This rationalization of comparative patterns of technical change represents an advance on the cruder form of the neo-classical model but it is still fundamentally unsatisfactory. First, as with the basic form, it is far too reductionist to provide a useful approximation to reality. Machine capital might reasonably be lumped into one category with the prevailing rate of interest being taken as a measure of its cost. Human capital, however, involves a range of skills operating at different levels of the labour market for which a given wage rate is a far from adequate proxy of cost. Furthermore, the models themselves are economy-wide abstractions that cannot capture the dynamics of economic growth which spring from technical change at the level of the sector, industry or firm.

Secondly, both analyses are essentially static in nature because they begin at the point where resources and factor endowments are given. Whilst things are what they are this does not directly provide the explanation of how they come to be so or why they should remain so. The crucial point is that resource and factor endowments (including the quality of entrepreneurship) are not God-given, though the former may prove more intractable than the latter, especially in the early forms of industrialization which were based on rudimentary technologies. The fact is, however, that the pattern of technological advance in the nineteenth century required corresponding improvements in the quality of human capital. Thus, to paraphrase a leading historian of technology, today's technical change possibilities are dependent on yesterday's actions in conditioning the quality of factor endowments.[10] The second model half recognizes this problem but, in effect, it fudges the issue. On the one hand, it is a static model to the extent that it claims that new techniques will not be sought in human capital intensive technologies until they become inferior to machine capital technologies at all relative factor costs. On the other hand, it incorporates a learning process as competitive conditions change, and it is difficult to see how this can be achieved without concurrent changes in resource and factor-price conditions. The real issue is not that certain conditions existed and therefore certain consequences followed, but one of why did those conditions exist. It is the difference between description and explanation.

A country's economic performance is not, however, simply the outcome of the supply of goods and services. It is the product of supply and demand conditions, though these are often difficult to disentangle. In particular, the pattern of income distribution has direct effects on the pattern of resource use. And demand conditions are no more God-given than those of supply, though the values they incorporate may well reflect the nature of the prevailing belief in God. In the late nineteenth century this belief was well imbued with the sense that a properly ordered society was one in which the rich man dwelt in his castle with the poor man at his gate; convictions that certainly had demand effects.

In sum, attempts by cliometric historians to elevate British businessmen of the late Victorian period from damnation to redemption by means of the devices of neo-classical economic analysis are not convincing. Alternatively, there is good reason to adopt at least a sceptical view of Britain's changing position in the world economy.

IV

To begin with, it is necessary to examine briefly some additional evidence on British economic performance and competitiveness during the period.

Comparative levels of capital formation are shown in Table 5.7. There are well-known difficulties in interpreting data of this type: the level of investment tells us nothing about the efficiency of capital use; the relationship between investment and growth may be either one of cause or effect; capital formation is related to a country's stage of economic development and to variations in capital/output ratios between sectors of the economy; and, finally, these data do not include human capital. This said, there is ample evidence to confirm that within reasonable tolerances there is a close positive association between levels of investment and rates of economic growth. Table 5.7 is, therefore, highly suggestive. Whilst it might be claimed that higher levels of capital formation in countries in comparison with the UK, in the period up to 1900, can be accounted for by the need to build up capital stock in the early phases of industrialization, such an explanation becomes far less persuasive for the subsequent period because of the level of industrial development that had by then been achieved. Furthermore, these countries had become accustomed to these higher levels of savings and investment over nearly half a century, and this was reflected in the institutional forms established in finance and business which were in sharp contrast to those which had grown up in Britain over a much longer period and which were based on accustomed low rates of capital accumulation. To the extent, therefore, that the development of advanced economies depended on increasingly capital intensive technologies, requiring higher investment ratios to sustain higher rates of growth and correspondingly higher absolute levels of income, there are clear signs that by 1914 Britain was falling behind the field.

A central test of an economy's competitiveness is its export performance but here, too, interpretation of the evidence requires care. See Table 5.8. At least part of the decline in Britain's overall position can be seen as reflecting the process of expansion in the world economy. More significant is the decline in its share of world exports of manufactured goods. But here, also, similar considerations apply, and it is worth noting that in proportionate terms Britain was still better placed than France. If, however, trade in manufactured goods is broken down into fast- and slow-growing sectors, Britain's position appears far less satisfactory, even in relation to France. See Table 5.9.

These trends correspond to the steady swing towards Empire markets. In 1870 the Empire absorbed 23 per cent of British exports; by 1914 this share had grown to 35 per cent. Moreover, the principal goods in this trade

Table 5.7 Comparative capital formation proportions late nineteenth to early twentieth century (% of GNP)

	Gross domestic capital formation	Capital exports or imports (−)	Gross national capital formation
United Kingdom			
1880–99	8.4	3.9	12.3
1900–14	8.7	5.3	14.0
Germany			
1871–90	18.9	2.1	21.0
1890–1913	23.0	1.1	24.1
Italy			
1881–1900	10.8	0.0	10.8
1901–10	15.9	1.4	17.3
Sweden			
1881–1900	11.2	−1.6	9.6
1901–20	13.1	−0.5	12.6
United States			
1869–88	20.6	−0.9	19.7
1889–1908	21.4	0.5	21.9
Japan			
1887–1906	10.1	−2.1	8.0
1907–26	14.1	−0.6	13.5

Source: S. Kuznets, *Modern Economic Growth. Rate, Structure and Spread* (Cambridge, Mass.: 1966), pp. 236–8.

Table 5.8 Shares of world trade, selected countries and years, 1880–1913 (%)

	Merchandise exports		
	1885	1900	1913
UK	16.7	15.0	13.9
Belgium	3.7	3.9	3.9
France	9.6	8.4	7.2
Germany	11.0	11.6	13.1
Switzerland	2.1	1.7	1.4
USA	11.2	15.0	12.9

Source: A. Maddison, 'Growth and Fluctuation in the World Economy, 1870–1960', *Banca Nationale Di Lavoro Quarterly Review*, 15 (1962), pp. 179–81. There are a number of estimates available but the figures above are broadly representative.

	Exports of manufactured goods		
	1880	1899	1913
UK	41.4	32.5	29.9
France	22.2	15.8	12.9
Germany	19.3	22.2	26.4
USA	2.8	11.2	12.6

Source: S. Pollard, *Britain's Prime and Britain's Decline. The British Economy 1870–1914* (London: 1989), p. 15. Pollard uses a range of estimates but the ones above are broadly representative.

Table 5.9 Shares of trade in manufactures grouped by rates of growth in 1899 and 1913 (% shares)

		Expanding	Stable	Declining
1899	United Kingdom	17.7	18.6	62.9
	USA	23.4	54.1	21.7
	Germany	11.2	45.8	42.5
	France	5.8	31.0	62.8
1913	United Kingdom	21.3	13.3	65.4
	USA	34.1	38.3	38.2
	Germany	28.5	33.3	38.2
	France	14.3	26.0	59.7

Source: S.B. Saul, 'The Export Economy', *Yorkshire Bulletin of Economic and Social Research*, 17 (1965), p. 15.

were produced by the traditional staple industries. Especially noteworthy is the increase in exports of coal which in terms of weight grew at 4.4 per cent per year between 1881 and 1913; and between 1910 and 1913 coal accounted for, on average, 9.4 per cent by value of total principal exports as compared with 5 per cent for the period 1881–90.[11]

Finally, the nature and extent of technical change can be briefly surveyed on the basis of the substantial literature on the subject. The widening range of manufacturing activities in which British firms failed to match international best practice in technical terms is well recorded. There is, of course, the danger of indulging in a form of chimney counting which gives an exaggerated picture of what was happening.[12] There is, too, another side to the picture which shows that Britain was in the forefront of technical advance in a number of areas. But the weight of negative evidence which grows with the years during the period, is too large to be ignored.[13] It is, in other words, a matter of the dynamics of technical change and the crucial and integral process of the rate and extent of technical diffusion.

All this, moreover, is to treat technical change rather narrowly as a 'nuts and bolts' affair, whereas in reality it should be widened to include commercial and managerial practices and business structure and organization. Here again, unless a God-given view of the world is adopted, conditions in Britain in these respects were failing to match what was occurring in other economies.[14] It is important to note, however, that this is not a matter of emulating best practice to be found predominantly in the USA, as some historians have tried to portray it, but one of devising new and different ways of realizing the potential of modern economic development.[15] Part and parcel of the British system was the quite widely shared belief between employers and labour – particularly craft and skilled workers – that radical changes in methods and practices were not only unnecessary but also undesirable. For the former they were frequently seen as a threat to profits with the corresponding loss of the desired level of current income; for the latter such changes posed a threat to jobs by undermining work practices and wage differentials that had been built up over a long period. The 'machinery question' cast a long shadow over nineteenth-century Britain. But whereas at the beginning of the century it had erupted into the violence of Luddism, by its end it had been transformed into a mainly unconscious alliance of 'short-termism' between masters and men. And the shadow has reached deep into the twentieth century.

V

Taken together, indicators of Britain's economic performance between 1880 and 1914 show a growing divergence from the broad trend among the major economies. In absolute terms, nevertheless, Britain was still strongly placed in the economic firmament, with the exception that the United States had clearly emerged as the world's leading economy. But whilst US trade accounted for an increasing share of world trade, Britain remained the major, though no longer the dominant force in international trade and finance right up to the outbreak of the First World War. Even so, an historical assessment of its position should be based on a perspective that seeks to understand the dynamics of change. It may be suggested that such an assessment can be based on two (not mutually exclusive) tests of the evidence. These may be defined as the test of interest and the test of sustainability.

The test of interest leads to the question: for whom did the economy succeed or fail? In answer, there seems little reason to conclude other than that the economy continued to perform well enough throughout the late Victorian and Edwardian periods, given the realities of political power. The record of the distribution of income and wealth bears out the fact that Britain remained a profoundly unequal society with little disturbance being experienced by the well-off minority (see Table 5.10). And this pattern is reinforced when the Empire is brought into account. The upper classes were the main beneficiaries of Imperial investment whilst for their younger sons the running of the Empire frequently provided a generous form of outdoor relief.[16]

Lower down the social structure the situation is less clear. For the middle classes the pattern varied, though more research needs to be done to establish a fuller picture. For the working classes, the most recent estimates show a sharp check in the rate of growth of real wages post-1899, the most likely explanation for it being a concurrent drop in productivity growth.[17] In turn, this pattern fits well with the qualitative evidence of the weakening nature of technical change. To some degree these movements were offset by the extension of social welfare provision as part of the Liberal government's reforms of this period. Overall, to the extent that economic welfare is judged by the degree to which it matches the expectations and demands of those who exercise political power, it is difficult to see how it can be claimed that the late Victorian and Edwardian economy failed.

The test of sustainability leads to the question: was the economy developing the capacity to meet rising standards and expectations, which were increasingly influenced by what was happening abroad? This test is much more difficult to apply. There is clear evidence, nevertheless, that in important areas the structure and operation of the economy were not showing sufficient degrees of adaptability and flexibility to match the requirements of modern economic development. Whilst the pattern and form of economic development differed among the major economies these were but alternative ways through which economic advantage could be taken of new technologies and market opportunities. And the development of new and alternative forms of organization were, themselves, essential elements in this process of adaptation, particularly in business structure and management organization. Moreover, for all its variation this process meant that the advanced industrial economies were becoming closer substitutes for one another. Net value-added in the process of production was accounting for an increasing proportion of the final value of manufactured goods, which in turn reflected the growing importance of raising the quality of human capital. Correspondingly, trading relationships were steadily more influenced by comparative advantage in the

Table 5.10 The Distribution of national income, 1880 and 1913

	1880						1913					
	Number of incomes		Total income		Average income		Number of incomes		Total income		Average income	
	m	%	£m	%	£		m	%	£m	%	£	
Wages	12.3	83.3	465	41.5	37.8		15.2	73.4	770	35.5	50.7	
Intermediate incomes under £160	1.85	12.5	130	11.5	70.3		4.31	20.8	365	17.0	84.7	
Incomes assessed for tax over £160, excluding wage earners	0.62	4.2	530	47.0	854.8		1.19	5.8	1,030	47.5	865.5	
Total	14.77	100.0	1,125	100.0	76.2		20.7	100.0	2,165	100.0	104.6	

Source: A.L. Bowley, *The Change in the Distribution of National Income 1880–1913* (Oxford: 1920), p. 16; reprinted in A.L. Bowley et al., *Three Studies of National Income* (Cambridge: 1938), p. 76.

production of manufactured goods rather than by the exchange of manufactured goods for primary products and raw materials.

The size of these changes can be seen in the rise of imports of manufactured goods, especially from Germany. Correspondingly, Britain's comparative advantage was driving it more into Empire markets. As yet, these were no more than ripples on the surface of trade flows, despite the somewhat hysterical reactions in some quarters at the time.[18] But in qualitative terms these changes represented a growing threat to the competitive sustainability of the British economy. The ultimate test cannot be drawn from the period itself, and in moving beyond it the complexities appear to multiply as the effects of the First World War on the British economy have to be taken into account. We have argued elsewhere, however, that as well as obvious losses, the war brought substantial benefits to major sectors of the economy, and businessmen in the staple industries were presented with new opportunities to adjust to the changing conditions in the international economy.[19] But in their response they demonstrated a dogged attachment to old methods and practices. At all events, their actions confirmed how strongly the roots of economic decline had taken hold.

Notes

1 For a broad coverage of the literature see M. Abramovitz, 'Catching Up, Forging Ahead and Falling Behind', *Journal of Economic History*, 46 (1986), pp. 385–406; B.W.E. Alford, 'British Economic Performance in the European Perspective – A Case of Catch-up and Convergence?', in Clemens A. Wurm (ed.), *Wege Nach Europa. Wirtschaft und Aussenpolitik Grossbritanniens in 20. Jahrhundert* (Bochum: 1992), pp. 17–30; C. Feinstein, 'Benefits of Backwardness and Costs of Continuity', in A. Graham and A. Seldon (eds), *Government and Economies in the Post-war World: Economic Policies and Comparative Performance 1945–85* (London: 1990), pp. 284–93.
2 So far as production indices are concerned the data for this period are heavily estimated and are not standardized as between one country and another. But an even larger problem is the calculation of relative prices and proxy purchasing power parities. A good example of the difficulties involved is provided by B. Van Ark, 'Comparative Levels of Labour Manufacturing Productivity in Europe. Measurement and Comparisons', *Oxford Bulletin of Economics & Statistics*, 52 (1990), pp. 343–74. The data in Table 5.2 differ significantly from Maddison's earlier estimates which are based on 1985 instead of 1990 as the price conversion year. See A. Maddison, *Dynamic Forces in Capitalist Development* (Oxford: 1991), pp. 6–7.
3 S.N. Broadberry, 'Manufacturing and the Convergence Hypothesis. What the Long-Run Data Show', *Journal of Economic History*, 53 (1993), pp. 772–95.
4 There are, for example, major problems in making comparisons for the 1980s because of the volatility of exchange rates in relation to underlying income trends. In such circumstances the estimation of purchasing parity rates becomes extremely hazardous.
5 Broadberry, *op. cit.*, pp. 773–6, outlines his methods of calculation. He relies on extrapolation from 1935 or 1937 as base years for which inter-country comparative data on the total *value* of output of manufacturing industry are

available. These data are drawn predominantly from censuses of production. The base-year data are then converted into output per person employed. The extrapolation for each of the previous years is obtained by adjusting the base-year figures by corresponding indices of *physical* output and numbers employed. The output indices have been built up from gross output indicators for individual industries and then weighted either by net output or employment shares.

6 Broadberry, *op. cit.*, p. 778.
7 H.J. Habakkuk, *American and British Technology in the Nineteenth Century* (Cambridge: 1962); D.N. McCloskey, 'Did Victorian Britain Fail?', *Economic History Review*, 23 (1970), pp. 446–59; McCloskey (ed.) *Essays on a Mature Economy* (Princeton: 1971); J. Foreman-Peck (ed.), *New Perspectives on the Late Victorian Economy: Essays in Quantitative Economic History 1860–1914* (Cambridge: 1991).
8 W.A. Lewis, *Growth and Fluctuations 1870–1913* (London: 1978), pp. 123–5.
9 The analysis is well surveyed in S.N. Broadberry, 'Technological Leadership and Productivity Leadership in Manufacturing since the Industrial Revolution: Implications for the Convergence Debate', *Economic Journal*, 104 (1994), pp. 291–302. See also P.A. David, *Technical Choice, Innovation and Economic Growth* (Cambridge: 1975).
10 N. Rosenberg, *Perspectives on Technology* (Cambridge: 1976), p. 253.
11 B.W.E. Alford, *Britain in the World Economy since 1880* (Cambridge: 1996), p. 34.
12 The optimistic picture is well presented in S. Pollard, *Britain's Prime and Britain's Decline. The British Economy 1870–1914* (London: 1989), pp. 18–57, 123–213.
13 D.C. Coleman and C. MacLeod, 'Attitudes to New Techniques. British Businessmen, 1800–1950', *Economic History Review*, 39 (1986), pp. 588–611.
14 Alford, *op. cit.*, pp. 23–32, 55–71 for a critical survey of this issue.
15 The dominant statement of US superiority in business organization is A.D. Chandler Jnr, *Scale and Scope. The Dynamics of Industrial Capitalism* (Cambridge, Mass.: 1990). Critiques of this approach are provided by, for example, B.W.E. Alford, 'Chandlerism. The New Orthodoxy of US and European Corporate Development?', *Journal of European Economic History*, 23 (1994), pp. 631–43; R. Church, 'The Family Firm in Industrial Capitalism: International Perspectives on Hypotheses and History', *Business History*, 35 (1993), pp. 17–43; L. Hannah, 'Scale and Scope: Towards a European Visible Hand?', *Business History*, 33 (1991), pp. 297–309; B. Supple, 'Scale and Scope: Alfred Chandler and the Dynamics of Industrial Capitalism', *Economic History Review*, 44 (1991), pp. 500–14.
16 See L.E. Davis and R.A. Huttenback, *Mammon and The Pursuit of Empire. The Political Economy of British Imperialism, 1860–1912* (Cambridge: 1986), especially pp. 195–217.
17 Feinstein, *op. cit.*
18 Best known in this respect are E.E. Williams, *Made in Germany* (1896) and F.A. MacKenzie, *The American Invaders* (1902).
19 B.W.E. Alford, 'Lost Opportunities: British Business and Businessmen during the First World War', in N. McKendrick and R.B. Outhwaite (eds), *Business Life and Public Policy* (Cambridge: 1986), pp. 205–27.

Part III

TECHNOLOGY AND INDUSTRY

6

THE AUDIT OF THE GREAT WAR ON BRITISH TECHNOLOGY

Correlli Barnett

In the twentieth century the capability of a nation's armed forces cannot be separated from that nation's technological capability and industrial resources, or even social fabric. This realization led me, as a military historian by professional origin, to the concept of 'total strategy', defined in my 1972 book *The Collapse of British Power* [1] as strategy conceived as encompassing *all* the factors relevant to preserving, or extending, the power and prosperity of a human group in the face of rivalry from other groups.[2]

Too often governments – or scholars – hive off into separate compartments such factors as foreign policy, defence policy, economic and industrial affairs, and, for that matter, education and training or R&D. But these are really all interrelated, inter-reacting parts of a whole. In a well-conceived 'total strategy', therefore, such factors are in due proportion one to another, while an ill-conceived total strategy will be marked by gross imbalances. To take an extreme case of such lack of balance: the former Soviet Union sought to maintain the role of super-power, with armed forces to match, on the back of a third-world industrial economy – with, in turn, catastrophic effects on that economy. Or if we look at Imperial Germany in the run-up to the Great War in terms of 'total strategy', we see tremendous industrial and military power fatally matched to crass political ineptitude.

It will be seen that 'total strategy' provides a different approach from that of the economic historian, and especially an economic historian in the Anglo-Saxon Adam-Smithian free-market tradition.

In the case of the Great War, its total-strategic demands served to test at proof the technological capabilities of late Victorian and Edwardian Britain, for munitions production for mass warfare depends not only on specialist armament firms but also on the general industrial resources which make for success (or otherwise) in peacetime world markets.

But first of all it must in fairness be remembered that in the first two years of conflict Britain in *her* industrial mobilization confronted problems of scale unique among the main belligerents. For the Continental states had all had mass conscript armies in peacetime, with inventories of weapons and ammunition to match. In contrast, Britain in peacetime had only maintained a small all-regular army, its main role that of imperial garrisoning and campaigning. Instead Britain had relied for her security on a 'two-power standard' Navy, for seapower was the foundation of a Victorian and Edwardian 'total strategy' consisting of the pound sterling, the City of London, global free trade and the British Empire.

This traditional British strategy was torpedoed by the partial success of the Schlieffen Plan in 1914, leading to the stalemate of the Western Front, which meant that for the first time in her history, Britain had to create a mass Continental Army – and do so in desperate haste. By the autumn of 1914 the target was 30 divisions; by spring 1915 it had grown to 70 divisions for all theatres of war.

The British political and military leadership was thus confronted with a unique industrial problem of scale: the problem, that is, of how to match such huge and breakneck expansion in personnel by output of weaponry, ammunition and equipment of all kinds. It must be remembered that the firepower of a 1915 infantry division comprised 17,000 rifles, four machine-guns, fifty-four 18-pounder field-guns, eighteen 4.5-inch howitzers and four 60-pounder medium guns.[3] Multiply all this by 70, and the size of the problem becomes clear. Its anatomy was well described by the official *History of the Ministry of Munitions*:

> bulk supply involves mass production, and mass production is only possible after stability of design and fixity of pattern have been arrived at. Inevitable loss, delay and disappointment are the consequences entailed by the premature organisation of an extensive manufacturing unit with its series of processes carefully balanced in sequence and velocity, which is then subject to a compulsory readjustment to a single stage in order to conform to a modification of design. That stage is practically certain at least to cause a 'bottle-neck', which will delay the flow of materials from machine to machine and process to process, and the efficiency of the whole organisation will thus be impaired.[4]

However, the very haste of expansion presented its own complex problems. It is a commonplace of mechanical industry that the full momentum of output can only be attained after a lengthy period of tuning up, even when the design of the article to be manufactured is settled and the accessories and special forms of equipment, such as tools, jigs and gauges, are at hand. When, as was often the case during the first year of the war, orders were given for articles, the design of which was merely provisional and the drawings and gauges for which were not available, there could be no real programme of supply. Thus the war imposed upon British manufacturing ingenuity the severest of all possible tests: the need for perpetual readjustments in process while maintaining or increasing output. There was no way of evading the necessity which demanded that the development of design should proceed *pari passu* with the development of manufacture.[5]

Such considerations signified that the existing specialist armaments industry simply could not be expanded fast enough in 1914–15 to meet the needs of Kitchener's 'New Army' or the sheer demands of the Western Front. For instance, orders given to British private firms for shells were doubled and doubled again until by the end of 1914 they had reached over 6 million. No wonder the firms were simply overwhelmed. Much the same gathering avalanche of orders happened with machine-guns and 18-pounder guns. On Vickers alone, 2,400 18-pounders were ordered for delivery by June 1915. The firm managed about half that quantity. Nonetheless, this was not bad for a company which produced fewer than twenty in 1914.[6]

It is interesting that the armaments firms were the first to come up against those basic industrial weaknesses with which the Ministry of Munitions had later to contend on the grand scale. For instance, sub-contractors new to armaments work could not manufacture to the fine tolerances required; and they consistently defaulted on their delivery promises. Then again, the armament firms themselves were shackled in expanding plant because they were unable to obtain the extra machine-tools they needed. To quote the official *History of the Ministry of Munitions* again:

> The provision of the machine tools required for the equipment of extensions to factories became a matter of concern early in the war. ... In consequence of the limited capacity of the home industry, and the scale of requirements, it was necessary to have recourse to the United States of America.[7]

When in September 1914 the Ordnance Department decided to substitute TNT for picric acid as a burster, the supplies of TNT from the chemical industry were so short that it had to be 'cut' with ammonium nitrate. There were more bottle-necks with fuses.[8] No wonder Britain had to place its biggest single orders for shell in America and Canada.

It was as a result of the notorious 'shell scandal' in spring 1915 that the Ministry of Munitions was set up under David Lloyd George to mastermind Britain's general industrial mobilization: the mobilization which was to test Britain's broad technological capabilities. As Lloyd George quickly appreciated, munitions production fell into two main categories. The first still necessarily remained the province of specialized armaments plants –

that is to say, kit like heavy guns and gun mountings, or warships of cruiser-size and upwards. Of this category I will only observe that the Battle of Jutland had demonstrated that German naval guns were superior to British, calibre for calibre, thanks to their steel-shrunk construction and steel made in electric crucibles, compared with British wire-wound construction and open-hearth steel; and that British heavy naval shells were defective both in their bursters and fuses.[9]

The second category relates to production of a vast range of weaponry and kit which depended on mobilizing Britain's *general* engineering, especially precision engineering – and her chemical industries. Since the Great War was an artillery war, shells for field and medium guns stood at the top of the list. But that list also included motor transport, aircraft and aero-engines, small arms and ammunition, telecommunications kit, drugs, and later, tanks and poison gas. It was here that 'the audit of war' (to coin a phrase) in 1914–1916 showed up the British industrial system as widely inadequate or obsolescent, even when allowances are made for the unique British problem of sheer scale of expansion of output.

To take the basic industrial sinew, British steel production in 1910 was little more than half the German total.[10] After 1914 Britain suffered particularly from weakness in special steels, such as for the cutting faces of high-speed machine-tools – steels largely imported from Germany before the war, and which now would have to be imported from Sweden. Even the quality of the general run of British steel-making and foundry-work was suspect. One major reason why it took so long to get the tank from prototype to mass deployment in the field was a wastage rate in track-link castings of up to 40 per cent because of blowholes.[11]

According to the *History of the Ministry of Munitions*:

> British manufacturers were behind other countries in research, plant and method. Many of the iron and steel firms were working on a small scale, old systems and uneconomic plant, their cost of production being so high that competition with the steel works of the United States and Germany was becoming impossible.[12]

In fact, this history draws the conclusion that in 1914–1916, 'it was only the ability of the Allies to import shell and shell steel from neutral America . . . that averted the decisive victory of the enemy'.[13] More than 50 per cent of shells fired off in the Battle of the Somme in 1916 were American and Canadian.

In trying to expand Britain's own shell output in 1915–16, Lloyd George faced fundamental difficulties. First, Britain was short of big, modern light-engineering factories that could be converted to finishing shell cases. She lacked precision engineering industries like mechanical toy- or clock-making, where Germany had been so strong in peacetime, and which could now be easily switched to mass production of finely accurate fuses. Fuses therefore became one of the major bottlenecks in shell production, until new 'national' fuse factories could be built equipped with American machine-tools.

The tools had to be American (though some came from Switzerland and Sweden) because Britain, the vaunted 'workshop of the world', lacked a modern machine-tool industry capable of fabricating the sophisticated semi-automatic machines needed to equip the production lines in the new government munitions factories being erected by the Ministry of Munitions on green-field sites. According to the *History of the Ministry of Munitions*: 'The British machine tool maker was conservative both as regards novelty of design and quantity of output.' Before the war Britain had relied on imports of German advanced tools. It was only the purchase of American, Swedish and Swiss machine-tools that prevented a complete breakdown in the munitions effort. Nevertheless, shortage of sophisticated machine-tools remained a constraint on production right through the war.

As Lloyd George wrote, a shell without the explosive filling is merely a harmless steel vase. Yet output of explosive proved a crippling bottleneck up to 1916. For, unlike Germany, Britain lacked the advantage of a great peacetime organic chemical industry. As the *History of the Ministry of Munitions* puts it: 'In August 1914, the Germans were in the fortunate position of being able to turn with ease the vast resources of a flourishing coal-tar industry to the production of high explosives.'[14]

Before the war Britain had depended on the *German* chemical industry for drugs like aspirin, novocaine and salvarsan, and for dyes (even khaki for the uniforms of the British army and navy-blue for the rig of the Royal Navy). The only place in England in 1914 where salvarsan and novocaine could be made was the Ellesmere Port works of a subsidiary of Farbwerke Hoechst.[15] Now in wartime, Britain was compelled to import German drugs through neutral countries until she could build new chemical plant of her own.

But British weaknesses in the first half of the war extended across a whole range of advanced technologies where she had previously relied wholly or largely on imports, most of them from Germany. Ball-bearings, that basic necessity of the motor age, serve as a notable example. Despite wartime imports from Sweden and Switzerland, shortage of ball-bearings shackled production of internal combustion engines for motor-vehicles and aircraft even as late as 1918; and held back tank production too, for that matter.[16] Or take magnetos, another vital component in the motor age, of which in 1914 the single British manufacturer produced a mere 1,140 of a simple type. By 1916 the shortage had become acute because pre-war stocks of German imports were near exhaustion and British production had met severe teething troubles.[17]

In any case, Britain had no aero-engine industry in 1914, and relied on French imports. It took until 1916 for British-built high-powered aero-engines to become available, and even in 1918 the lack of enough engines was holding up the creation of Britain's first strategic bomber force, the so-called 'Independent Air Force'.

Machine-tools, ball-bearings, magnetos, internal combustion engines, drugs – it is hard to name a basic necessity of advanced technology in which Britain was self-sufficient in 1915. Take measuring equipment and instrumentation – another pre-war import. Or industrial gauges and other gauges. Or optical glass for instruments, where 90 per cent had been imported from Germany before the war. Or glass bulbs and tubes for electric lamps – 75 per cent from Germany and Austria.[18]

Thus the audit rendered by the first two years of the war on Britain's own capabilities in newer technologies proved harsh enough.

Nonetheless, economic historians might object that Britain's Victorian and Edwardian 'total strategy' actually served her well enough in wartime. Thanks to her accumulated wealth and her credit as the centre of a global free trade economy and thanks also to British seapower, she could buy in all the technological imports that she needed – largely from North America. But there are two snags here. First, wealth and credit are wasting assets when spent, while the spending only serves to profit other countries' manufacturers and build up their industries. In contrast, up-to-date export industries of your own are long-term earners. Secondly, the high degree to which free trade had rendered Britain dependent on imports of food and raw materials actually brought her near to complete national defeat in 1917 at the hands of the U-boat. Germany suffered from no such acute economic vulnerability. Moreover, even though the U-boat was narrowly beaten, Britain had to devote immense naval resources to the merely defensive purpose of keeping open her sea lifelines. This pattern was to be repeated in the Second World War.[19]

Cobden in his boundless mid-Victorian optimism about free trade could no more have imagined such a plight than Adam Smith could have imagined refrigerated cargo ships bringing meat from the New World to undercut British livestock farmers. Perhaps their intellectual descendants today are at times too preoccupied with peacetime world trade and the advantages of economic specialization between nations, to the neglect of the total-strategic implications in wartime of such specialization. But at least Adam Smith himself recognized that, in his words, 'defence, however, is of much greater importance than opulence'.[20]

The audit of the Great War showed up widespread human weaknesses in British industry. Too many British capitalists in their boardrooms were simply self-trained 'practical men' smugly content with old products, old equipment and old markets, guided by a concern for short-term profits rather than for the long-term development of their businesses.[21] The trade unions, for their part, were resolutely resistant to new technology, while also holding back productivity by a maze of demarcations and restrictive practices. Whereas pre-war Britain had more than a thousand separate unions, most of them claiming exclusive ownership of some corner of the production process, Germany had only 47. In Britain there were 75 separate unions in the engineering industries alone.[22] One of Lloyd George's worst problems as Minister of Munitions lay in strike-prone union resistance to 'dilution' – i.e., putting unskilled or semi-skilled labour, often female, on to new American machines to do what traditionally had been done by crews of expensive skilled craftsmen.[23] Nor did the British institution of the disruptive strike suffer any decline in wartime. Governments had to negotiate with the trade union movement as with a foreign power.[24] The so-called 'Treasury Agreement' of March 1915, supposed to settle all these issues for the duration of the war, proved a dead letter. Lloyd George's Munitions of War Act of June 1915 sought to deal with the problem, but, as it turned out, with only limited success, except in the new national factories.[25]

The urgent challenge of winning a total war against so formidable an enemy as Germany, indeed the peril of national defeat, jolted Britain as an industrial society far more effectively than mere peacetime world-market competition, to which she had failed to respond as she should have done according to classical economic ideas. A remarkable technological revolution began in Britain in 1915 and was consummated by 1918 – remarkable not only because of all the deficiencies that had got to be made good, but also because the revolution was accomplished under wartime conditions and at utmost speed. It is also noteworthy that it was masterminded by the *government*, and that many of the new American-style factories were actually owned and operated by the state.

All the newly created resources and capabilities naturally constitute a mirror-image of what Britain had lacked, or had failed fully to exploit, during the Edwardian era. For a start, British universities and technical institutions, their staffs and laboratories, were mobilized in the service of the nation's industry virtually for the first time in their history – not only in order to develop urgently needed new technologies, but also to expand the output of skilled scientific and technical personnel, which had been another field of relative British neglect before the war.[26] In the words of the report of the Board of Education for 1915–1916: 'The War has brought the professor and the manufacturer together with results which neither of them are likely to forget.'[27]

It was thanks to University College, London, that Britain developed a process for fixing nitrogen, a basic ingredient of TNT. This enabled the government to build a main production plant at Billingham, to be taken over by ICI in the 1920s. Other universities provided rigorous scientific tests on the quality of propellants and bursters. It was Chaim Weizmann at Manchester who discovered how to mass-produce acetone by fermenting starch – essential to the production of cordite and for 'doping' aircraft fabric. The effectiveness of the British gas-mask owed itself to experiments at Oxford and Bristol universities. Research at Manchester and Cambridge led eventually to a process for producing mustard gas which by the end of the war gave Britain an output thirty times larger than Germany's, and at one-thirtieth of the cost. It was owing to close collaboration between university research and industry that Britain also caught up in the production of drugs, so essential to the treatment of the sick and wounded. To cite but one example, St Andrews University devised a means of producing novocaine at half the cost and a fifth of the time of the German Hoechst method.

In aeronautics too, the universities played a truly vital role with work on light alloys, on aerodynamic design and on instrumentation. It was mathematical studies on aircraft structure that led to British combat aircraft like the SE5 being much more stable than the German equivalents, with consequent advantage in the dog-fights over the Western Front.

Then again, the development of British-made magnetos owed much to Bangor University; of radio to Royal Holloway College, which developed the thermionic valve adopted by the Royal Navy while Birmingham University completely designed the morse radio used for communicating with submerged submarines. The hydrophone, that major step forward in detecting the submerged U-boat, was developed thanks to research by Queen Mary College, London.

It is significant that the present-day Department of Scientific and Industrial Research was founded in 1916: a mark of the government's recognition that the state must assume direct responsibility for sponsoring, financing and co-ordinating research; and equally an implicit acknowledgement that British industry had failed in peacetime spontaneously to match the efforts of German or American industry.

Nevertheless, all the brilliant wartime R&D would have been barren of result on the battlefield without the accompanying massive expansion of manufacturing resources masterminded by the Ministry of Munitions. In the first place, huge additions were built to existing privately owned plant thanks to government funding. But secondly, and even more revolutionary in terms of traditional Victorian *laissez-faire*, no fewer than 218 national factories were built on green-field sites to manufacture products ranging from ball-bearings, aircraft, fuses, explosives, chemicals, tools and gauges to concrete slabs. These were laid out on a grand scale then novel to British industry, as a newspaper reported in November 1915:

> One of the new factories has grown up on a spot which last November was green fields. Now there are 25 acres covered with buildings packed full of machinery. Most of the machines are of American make, and some are marvels of ingenuity. Herein the war will prove a permanent benefactor to Birmingham. For it would be flattery to pretend that the prevailing Birmingham type of workshop is anything to boast about. It is on the whole conspicuously antiquated.

Novel too was the whole approach to production. Again I quote from the *History of the Ministry of Munitions*: 'Standardised repetition work or mass production took the place of the varied and variable output characteristic of much British manufacture before the war.'[28]

Much of this new plant also enjoyed high potential for peacetime. In order to produce drugs and supply chemicals for explosives and then poison gas, the foundations of the modern British chemical industry were laid, not least thanks to seized German patents. When Imperial Chemical Industries was set up in 1926, it owed an important part of its assets to the wartime creation of the British Dyestuff Corporation.

Electrical generating capacity doubled between 1914 and 1918, and the average output of a power station increased fourteen times.[29] British ball-bearing production also doubled during the war; production of electric bulbs quadrupled. The output of optical and scientific instruments increased twenty times in value; of optical glass sixty times. According to the *History of the Ministry of Munitions*,

> It became possible to manufacture for the first time in England a large number of instruments, such as panoramic dial sights, periscopes, rangefinders for aeroplanes, height finders for aeroplanes, sound ranging apparatus, and several other instruments used in the detection, location and handling of aeroplanes. The introduction of tanks also necessitated the manufacture of periscopes of suitable types, and gun sighting periscopes.[30]

But in terms of new technology on the largest scale, aircraft manufacture stands out, along with all the subsidiary industries which served it. To quote again from the *History of the Ministry of Munitions*:

> Aircraft construction was in its infancy in 1914, and the aero-engine building industry was practically nonexistent. . . . At the end of the war aero-engine production was a huge industry . . . and British engines had outstripped the productions of all other countries as to quality and quantity.
>
> The advances made by subsidiary industries were remarkable. The production of magnetos was multiplied a hundred-fold; the research on alloy and steel, the development of strong and light-weight metal tubing, and of petrol-resistant rubber tubing, and the improvement in the quality of oil and petrol are all of permanent value to industry.[31]

In this wartime industrial revolution, women played a key role. By August 1916 some 520,000 women were employed in the metal and engineering industries. By July 1917, six months after the introduction of universal adult liability to National Service, the number had risen to over 800,000; and the last year of the war added another 100,000. In industry as a whole the number of women workers increased by about 800,000 between 1914 and 1918.[32] The largest single concentration of women on munitions work was at the national cordite factory at Gretna – no fewer than 11,000 of them.[33]

It hardly needs emphasizing that this wartime technological revolution marked a complete departure from Victorian and Edwardian *laissez-faire* orthodoxy. Given time for consolidation and further development – probably under some form of protection such as fostered the growth of American, German and Japanese industry – Britain's wartime achievements might have served as the starting-point for a root-and-branch modernization of Britain as an industrial society. Indeed, the 1918 report of the Committee on Commercial and Industrial Policy virtually recommended this.[34]

More fundamentally still, the wartime revolution could have served as the prototype for a new British 'total strategy', based on Britain's own technological strength: in other words, the German or Japanese version of capitalism, a partnership between state and industry, rather than the Anglo-Saxon version. But instead Britain tried after the war to revert to her Victorian and Edwardian total strategy based on *laissez-faire*, the City of London, the gold-standard pound sterling and the Empire – with consequences which would only be fully revealed when the Second World War submitted Britain to yet another audit of industrial capability.[35]

Notes

1 Hardback published in 1972 by Eyre-Methuen (London); paperback by Sutton Publishing (Stroud) in 1984; reprinted in 1987, 1991, 1993 and 1997.
2 'Total strategy' has served me as a basic conceptual tool in writing my 'Pride and Fall' sequence on Britain as a political and military power in the twentieth century: *The Collapse of British Power* (London, 1972 and 1984), *The Audit of War* (London, Macmillan, 1986; Pan Books, 1987) and *The Lost Victory: British Dreams. British Illusions 1945–1950* (London, Macmillan, 1995; Pan Books, 1996). A fourth and final book, covering the period from the outbreak of the Korean War in 1950 to the Suez adventure in 1956, is in preparation.
3 *History of the Ministry of Munitions* (London, HMSO, 1922), Vol I. Pt. I, ch. 1, p. 15; hereafter cited as *Hist. Min. Mun.*
4 *Ibid.*, p. 31.
5 *Ibid.*
6 J.D. Scott, *Vickers: A History* (London, Weidenfeld and Nicolson, 1963).
7 *Hist. Min. Mun.*, Vol. I, Pt I, ch. 5, p. 125.
8 *Ibid.*, ch.6.
9 See C. Barnett, *The Swordbearers: Studies in Supreme Command in the First World War* (London, Eyre and Spottiswoode, 1963; New York, William Morrow, 1964; Bloomington, University of Indiana Press, 1975; paperback: London, Hodder and Stoughton, 1986), pp. 187–91; A.J. Marder, *From the Dreadnought to Scapa Flow: The Royal Navy in the Fisher Era. 1904–1919*, Vol. III, *Jutland and After* (London, Oxford University Press, 1966), pp. 166–75, 213–21.

10 7,613,000 tonnes. J.H. Clapham, *Economic Development of France and Germany 1815–1914* (Cambridge, Cambridge University Press, 1923) p. 285.
11 *Hist. Min. Mun.*, Vol. XII, Pt. III, pp. 42–9.
12 *Ibid.*, Vol. VII Pt II, pp. 1–2.
13 *Ibid.*, Vol. II, p. 58.
14 *Ibid.*, Vol. VII, Pt. IV, p.11.
15 M. Sanderson, *The Universities and British Industry, 1850–1950* (London, Routledge and Kegan Paul, 1972), ch. 8.
16 *Hist.Min.Mun.*, Vol. VII, Pt. I, p. 108.
17 *Ibid.*, p. 103.
18 See Barnett, *The Collapse of British Power*, pp. 86–7 and cited sources (mostly volumes of the *Hist. Min. Mun.*) for a summary of what 'the workshop of the world' could not make in terms of products of the 'second' industrial revolution; see also Sanderson, *Universities*, Chap. 8.
19 See Barnett, *Engage the Enemy More Closely: the Royal Navy in the Second World War* (London, Hodder and Stoughton, 1991), pp. 8–9, and ch. 9, 14, 15 and 19; John Terraine, *Business in Great Waters: The U-boat Wars 1916–1945* (London, Leo Cooper, 1989), *passim*.
20 Adam Smith, *The Wealth of Nations* (London, Dent, 1929), p. 408.
21 This large topic is central to other contributions of the Montpellier symposium. My own reading of the evidence in regard to British management in the nineteenth century and after is summarized in *The Collapse of British Power*, *passim*, but especially pp. 94–106. Since writing that book, I have been particularly impressed by Robert R. Locke, *The End of the Practical Man: Entrepreneurship and Higher Education in Germany, France and Britain, 1880–1940* (Greenwich, CT; London, The Jai Press, 1984).
22 R. Seidel, *The Trade Union Movement in Germany* (London, Fabian Tract, 1916).
23 See *Hist. Min. Mun.*, Vol. I, Pt. II, ch. 1 and 2; and Pt. IV.
24 See *ibid.*, ch. 2.
25 Keith Layburn, *British Trade Unionism c. 1770–1990: A Reader in History* (Stroud, Alan Sutton, 1991), pp. 104–31.
26 The following summary of the contribution made by British universities and technical institutions to the war effort is based on Sanderson, *Universities* ch. 8, 'The Universities and the War 1914–18'.
27 Cd.8594 (London, HMSO, 1917), p. 70, 'University Institutions in Relation to Industry and Commerce', cited in Sanderson, *Universities*, p. 214.
28 *Hist.Min.Mun.*, Vol. IV, Pt. IV, pp. 74–5.
29 *Ibid.*, Vol. VIII, Pt. III, p. 105.
30 *Ibid.*, Vol. XI, Pt. III, p. 9.
31 *Ibid.*, Vol. XII, Pt. I, pp. 174–5.
32 Figures from Arthur Marwick, *Women at War 1914–1918* (London, Fontana Original, 1977) p. 73.
33 *Ibid.*, pp. 68–9.
34 Cd.9032, pp.11–12, cited in Barnett, *The Collapse of British Power*, pp. 116–17.
35 See Barnett, *The Audit of War*, passim.

7

THE BALANCE OF TECHNOLOGICAL TRANSFERS 1870–1914

James Foreman-Peck

The late Victorian British economy attracted a good deal of attention in the 1980s. Those who believed American economic and political hegemony was threatened in the waning twentieth century saw analogies with Britain's supposed earlier circumstances (Elbaum and Lazonick 1986: 1). British 'ungovernability' during the preceding decade, when relative decline accelerated, persuaded even scholars and observers unconcerned with the American analogy that they should look for the historical roots of Britain's failings (Barnett 1986). Not quite matching Edward Gibbon's tale of Roman imperial degeneration over a millennium, their narratives are nonetheless prone to tell a story of continuous British economic decadence over a century or more.

Though a great deal of the debate over 'economic decline' is based upon conflations of political power and economic productivity, a thumbnail sketch of technological history does suggest a loss of leadership. Britain was clearly the innovator and exporter of the industrial revolution technologies of the steam engine, coal and iron, which were ascientific and mechanical. In the new wave of technology from the 1870s, in electricity, organic chemistry and the internal combustion engine, scientific principles played a far greater role (Landes 1969: 321). In these industries, the British economy was apparently very much a follower, an importer of technologies developed elsewhere. Moreover, entrepreneurs have been accused of failing even to use new technology in established industries. Since the ability to generate and absorb new technology underlies the high and growing productivity that has created unprecedented Western living standards, a reduction in technological capacity has serious implications. An industrial society that begins losing the ability to take advantage of new technology is certainly on a path to decline. An economy does not have to generate innovations as long as they can be borrowed. But many would judge that a society that can only imitate has lost some of its vitality and productivity potential.

TECHNOLOGICAL TRANSFERS

This chapter looks at the technological dynamism of the British economy between 1870 and 1914 paying particular attention to the exchanges with the rest of the world. To remedy the impressionistic approach of much of the literature I first discuss the evidence of trade statistics. The questions addressed are which sectors were importers and which exporters of new technology and why? I then probe key sectors with the case study approach.

Of course, case study surveys are not new. Dintenfass's (1992) concise survey of the literature on British industrial performance accepts Sandberg's (1974) exemption of the cotton industry. On the other hand, he condemns the technological choices made by the iron and steel industry, giving little weight to Elbaum's (1986: 73) conclusion that ore costs could have been decisive. Wilson points out for the industry with which he is especially familiar, electrical engineering, that the constraints were immovable. But he accepts Saul's (1962) condemnation of motors through the baleful influence of the consulting engineer in constraining mass production (Wilson 1995: 93–4). The problem they all face is the availability of sufficient relevant information about each industry, and perhaps even firm, to explain why it was sensible not to imitate what was done in the different conditions of the United States (or when it suits, Germany).

A related issue is the probabilistic nature of generalizations. No doubt many entrepreneurs made inappropriate technological choices and selection of individual examples can easily suggest failure. But in sectors with many competing suppliers, the general state of British industries between 1870 and 1914, those that do make the right choices should flourish. And if all domestic entrepreneurs are hamstrung by their social background, in an open economy like Britain's, foreign entrepreneurs who are more competent are likely to enter the industry. That is not to say that industries into which foreigners enter are necessarily those in which domestic entrepreneurs have failed, as the Rothschilds' and Engels' cotton factories demonstrate.

There is a more fundamental methodological problem. 'Entrepreneurial failure' is a residual hypothesis, like 'chance'. A systematic explanation can be found, endogenizing entrepreneurial behaviour, showing it to be determined by other constraints. That does not necessarily mean the behaviour becomes optimal, for there is no necessary reason to accept these constraints as inevitable. But it can shift history in a more scientific direction, allowing the calculation of the costs of particular constraints. For instance, the timing of United Alkali's adoption of the Solvay process was not consistent with profit maximization (Lindert and Trace 1971). But the lag in adoption, explicable by the protection afforded by monopoly power, is insufficient to explain any major failure in the economy even if all British monopoly firms behaved the same way. Moreover, some constraints are more shiftable than others. It would be foolish to blame entrepreneurs around the turn of the century for not developing competitive electric cars, when even today the physics and engineering of battery technology suggests the constraint of cheap electrical power storage is still binding.

Trade and the balance of technological transfers

A major difficulty in studying technology transfer is the measurement of what is transferred. Patent registration propensities vary between industries and patenting has more than one motive. Royalty fees are difficult to establish and may not capture the value of what is sold. Hi-tech goods may only transfer the use of those goods, not an understanding of what they embody. Multinational companies may export technological knowledge to a new national site but maintain exclusive ownership so that domestically based entrepreneurs and businesses never gain access.

Some items of trade are more technology-intensive than others; some are capital goods, the means of applying technological expertise. Official statistics are not all they should be. The 1886 Royal Commission on the Depression in Trade and Industry set the trend for those looking for late Victorian failure when they complained of a falling off of energy amongst manufacturers. Consideration of their analytical contribution suggests they should have removed the beam from their own eye before commenting on the mote in the eyes of manufacturers. More obviously justifiably, they went on to bemoan the absence of any official series on production by industry or on wage bills. Similarly, trade statistics were grossly inadequate until 1901. In that year for the first time imports of machinery were classified, whereas they were already distinguished for exports.

Inspection of the trade accounts for 1880 suggests no hi-tech imports; exports identify machinery by type and telegraph wires and apparatus. (They also distinguish muskets consigned to West Africa.) Apparently Britain was self-sufficient in technology or had not noticed any deficiency.

By 1901 Britain is revealed as importing even textile machinery and steam engines – though the balance in textile machinery is massively in Britain's favour (Table 7.1). In both steam and non-steam machinery Britain obviously maintains a strong comparative advantage – least so in agricultural machinery, having shifted resources out of agriculture over the preceding twenty years. Telegraphy is a strong export earner, thanks to strong British demand from a subsidized domestic network and dominating international communications. But apart from that, Britain does not seem (wrongly) to export electrical goods, despite considerable imports.

The absence of scientific instrument (vital to electrical engineering) exports is noteworthy, though to some extent that may be due to inadequate classification. The considerable imports from and dependence on Germany reflect Germany's sustained and extensive historical interest in science. Watches and clocks are imported on a large scale but hardly exported. Ships are second only to non-steam machinery as an export earner and none are imported.

Table 7.1 British trade in higher technology products 1901 and 1913

	1901		1913		
	Exports	Imports	Exports	Imports	
Steam engines					
locomotives	1.911	0.062	2.784	0.003	(rail)
	—	—	0.628	0.013	(road)
agricultural	0.621	0.004	1.361	0.008	
other	1.726	0.423	5.216	0.235	
Total	4.258	0.489	9.989	0.259	
Prime mover excl. electric					
Ships	9.149	—	11.031	0.034	
Non-steam machinery					
agricultural	0.733	0.369	1.628	0.728	
sewing	1.552	0.350	2.360	0.412	
mining	0.509	0.046	1.018	0.114	
textiles	4.726	0.112	8.281	0.366	
other	6.034	2.595	23.736	5.663	
Total	13.554	3.472	37.023	7.283	
Machine tools	—	—	1.012	0.361	
Scientific instruments	—	0.711	0.770	0.710	
complete				(Ger. 0.363)	
(incl. parts and photo	—	—	1.839	3.083	
cinema films)				(US 1.256)	
Arms & ammunition	2.693	—	4.707	—	
Cycles	0.577	—	2.087	0.244	
Typewriters	—	—	0.032	0.512	
Watches	—	1.548	0.012	1.746	
Clocks	—	0.526	0.045	0.499	
Motorcycles }	0.172*	1.103*	0.991	0.267	
Motorcars }			4.359	7.411	
Aeroplanes and balloons	—	—	0.047	0.244	
Telegraph wire and	3.148	—(eqpt)	0.711	0.252	
apparatus					
Submarine cable	—	—	1.904	0	
Telegraph & telephone wires	—	—	0.711	0.059	
Electric wires & cable	—	—	0	0.379	
Total electrical goods	3.148	0.849	5.386	1.587	
Electrical prime movers	—	—	2.275	1.345	
and machinery					
Chemicals inc. medicine	8.942	6.129	22.012	12.906	
Manure			2.401	}	
Indigo			0.542	} 1.542	
Alzarine, aniline, etc.			0.720	}	
				incl. napthalene	
Coal products	1.152		(2.665)	incl. chemicals	

Source: Trade and Navigation Accounts of the United Kingdom.
Note: *=1902.

In chemicals the substantial trade is much more closely in balance but that conceals the tendency to import raw materials such as indigo for natural dyes and synthetic dyestuffs, and export manufactured chemicals, especially for 'manure' (fertilizer). Coal products are later classified as chemicals. They demonstrate the natural resource basis of Britain's broader specialization in chemicals.

By 1913 an even more detailed classification shows a continuing British weakness in watches, clocks, and now typewriters, motor cars and aircraft (Table 7.1). However, motor cycles, presumably by virtue of their close technological relationship with bicycles, have been added to the competitive group. But more surprising is the apparent increasing strength in electrical goods (a positive balance) and scientific instruments relative to 1901, though the rise of popular cine films boosted US imports. The non-steam machinery balance, even excluding machine tools, has risen from £10 million in 1901 to £30 million in 1913. Even the chemical balance improved from £2.8 million in 1901 to £8 million in 1913.

So trade data suggest Britain as a follower economy in the new sectors but following fairly rapidly. Multinationals interested in exporting to the British Empire were important, especially in electricals. In such cases there is a question of whether the underlying pattern of technology generation and absorption is entirely different, with possible adverse consequences for the economy. In the case of Siemens at least, we shall see that Britain had little reason for concern.

Japanese import figures for British electrical goods can in part remedy the shortcomings of British trade classification and cast some light on British electrical strengths and weaknesses. Between 1893 and 1895 47% of the total value of Japanese imported electrical machines were British. By 1911–13 this had fallen to 24%. In the early phase, much of the British machinery was electrical motors to drive cotton textile plant. Later, US and German large capacity generating equipment for hydroelectric stations dominated, though Ferranti and Fowler maintained a foothold and electric wires and cables were a British speciality. British technology was likely to have been handicapped in the same way as Japanese (but with far less excuse), as machinery became more sophisticated (Uchida 1991).

In railways British imports to Japan lost out to the Americans and Germans, though not until after 1902 did the proportion of British locomotives fall below one-half. Even then Britain continued to be the largest single source of rolling stock (Yuzawa 1991).

Principles of technology transfers

What causes technological transfers? In an international economy different resource endowments give rise to trade and specialization. Movement of goods (including books and journals) transmits knowledge of different technologies

Table 7.2 Population, industrial output and US patents in the G4, 1913

	Population (m)	Index	Industrial prodn.	US patents (1910–12)
Germany	66,978	147	114	3,961
Britain	45,649	100	100	2,970
USA	97,227	213	257	95,022
France	39,770	87	43	1,031

and even more effectively so does movement of people. Reverse engineering was known by the beginning of the century. Henry Ford extracted a component of a crashed French car in 1905. He established that the recovered valve strip stem was made of light and strong French vanadium steel which no US steel company could manufacture. So an Englishman, who knew how to produce the material commercially, was imported (Ford 1923: 65–6). As this example shows, up to a point metallurgy and engineering could develop differently in different countries. There were often advantages to be gained from international arbitrage, if someone in either country had sufficient technical knowledge to perceive the opportunity.

Followed by many other subsequent writers, Landes (1969) asks, 'Why did industrial leadership pass from Britain to Germany in the closing decades of the 19th century?' The international distribution of population and industrial production in 1913 offers a simple answer – 'because Germany was bigger'. Table 7.2, moreover, suggests that judged by the criterion of industrial output, 'leadership' had passed to the United States, rather than to Germany. Chandler's (1990) views of the primacy of large corporations in industrial progress are consistent with this position. Recent productivity calculations suggest that the US held a manufacturing lead over Britain from 1870 or earlier (Broadberry 1994). The research question is then why was the United States so productive compared with all other industrial economies, not just Britain? To this Wright (1990) and Nelson and Wright (1992) have answered 'natural resource abundance and the size of the market (economies of scale)'.

Path dependent technological and institutional change

Measured by share of world production, British technological 'leadership' in some sectors persisted. At the end of the 'long nineteenth century', Britain dominated world production in ships and cotton textiles, while supplying one-fifth of the world's coal and a good deal of the iron and steel. Although undoubtedly conferring gains, the remarkable concentration of production through international specialization left the economy vulnerable to external shocks, such as those initiated by the First World War.

Quite independently of subsequent shocks, this particular specialization pattern might have inhibited subsequent British economic development for institutional and technological reasons. Some sectors offered greater scope for productivity increase than others. Given that technological experience, learning by doing or acquired advantages played a key role in industrial competitiveness, in principle it is quite possible for an economy to become 'locked in' to a low productivity growth path. Is that what happened to Britain in the twentieth century?

Landes did conclude from his survey that the British economy was locked in to outdated technologies. The tie between science and practice accelerated the pace of invention. Germany was markedly superior in science and its applications (Landes 1969: 328). The proportion of Nobel prizes awarded to Germans (29%, Britain 8%) in the years 1900–1915 certainly confirms German scientific precocity. But Germany was more precocious than the United States as well, which Table 7.2 shows to be the world industrial leader on an output per head basis. Different leadership criteria and explanations give contradictory indications.

Certainly a good proportion of British hi-tech exports can be linked to domestic demand conditions, given by 'history'. Britain supplied so much of the world's textile machinery because she acquired the knowledge and the demand from pre-eminence in world cotton textile production. An early start in cotton textiles also created a pool of skilled labour and specialized markets, especially in raw cotton. In shipbuilding, domination of world coal exports, as well as being the world's largest trader, ensured a strong British demand for ships which called forth a great deal of expertise, and an extraordinary concentration of world shipbuilding. Once technology shifted towards oil, Britain began to lose out.

Coal availability and mining established the environment in which experimentation with first stationary, and then mobile, steam engines was profitable. Coal also underwrote Britain's heat-intensive approach to the chemical industry, as the industrial focus in Newcastle upon Tyne showed in the 1860s.

German concern with science, perhaps driven by the multiplicity of long established universities, in turn a consequence of multiple German states, contrasted with Britain. Attending a lecture in Heidelberg in 1834, Cooke appreciated how a commercially successful electric telegraph could operate in England. In electricity and telecommunications, trade and empire ensured British domination in submarine cable, with help from the Glasgow University professor, Lord Kelvin. Apart from this bright spot, for other advanced technology electrical products, including telephony, Britain remained a colony of the United States and Germany. As will be shown below, British regulation of road vehicles ensured French dominance of the internal combustion engine before 1904 and in Europe before the First World War.

Contrast the US domination of shipbuilding while the technology was based on wood and sail, when Britain clearly was at a disadvantage where wood availability was concerned. Natural resource abundance played a neglected role in the development of the internal combustion engine. The pursuit of steam cars in the United States stemmed from abundant oil whereas the more economical internal combustion engine was developed earliest in Germany and then France.

Other forces pulled in a different direction. Circulation of ideas, people and capital around the world economy were remarkably free by 1913. And Britain was at the centre of the world wide web of finance and trade. She was a natural location for international industries that were not substantially dependent on untransferable technological and other advantages. Though early specialization, or other causes, may have stifled the development of certain new industries, they might be attracted later when they had demonstrated their profitability. Generation and absorption of new technology drives economic development but it does not have to be generated by the national economy that absorbs it. On the other hand, in some cases there were 'first mover advantages'.

Differences between British and American technology have been represented as the tendency to adopt labour-saving techniques in the US relative to the UK and the propensity to generate new labour-saving technology (Habbakuk 1962, Broadberry 1994). In the frictionless world of neoclassical economics two economies with different endowments of natural and human resources would adopt different techniques of production, defined by the proportions of factors of production employed. So ring spinning of cotton required less skilled labour than did mule spinning, and was generally preferred in the US where skilled labour was scarce. In the UK mule spinning predominated because skilled spinners were abundant. These techniques might be equally efficient technically, in the sense that neither economy is better off adopting the other's technique. But each has lower costs with the chosen technique because it is better adapted to the economy's particular combination of resource endowments. Under normal circumstances such differences in technique did not warrant technological transfers. Since knowledge was acquired by experience, technical progress tended to be incremental rather than making jumps.

Completely new technologies that did entail leaps, such as electrical lighting and power in the 1880s, typically did not at first confer a massive advantage over the old techniques (in the case of electricity, gas and oil lighting, and steam power generated by coal and oil). As experience with the technology was acquired, the technology's 'trajectory' carried it past the older vintages, if factor prices were right. At this point transfers were warranted. National styles of technological development thus depended on both resource endowments, which determined an 'initial technological position', and on national circumstances, which determined the experience that would be gained on particular technologies.

The purpose of this chapter is to show how those differences came about, and in the British case, how advantage was taken of them and with what consequences. The argument here is that factor endowments, industrial evolution and regulation of final use retarded British technical progress in a few new industries, and thus slowed growth by a very small but indeterminate amount. Subsequent technological transfer partly compensated, allowing the new technology to be absorbed, albeit more slowly. This absorption showed itself in the turnaround from a negative trade balance in the earliest phase to a positive balance later. The multinational companies that were responsible for this reversal were not sufficiently tightly controlled that, in the modern sectors, Britain became a *mere* branch plant economy.

New technology

David Landes's classic account (1969) of the development of new technology in this period is the framework for discussion of generation, absorption and transfer in individual industries. Landes distinguishes three categories of new technology: new materials, new power sources and new forms of mechanization.

New materials

The 1870s inaugurated the age of steel. Continental producers leased patents for 'basic' steel manufacture from the British inventors Gilchrist and Thomas very cheaply. The Gilchrist–Thomas process in particular allowed German steel producers to utilize their native ores, growing rapidly to overtake British output. In German and US cases of overtaking, it should be noted that population growth and population levels exceeded those of Britain by a substantial margin, allowing technical developments to be embodied more rapidly in these competitor industries. The overall impact of this advantage on productivity has been judged small by subsequent commentators (Elbaum 1986). In a liberal world economy steel is a good example of the international division of labour working well – except perhaps for Thomas the inventor, who died at the age of 35 exhausted by the need to earn a living in a job (a police court) unrelated to his field of expertise. The steel industry is often accused of neglecting the ores that the Gilchrist–Thomas 'basic process' would have made profitable, but transport costs and the quality of the ore are probably the explanation (McCloskey 1973: 56–72). In special steels we have already seen that Ford found British expertise essential in 1905. By the 1880s German steel was reckoned to be cheaper than British. Greater efficiency in running US Bessemer plants in the 1880s beat the British output but did not overtake British productivity until the end of the century. Elbaum (1986) has lowered Allen's (1979) estimate of the productivity lead from 1.8 to 1.4.

At roughly the same time as the age of steel began, so did the new chemical industry, based on organic chemistry. Here the conventional judgement is that the British industry was backward and dependent on foreign knowhow. However, to be evenhanded with steel, this is merely a different pattern of international specialization, of transfer of technical knowledge. Chandler (1990) remarks that in chemistry, only in dynamite and synthetic soda ash, both made commercially viable by foreign innovators, did British chemical industrialists make the necessary investment to remain competitive. Moreover, 'By any criterion British dyestuffs should have dominated world markets' (Chandler 1990: 278). 'Burroughs Wellcome was the only enterprise to process and distribute pharmaceuticals or fine chemicals comparable to Monsanto or Merck' and it was founded by two Americans (Chandler 1990: 279). The evidence of Burroughs Wellcome will be examined more closely below. Pollard (1989) countered with the observation that dyestuffs was a very small sector. Moreover, the British synthetic dyestuffs industry, minuscule as it was by German standards, was larger than the US industry, which strangely has not been subject to similar accusations.

Continuing backwardness in the dyestuffs industry owes at least something to the early use of blocking patents. Patents were taken out to prevent competitors' products emerging rather than to protect investment in new technology. Until the legislation of 1907, the German industry's products were exported but German dyestuffs patents in Britain blocked technological transfers. Before 1877 in Germany, organic chemical firms were able to imitate products invented in Britain and France, unconstrained by any patent legislation. Having caught up, the German Society for the Protection of the Interests of the Chemical Industry successfully pressed the government for a rigorous patent law that, unlike the French legislation, protected chemical processes and not substances (Reed 1992). This stimulated the search for new and better processes for the same product.

Once Britain had lost her technological lead to Germany, her patent legislation exacerbated the lag. Foreign firms taking out patents in the UK were not obliged to work them in the country. Between 1891 and 1895, 600 patents for coal tar dyes were granted to foreigners, but not one was worked in Britain. German manufacturers were able to block innovation in Britain. The Patent Amendment Act of 1907, obliging foreigners to work or license patents in Britain, demonstrated the impact of earlier legislation by the response the Act evoked. Hoechst set up an indigo plant at Ellesmere Port (Lucius & Bruening), BASF assigned 270 of its patents to the new Mersey Chemicals Co., and Bayer began production on a small scale in Liverpool. However, two years later a court decision effectively nullified the law.

The interface between chemistry and new materials was tolerably well probed and exploited in Britain, culminating in Courtaulds' exploitation of rayon and Pilkingtons' development of plate glass. J.B. Dunlop, a 'tinkerer' vet in the traditional British mould of inventor, used rubber to make a pneumatic tyre in 1888 that would smooth the passage of a child's bike over the cobbles of Belfast. Though Dunlop was not greatly interested in commercial exploitation, a racing cyclist, Du Cros, bought the rights and quickly created a major British multinational company. Joseph W. Swan in 1883 patented an artificial fibre from nitrocellulose, and three British chemists discovered viscose rayon in 1892.

Pharmaceuticals

Together with dyestuffs and electrical engineering, pharmaceuticals have been a key item of evidence in the case against the British economy from the late nineteenth century onwards. One of the few recent historians of the pharmaceutical industry, Jonathan Liebenau (1984, 1990) fits the mould nicely. He paints a picture of an industry slow to evolve from its eighteenth- and nineteenth-century structure of small firms, dependent on raw material imported from the tropics or upon standard chemicals, with little commitment to scientific inventiveness. The industry preferred to license German and Swiss products and shelter behind the barrier of cartels. By the outbreak of the First World War, the pharmaceutical industry was 'unable to supply the domestic market with many of the products that had so changed industry abroad'. It possessed no substantial industrial laboratories and the armed forces were obliged to place major contracts with US corporations. With the exception of Burroughs Wellcome, the industry is presented as the epitome of late Victorian economic inertia and relative decline in the face of new, technologically based competitors in continental Europe and the United States.

The error of this view arises from defining the industry of 1900 in terms only appropriate to recent decades. Liebenau opts for a very narrow definition based on a technology that had little economic impact until the 1940s. There has been excessive emphasis on a small number of drugs which at the time were not of vast significance, but which the First World War revealed to have some strategic importance. A broader definition, of the type used by contemporaries, together with some quantitative evidence, offers a less misleading long-term perspective. It does, however, require some licence in the name of the industry.

Most effective drugs throughout the late Victorian period were alkaloids isolated from plant sources. In 1806 morphine was extracted from opium. Cocaine, isolated in 1860, was the only potent local anaesthetic until 1900. Quinine was extracted from cinchona or Peruvian bark. Britain's key position in international trade ideally suited her to gaining access to the necessary exotic raw materials, not only in pharmaceuticals, but in dyes (indigo), and electrical insulation (gutta percha, rubber). Germany's commitment to chemistry joined with her lesser access to these materials encouraged a drive to produce synthetics.

Examination of Liebenau's contentions more closely requires some objective performance indicators. One measure of competitiveness is the national share in trade. Alternatively, international competitiveness might be judged by the balance of trade, perhaps as a proportion of home sales or imports. These indices are relevant to the competitiveness of an economy as a location. But when the bulk of production is undertaken by multinational companies, as in the 1980s, they are not necessarily measures of the competitiveness of national firms. Such businesses may produce overseas, or foreign owned firms may export from the economy to a third country.

The much remarked German pharmaceutical success before the First World War, according to one calculation, was reflected in a 30% share in world trade by 1913 (James 1977: 19). The corresponding figures for Britain and the US were respectively 21% and 13%. Germany's achievements turned on chemists who were universally recognized as the world leaders throughout the nineteenth century. William Perkin was working in the laboratory of Augustus Wilhelm von Hofman when he synthesized aniline in 1856, the most trumpeted British success in organic chemistry (Reader 1970: 13). Hofman, who studied under Justus von Liebig at Giessen, was appointed the first director of the new Royal College of Chemistry in 1845. He returned to Germany in 1864.

The German lead did not prevent the export of something like two-fifths of British total output of drugs and medicines in 1912. Admittedly, a high proportion was also imported but that might be expected in an open economy such as Britain's, dependent on foreign raw materials. An industry's 'success' is a relative term, for specialization is highly desirable in an international economy, and if an economy exports, it must also import. Some sectors are necessarily net importers if others are to be net exporters. Nonetheless, specialization entirely in products with limited scope for productivity and revenue gain might justify some concern.

More surprisingly, UK exports were far greater than those of the US, the other industry that was supposedly exposing British shortcomings. When the abundance of US natural resources that determined her comparative advantage is recalled – her enormous exports of raw cotton and wheat for instance – the US market share in 1913 is more easily understood.

Revealed comparative advantage (RCA) indices standardize pharmaceutical trade share by the national share in world trade. The RCA index for the United States in 1913 is lower than Britain's since her world trade share was comparable but her pharmaceutical trade share was lower. That is to say, the US pharmaceutical industry was less competitive relative to other US industries than the British pharmaceutical industry was to other British industries.

Britain's balance of trade in drugs and medicines (Table 7.3) shows an increasing surplus of unenumerated exports over unenumerated imports. Imports include re-exports of raw materials such as Peruvian bark for quinine, and opium.

Table 7.3 UK trade in drugs, medicines and medical preparations, 1880–1913 (£000)

Year	Imports			Re-exports			Exports
	Unenum.	Peruvian bark	Opium	Unenum.	Peruvian bark	Opium	
1880	665	1,183	359	510	611	191	814
1890	863	341	282	430	232	232	1,060
1900	1,199	92	427	587	116	216	1,263
1910	1,127	39	434	422	19	155	1,875
1913	1,303	58	507	444	55	285	2,352

Source: Trade and Navigation Accounts of the United Kingdom.
Note: Re-exports for 1910 and 1913 exclude quinine (6 and 12 respectively). Imports for 1913 exclude cocaine (14) and quinine (102). In 1910 quinine imports were 91.

A test of the hypothesis that the British economic environment rather than British entrepreneurs or business styles was constraining pharmaceutical development is to examine the performance of the most dynamic, research-oriented, early pharmaceutical business, Burroughs Wellcome (BW). If it was outstandingly successful in the British market this would refute the environmental hypothesis.

The two American pharmacist entrepreneurs were both graduates and both interested in international travel. Wellcome gave the business a commitment to research, establishing laboratories in 1894 and 1896 with a professionalism not noticeable in native British companies at the time. Both founders were also committed to overseas salesmanship.

Like other British pharmaceutical companies, BW began trading in a low technology business concerned with tonics and health foods. The official history notes Burroughs and Wellcome decided to set up on their own in Britain to take advantage of American improvements in compressed pill manufacture. In 1884 Wellcome coined the trademark 'Tabloid'. But first Burroughs and Wellcome became directors of the Kepler Malt Extract company. By July 1881 problems were being reported with the crystallization of the malt extract obtained from the Condensed Beer Works by another director, P.E. Lockwood. Customers were returning their goods. Burroughs and Wellcome ousted Lockwood from the company and continued to sell the products under their names for many decades (Foreman-Peck 1995).

Salesmanship, not research, was the first principle of BW, as with other British companies in this line of business. In 1881 Burroughs left with a large supply of samples to build up the business overseas. Branches were founded in Australia in 1886, South Africa in 1902, Italy 1905, Canada and the US the following year, Shanghai in 1908 followed by Argentina 1910 and India 1912.

Exports offered a means of spreading the fixed costs of pharmaceuticals over a greater volume of sales. Pushing these sales was often a major effort in overseas political, legislative and climatic environments, but these provided the growth for BW, not the home market, despite the corporate research commitment. If R&D, or a science based pharmaceutical company, was the missing ingredient for pharmaceutical success in the British market before 1914, we should expect to see BW increasing market share. In fact, sales more or less tracked rather stagnant British health care expenditure. Only wartime expansion of the domestic market, and peacetime overseas sales before the Great Depression, provided growth.

New power sources and energy

Turning to new power sources and energy, these included the triple expansion steam engine, Parsons steam turbine of 1884, subsequently licensed to Westinghouse in the US and Brown Boveri on the continent (itself originally an example of British technology transfer to Switzerland), the internal combustion engine, and above all, electricity.

Electricity supply and electrical engineering

British experiments with arc electricity for lighthouses were prominent from 1858. But a French company, the Société Générale d'Electricité de Paris, brought the first public electric lighting to Britain. By 1878, when Joseph Swan (1828–1914) demonstrated his incandescent lamp at the Newcastle Chemical Society, there were a considerable number of electric light installations based on arcing or the Jablochkoff candle. Swan set up the Swan Electric Lighting company in 1881 with R.E. Crompton as chief engineer. Crompton was responsible for lighting the Vienna Opera House in 1883 on an unprecedented scale. Between them Brush, Siemens and Crompton dominated British electrical engineering in 1881.

Thomas Edison made a satisfactory lamp in 1879, the year after Swan's demonstration. Edison was awarded a British patent in 1879 for a lamp in the broadest terms and a few months later Swan obtained one to evacuate the lamp while incandescent. In 1881 the Swan and Edison English companies merged. Patent litigation in the industry continued though. In the US by 1892 the patent position was so chaotic that all the large manufacturers except Westinghouse merged to form General Electric.

The German multinational Siemens had been precociously interested in electrical technology from the introduction of the telegraph. The Siemens family was an example of technology transfer from Germany, and assimilation in the case of Sir William, when Britain was 'workshop of the world', and when nationalism and national rivalries were less apparent. Alexander Siemens was one of the British representatives at the 1893 Chicago International Electrical Congress (Dunsheath 1962: 302). Siemens experimented with an electric train in Berlin in 1879. It opened the first small

British hydro-electric public power station at Godalming two years later. About the same time the Swan Edison Holborn Viaduct station began supplying the public a few months before Pearl Street, New York.

Sebastian de Ferranti's career disproves a number of explanations for the limited scope of Britain's late Victorian electrical engineering industry; that enterprise and technical innovation were lacking (Deptford power station and the 10,000 volt cables), that finance was hard to come by (Parr's Bank for liquidity and stock subscribers like Lord Wantage), that British technical and scientific resources were not adequately mobilized for commercial use (Lord Kelvin, the Siemens connections, the link with BIC), or that business organization was backward (the receiver's first report on departmental organization) (Wilson 1988). Ferranti was certainly an individualist, concerned with the product and the technology, not with finance. But the character of the market, the established position of gas for lighting and the first mover advantages in Germany and the US together with regulation are better explanations for the general backwardness of the industry.

Sebastian de Ferranti was born in Liverpool in 1864 and made and sold his first dynamo at the age of 17. He began work as a research assistant in Siemens in 1881. By 1882 he was independent and patenting an improvement to the Siemens alternator. The Ferranti-Thomson alternator was 50% more efficient than the Siemens original. Deptford power station (the largest in the world) on the right side of the battle of the systems, began supply in 1889 but the cables running through the underground railway tunnels would not take the voltage. Edison in 1889 disapproved of Deptford and J.E.H. Gordon favoured AC. Ferranti appreciated the need for rigid concentric cable construction in his 10,000 volt cable to link the new Deptford station with Grosvenor Gallery. His cables brought in large royalties in the 1890s. The Marindin safety inquiry hamstrung Deptford's commercial viability. Finally, a fire at the Grosvenor Gallery and ensuing losses precipitated a break between Ferranti and the London Electricity Supply Corporation, who built and operated the station (Wilson 1988: 40–1). LESCo began paying dividends only in 1905. Hughes (1983) criticized Deptford as excessively technologically ambitious while at the same time castigating the British industry for lack of enterprise. Deptford used single phase but by 1891 Tesla's polyphase was demonstrated in the US. The general principles were similar.

Ferranti sold the licence to his 1885 meter to Compagnie Générale d'Electricité for Belgium and France for £5,000 over three years (Wilson 1988: 26–7). Sir William Thomson's (Lord Kelvin) co-operation with Ferranti was vital for the success of his meter and his cables. Ferranti co-operated with Atherton of Liverpool who formed British Insulated Wire Co. at Prescot 1891 for low and high voltage cable. Atherton became interested in lead sheathing during a US visit in 1889.

The principal submarine telegraph cable firm Telcon established its first power station, with J.E.H. Gordon's expertise, at Paddington for the Great

Western Railway in 1886. This used three 45 ton alternators. Gordon himself lost faith in AC and concentrated on DC. DC was cheaper to supply because it was more easily storable (in batteries or accumulators) but it needed more copper for transmission lines. AC needed less copper and was more suitable for long distance transmission. Hence AC favoured large central generating stations with scale economies. Gordon, a Cambridge graduate, also installed a station at Manchester Square where the residents took legal action to suppress the vibration. Parsons provided the solution.

The Honourable Charles Parsons, also a Cambridge graduate, constructed the first power stations on the banks of the Cam in 1892 using turbo-alternators on rubber blocks. The engineering laboratory of the University of Cambridge the same year carried out extensive tests on the installation with complimentary conclusions. Parsons' position in world electricity supply was such that he secured an order at the turn of the century to supply the largest turbo-alternators in the world for the German city of Elberfeld.

Possibly more electricity was consumed in Britain until the First World War than in Germany (Landes 1969: 289). But electrical engineering manufacture in Germany was more than double British output and almost equal to the United States. Germany's exports were 2.5 times the UK's, which in turn were larger than the United States'. Two-thirds of British electrical output was produced by subsidiaries of Westinghouse, General Electric (British Thomson Houston) and Siemens by 1913.

Landes points out that nonetheless coal continued to supply most of Europe's primary power; in Britain 92% of primary power came from steam in 1911, in Germany 82% and in France 73%. Shortcomings in electrical technology were not going to damage the economy greatly.

The regulatory constraint on electricity

During 1878, 34 applications for private bills were made to parliament to open up the streets for public electricity supply. The Electric Lighting Act of 1882 allowed the Board of Trade to grant companies seven-year licences if the relevant municipalities agreed. Municipalities by now often controlled the competing gas works and therefore could have an interest in protecting their revenue. If they did not consent, electricity companies needed an order from the Board of Trade confirmed by parliament. The 1882 Act prescribed that the area of supply should be coterminous with the local authority and provisional orders to break up the streets were subject to cancellation after twenty-one years on terms settled by the authority. The compulsory purchase price included no allowance for good will or future profits. Two years after the Act, seventy-three orders had been granted but in not one case had electricity supply begun. This continued to be the case until 1888 when an amending Act extended the period to forty-two years and capital began to flow. But the British industry had lost a crucial decade of development, which affected not only electricity supply but also electrical engineering.

Moreover, the constraint imposed by local authority areas persisted. Local authorities were encouraged to establish many small electricity stations. After an 1898 Joint Select Committee a number of power companies were authorized by private Acts of Parliament to supply electricity in bulk over wide areas, exempt from the purchase provisions of the 1888 Act (Committee on Industry and Trade 1928: 315–16; Dunsheath 1962).

By and large the legal constraints of the Acts of 1882 and 1889 held back electrical engineering and electrochemistry as a consequence of restraining electricity supply. It is difficult to produce successfully equipment on the frontiers of technology for export when the domestic market requires something less sophisticated. If electricity is expensive because of low thermal efficiency stations then electricity-intensive metallurgical projects, such as aluminium smelting, will be unprofitable. Until 1888 there was only one electricity supply company, whereas Edison had installed 149 generating central stations in the US by then.

Hannah (1979) denies regulation mattered. Twenty-one years was long enough for a commercial return and only in the 1890s did electrical engineers construct intermunicipal works (presumably with the exception of LESCo's Deptford–Grosvenor system). But at 5% (and these were years of low interest rates) £10,000 in twenty-one years' time is worth as much as £3,500 today. Given that immediate returns may be zero, as witnessed by shareholders in the Deptford power station project waiting sixteen years for their first dividends, endweighting could well be important. Wilson (1988) maintains the key obstacle was the aftermath of the 1882 speculative frenzy known as the 'Brush Bubble' which raised over £7 million for the electricity industry, though little was used productively. Even with the new incandescent lamps, electric lighting remained up to one-third more expensive than gas (Byatt 1979). Byatt notes there were only 1 million lamps in London by 1890 but ignores the Marindin restrictions. Regulation also contributed to persisting with DC.

Telecoms

Telephony was a specialized branch of electrical engineering, the stifling of which by the Post Office monopoly of telegraphy has been discussed elsewhere (Foreman-Peck and Millward 1994). The knock-on effects for British telephone engineering development were disastrous but there were minor compensations in telegraphy, and anyway cable technology continued to be dominated by Britain. A British technological lead in radio stemmed from openness to outsiders and naval requirements.

With the second Atlantic cable completed and operating, Britain in 1866 not only owned the world's submarine cables but also had a virtual monopoly of submarine telegraph expertise and cable manufacture. The British cable-making industry expanded rapidly, with two new cable core suppliers entering the industry. A Pacific Cable Board, a consortium of Empire governments, was established in 1898. The cable agreement for completion in two years was signed in 1900, by which time the military demands of the Boer War were reinforcing the political support for rapid Imperial communications.

Telcon constructed and laid 80% of the world's submarine telegraph cable and therefore might have been expected to carry out research commensurate with its position at the leading edge of technology at the time. It did not. Before 1890 there was a room on the third floor at the Wharf Road factory called 'the Chemistry' into which only three people were allowed. After the First World War a team of qualified chemists and physicists expanded the department to two floors of laboratories.

Because of the link with telegraphy, in which Britain increasingly acquired an advantage as the United States moved over to the telephone, high speed tele-printer innovation was more likely in Britain. An electric typewriter, consisting of a printing wheel, was invented by Thomas Edison in 1872 and developed into the ticker tape printer. Extel originally planned to import tape machines from the United States in 1872 but cheaper, equally satisfactory, British machines turned out to be available (Scott 1972: 16). Fred Higgins, the Exchange Telegraph Company's engineer (formerly Superintendent of Telegraphs for Mauritius), developed a type printing system, described in a paper to the Society of Telegraph Engineers in 1877. The system could print a massive volume of information by contrast with the earlier techniques. From 1883 the column printer with type wheel was available for long telegraph messages. Extel's use of column printers increased as they proved themselves and as business grew; in 1890 there were 4, in 1891 46 and in 1892 74, which could produce 2,000 words per hour. In 1895 317 million words were transmitted and half a million calls passed through Extel's headquarters. By 1902 machines were printing 35–40 words a minute compared with about 6 when Higgins joined Extel in 1873. In the year ending 30 June 1911 Extel transmitted 607 million words (Scott 1972: 92). Only 5.5 minutes were required for New York stock prices to appear before Extel's public in 1910, served on 1,100 instruments.

Surprisingly, the introduction of the automatic telephone exchange, perhaps the most sophisticated technology of the early twentieth century, looks like a case of US or Bell entrepreneurial failure, rather than primarily a British deficiency. However, it was not one that apparently stifled the US economy nor one that has been widely noted. The replacement of the manual by the automatic exchange substituted capital for labour. The automatic could also speed up the arranging of a call.

Dane Sinclair invented the first automatic switchboard used in Britain in 1883, but it was not developed further even though Sinclair became engineer in chief to the National Telephone Company in 1882 and general manager of British Insulated & Helsby Cables in 1902. Later AT&T examined Sinclair's apparatus and compared it with its own experimental switches. These used cheap clockwork whereas Sinclair's more effective version was a costly £35. The author of the AT&T report remarked that a cheaper and more effective solution to providing an exchange for the small number of subscribers that a rural community might support (and one used in the Birmingham district) was to employ the daughters of a respectable local family in return for supplying them with a house (and telephone exchange) rent free (Foreman-Peck 1992).

Although Kansas undertaker Almon Strowger produced his first 'step by step' exchange in 1889, his idea that the subscriber sent current impulses by wire to move an arm over contacts required a great deal of innovation before it could come into widespread use. Chief Engineer W.H. Preece reported unfavourably on automatics to the Post Office. The National Telephone Company (NTC) had no incentive to invest in new technology, knowing it was to be bought out by the Post Office. Not until 1912 did Britain get its first experimental automatic exchange, fourteen years after Amsterdam.

The US Bell Chief Engineer J.J. Carty contended that the number of people needed to operate and maintain an automatic system was not much less than a 'manual' system and the capital costs were considerably greater. Anyway, so-called manual systems were largely automatic. Bell's 1910 assessment of exchange costs for 100,000 subscribers in New York was that 13,000 staff were needed for 'manual' working and 10,000 for 'automatic'.

The technological costs of this delay were apparent from the foreign sources of all key patents when the Post Office began introducing different automatics to gain experience in their working. US Strowger patents were held by the Liverpool based Automatic Telephone Manufacturing Co. (ATM) formed in 1911 and occupying British Insulated & Helsby's former factory. ATM supplied the Epsom switch. Western Electric, the manufacturing arm of AT&T, installed a rotary based automatic in Darlington in 1914. Siemens, which gained access to Strowger technology through the German rights of Siemens & Halske, supplied a step by step exchange at Grimsby in 1918. Marconi's Wireless Telegraph Company acquired the Swedish Betulander patents in 1913, forming the Relay Automatic Telephone Company to exploit them in 1915.

Siemens in Britain benefited from German automatic exchange research. But it had by 1912 recruited its own staff of British telephone engineers, headed by E.A. Laidlaw, formerly of the NTC (the Post Office was unable to pay comparable top salaries for NTC officials). Laidlaw, with his lieutenant W.H. Grinstead, was a believer in the future of the automatic exchange, unlike the NTC (Scott 1958: 170). Grinstead had been making original contributions in probability theory as a private interest from 1907 while working for the NTC. His expertise put Siemens ahead of the

Americans and Siemens & Halske. The Siemens ten-point pre-selector was the basic difference between European and American automatic exchanges.

Guglielmo Marconi was an example of Britain's ability to attract foreign technological talent at the end of the nineteenth century, although in fact his mother was Irish. Pocock's (1988) study shows that the British Post Office was not initially favourably inclined to Marconi's wireless invention but the communication needs of the Royal Navy provided the justification for development support.

In 1901 Marconi managed to receive in Newfoundland the Morse signal for *S* transmitted by wireless from Cornwall. In February 1908 he opened a public wireless telegraph service between Britain and Canada but it proved inferior to cable. Marconi established a formal research department in 1912.

Internal combustion engines

In 1901 far more US steam and electric cars were produced than internal combustion engined vehicles (Foreman-Peck and Hayafuji 1995). This apparently clear case of US entrepreneurial failure to make the right choice of technique has not been identified as such by historians. The reason highlights the methodological error of so much of the 'decline of the British economy' literature; any deviant pattern in the British economy is a potential cause of 'failure'. By contrast, since it occurs in the US the observation is cited as a case of the path dependence of the development of the internal combustion engine and the role of chance in technological history (Arthur 1989). By following the French, the British did not make the same mistake, though their early experiments were constrained by a tighter regulatory environment than in France. When Coventry bicycle-maker J.K. Starley wished to test his electric powered tricycle in 1888, he was obliged to take it to Deauville.

Concern with public safety during the 1860s and 1870s so restricted the use of motor vehicles on the public road that the incentive to invent in Britain was markedly reduced until the repeal of the 'Red Flag Act' in 1896. Although when agitation against the 1878 Highways and Locomotives Act arose, the legislation was quickly repealed, the Act may well have constrained innovation while in force. An entrepreneur is not inclined to consider supplying a new market restricted by legislation unless that market has been clearly identified. By that time, entrepreneurs in other countries will have achieved a lead. In the absence of restrictive legislation it is not clear why Britain, a highly urbanized, industrial society, should have been backward. If a general entrepreneurial failure was at the root, we would not have expected to see such a dynamic British bicycle industry.

Despite the absence of a high-income mass market, British manufacturers were as anxious to extend motoring as businessmen in North America. The evidence comes from the motorcycle, the cycle car and the light car. Each was a way of bringing down prices in an environment where the scope for volume production was limited. The cycle car originated in Paris in 1909 with the Bedelia, a two-seater air-cooled engine model. Morgan and GN cycle cars began production in Britain in 1911. By the following year, at least sixty British manufacturers were engaged in making cycle cars. They were defined as small motor cars of narrow wheel gauge, but light in construction, selling at a lower price and costing less to operate than the usual motor car, with a possible speed of 30–40 m.p.h. These cars might have three or four wheels, a track of 36–40 inches and 2–4 seats. The cycle car had to be less than 1,100 cc engine capacity and 784 lb weight; above these limits a reverse gear was needed. It was thought that at least 350,000 people in the UK could afford them. *Motor* magazine claimed that their output was well over 20,000, with home manufacturers supplying two-thirds of home demand. The cycle car boom may well have been encouraged by the rising price of petrol which began the year at 1/0d a gallon rising to 1/7d a gallon, far above US prices (Foreman-Peck, Bowden and McKinley 1995).

The cycle car was essentially a crossbreed of a motorcycle with a car, with all the discomfort that combination implied. The more successful species was the light car, or *voiturette*, a category that had been identified by the French motoring magazine *l'Auto* in 1905 inaugurating a special race for them. In 1908, the category was extended to include four-cylinder engines, as well as those with one and two cylinders. From this event, Bugatti designed a model which, when sold to Peugeot, propelled that company to the top of the French car-makers league in 1913. Light cars soon crossed the Channel. Singer's 1912 Ten and the Morris Oxford of 1913 were to set the trend for the new era of the British motor industry. Comparatively good roads and the horsepower tax favoured such cars in Britain, in contrast to the US.

Immediately after the repeal of the Red Flag Act removed one barrier to development of the internal combustion engine another appeared. Harry Lawson attempted to establish a monopoly right to produce or license all petrol-driven cars. Lawson formed the British Motor Syndicate in 1895 with the intention of acquiring the original German Daimler and other major patents. The Syndicate then expected to be able to exploit its position by charging substantial royalties. The Daimler Motor Company was established the following year as a subsidiary of the Syndicate and maintained a dominant position in the pre-1914 industry (from 1909 helped by one of the most creative British motor engineers, Frederick Lanchester). A court decision of 1901 put paid to Lawson's monopolistic aspirations, giving British engineers a stronger reason to favour the internal combustion engine than Americans. Technical progress was making the patents obsolete in any case, but in Britain and America such a monopoly, even for a few years at such a crucial stage, was almost certain to retard development. Herbert Austin abandoned development of the first Wolseley he built because it so closely resembled a model the patent for which was held by Lawson's Syndicate.

The emergence of the motor vehicle illustrates a principle of technological development; in the freer economic environment innovation will be stronger. As soon as state virtual prohibitions were abolished in 1896, Lawson's own profit-oriented restrictions were introduced. The beneficiaries were the French manufacturers, whose demonstrations effects were stronger in Britain than in the United States.

New forms of mechanization

In light machinery Chandler (1990) claims British entrepreneurial and technological failure was understandable. Sewing machines, typewriters, cash registers and electrical appliances benefited from first mover advantages. On bicycles he is silent.

The United States had been highly precocious in mechanization and the division of labour through much of the nineteenth century, especially with the technology of interchangeable parts, exemplified by the Singer sewing machine and the Colt revolver. The extension to machine tools was a continuation of the same trajectory. In this field a loss of 'industrial leadership' by Britain is hard to demonstrate because it was never a unique British strength. Nonetheless, William Brown of Birmingham's 1877 patent for ball bearings and the bicycle boom of the 1890s showed that Britain maintained strengths in this field as well.

Bicycles and small arms were connected in Birmingham Small Arm's (BSA) diversification strategy. British specialisation in bicycles reflected a strong domestic demand – for which tolerable roads were necessary but lacking in the US – and the skills of the West Midlands metalworking industry. By contrast, Remingtons, the US arms manufacturer, specialist in the technology of interchangeable components, diversified into typewriters for which US demand was strong, reflecting the more expensive American clerical labour.

Conclusion

Late Victorian generation and absorption of new technology (and therefore productivity) was strongly influenced by regulation – and by past history and factor prices. Contrary to Chandler there are no widespread obvious entrepreneurial failures. The case for political failure is rather stronger, casting new light on the 'institutional sclerosis' thesis proposed by Olson (1982).

A large domestic gas industry offered strong competition to electricity for lighting. Together they slowed the development of electrical engineering, of electricity supply and thus of industrial uses of electricity. A subsidized telegraph industry and regulation constrained telephony so telecommunications engineering was held back even though little electricity was needed. The internal combustion engine was constrained again by regulation, this time in the interests of safety.

In new branches of chemistry, dyestuffs were a small sector, as shown by the failure of the US to develop even as much as the UK, without apparent adverse consequences. That was also true of what was to develop into the pharmaceutical industry. Most drugs employed and traded were extracted from natural products and British trade performance in the sector as a whole was ahead of the US, though behind Germany. Research deficiencies in this field are no explanation for slow growth, as Burroughs Wellcome shows.

Highly developed markets and rather low moral hazard discouraged large integrated firms even for advanced technology. In low technology cotton textiles, where British comparative advantage was most extreme (with labour productivity in spinning almost double US levels), the arrangement obviously worked well (Levnig 1998). In high technology, where British entrepreneurs gained a foothold, it may not have done. So C.A. Parsons licensed turbine production by Westinghouse in the US and Brown Boveri on the continent rather than producing for export or developing a multinational enterprise himself. With hindsight, this may have been an error. The costs of negotiating a contract for advanced technology and continuing to develop it in fact may have meant Parsons would have gained more from the US route. But it was not so apparent at the time. The US large corporation solution was a fortuitous response to distinctive and different US problems – imperfect markets and the high moral hazard of a more mobile society. Other US responses to the distinctive US environment – the steam car, and the commitment to the manual telephone exchange – were not so obviously suitable for the twentieth century.

Writing history backwards emphasizes before their time institutions that will eventually become important. The efficiency with which railways operated mattered a great deal more to late Victorian and Edwardian Britain than did the dyestuffs sector or large integrated corporations. Regulatory failures also hamstrung railways but, because there had been a period of untrammelled growth, product suppliers – in particular railway locomotive manufacturers that remained unintegrated with operating companies – were able to perform creditably in export markets, such as Japan, until 1914.

References

Allen, R. C. (1979), ' International Competitiveness in Iron and Steel, 1850–1913', *Journal of Economic History*, 39, pp. 911–37.
Arthur, W.B. (1989), 'Competing Technologies, Increasing Returns and Lock-In by Historical Events', *Economic Journal*, 99, pp. 116–31.
Barnett, C. (1986), *The Audit of War: The Myth and Reality of Britain as a Great Power*, London, Macmillan.

Broadberry, S.N. (1994), 'Technological Leadership and Productivity Leadership in Manufacturing since the Industrial Revolution: Implications for the Convergence Debate', *Economic Journal*, 104, pp. 291–302.

Byatt, I.C.R. (1979), *The British Electrical Industry, 1875–1914*, Oxford, Clarendon Press.

Chandler, A. (1990), *Scale and Scope: The Dynamics of Industrial Capitalism*, Cambridge, Mass., Harvard University Press.

Committee on Industry and Trade (1928), *Report*, London, HMSO, vol. 2.

Dintenfass, M. (1992), *The Decline of Industrial Britain 1870–1980*, London, Routledge.

Dunsheath, P. (1962), *A History of Electrical Engineering*, London, Faber.

Elbaum, B. (1986), 'The Steel Industry Before the First World War', in B. Elbaum and W. Lazonick, *The Decline of the British Economy*, Oxford, Oxford University Press.

Elbaum, B. and Lazonick, W. (1986), *The Decline of the British Economy*, Oxford, Oxford University Press.

Ford, H. (1923), *My Life and Work*, London, Heinemann.

Foreman-Peck, J.S. (1992), 'The Development and Diffusion of Telephone Technology in Britain 1900–1940', *Transactions of the Newcomen Society*, 63, pp. 165–79.

Foreman-Peck, J.S. (1995), 'The Long Run Competitiveness of British Healthcare Businesses', Aberdeen Conference on the History of Medicine.

Foreman-Peck, J.S. and Hayafuji, M. (1995), 'Lock-in versus Panglossian Selection: The Choice of Power Source for the Motor Car', Paper presented to the Business History Association conference, Florida.

Foreman-Peck, J.S. and Millward, R. (1994), *Public and Private Ownership of Industry in Britain 1820–1990*, Oxford, Clarendon Press.

Foreman-Peck, J.S., Bowden, S. and McKinley, A. (1995), *The Motor Industry*, Manchester, Manchester University Press.

Habbakuk, H.J. (1962), *American and British Technology in the Nineteenth Century*, Cambridge, Cambridge University Press.

Hannah, L. (1979), *Electricity before Nationalisation*, London, Macmillan.

Hughes, T.P. (1983), *Networks of Power: Electrification of Western Society 1880–1930*, Baltimore, The Johns Hopkins University Press.

James, B.G. (1977), *The Future of the Multinational Pharmaceutical Industry to 1990*, Ass. Bus. Prog., London.

Landes, D.S. (1969), *The Unbound Prometheus: Technological Change and Industrial Development in Western Europe from 1750 to the Present*, Cambridge, Cambridge University Press.

Lawford, G.L. and Nicholson L.R. (1950), *The Telcon Story 1850–1950*, The Telegraph Construction and Maintenance Co. Ltd, London.

Levnig, T. (1998) 'Summary of *The Myth of the Corporate Economy*', *Journal of Economic History*, 58, pp. 528–31.

Liebenau, J. (1984), 'Industrial R&D in Pharmaceutical Firms in the Early Twentieth Century', *Business History*, 26, pp. 329–46.

Liebenau, J. (1990), 'The Twentieth Century British Pharmaceutical Industry in International Context', in J. Liebenau, G.J. Higby and E.C. Stroud (eds), *Pill Pedlers: Essays on the History of the Pharmaceutical Industry*, American Institute of the History of Pharmacy, Madison Wisconsin.

Lindert, P.H. and Trace, K. (1971), 'Yardsticks for Victorian Entrepreneurs', in D. N. McCloskey (ed.), *Essays on a Mature Economy: Britain after 1840*, London, Methuen.

McCloskey, D.N. (1973), *Economic Maturity and Entrepreneurial Decline: British Iron and Steel 1870–1913*, Cambridge, Mass., Harvard University Press.

Nelson, R.R. and Wright, G. (1992), 'American Technological Leadership', *Journal of Economic Literature*, 30, pp. 1931–64.
Olson, M. (1982), *The Rise and Decline of Nations*, New Haven, Yale University Press.
Pocock, R.F. (1988), *The Early British Radio Industry*, Manchester, Manchester University Press.
Pollard, S. (1989), *Britain's Prime and Britain's Decline: The British Economy 1870–1914*, London, Edward Arnold.
Reader, W.J. (1970), *Imperial Chemical Industries: A History*, vol. I: *The Forerunners 1870–1926*, London, Oxford University Press.
Reed, P. (1992), 'The British Chemical Industry and the Indigo Trade', *British Journal for the History of Science*, 25, pp. 113–25.
Royal Commission on the Depression in Trade and Industry (1886), British Parliamentary Papers.
Sandberg, L.G. (1974), *Lancashire in Decline*, Columbus, Ohio State University Press.
Saul, S.B. (1962), 'The Motor Industry to 1914', *Business History*, 5, pp. 22–44.
Scott, J.D. (1958), *Siemens Brothers 1858–1958*, London, Weidenfeld and Nicolson.
Scott, J.M. (1972), *Extel 100: The Centenary History of the Exchange Telegraph Company*, London, Ernest Benn.
Uchida, H. (1991), 'The Transfer of Electrical Technologies from the United States and Europe to Japan 1869–1914', in D.J. Jeremy (ed.), *International Technology Transfer: Europe, Japan and the USA 1700–1914*, Aldershot, Edward Elgar.
Wilson, J.F. (1988), *Ferranti and the British Electrical Industry 1864–1930*, Manchester, Manchester University Press.
Wilson, J.F. (1995), *British Business History 1720–1994*, Manchester, Manchester University Press.
Wright, G. (1990), 'The Origins of American Industrial Success 1879–1940', *American Economic Review*, 80, pp. 651–68.
Yuzawa, T. (1991), 'The Transfer of Railway Technologies from Britain to Japan, with Special Reference to Locomotive Manufacture', in D.J. Jeremy (ed.), *International Technology Transfer: Europe, Japan and the USA 1700–1914*, Aldershot, Edward Elgar.

8

REGIONAL VS. NATIONAL PERSPECTIVES ON ECONOMIC 'DECLINE' IN LATE VICTORIAN AND EDWARDIAN BRITAIN

W.R. Garside

The economic development of the modern world is usually written in terms of national units. In effect, however, the national growth rates are merely the outcome of averaging out, or adding together, the growth of industrial regions. That is more than a statistical convenience. Growth was not merely registered, it essentially also took place in regions. Governments . . . in the end . . . depended on what took place on the ground, and on the ground were the regions.[1]

Much of the debate about economic performance in late Victorian and Edwardian Britain has concentrated on the country's overcommitment to a narrow range of staple export industries catering for relatively low income markets and the subsequent retardation in the development of potential growth sectors such as vehicles, chemicals and electrical engineering. The consequences, whatever the precise sources of the relative decline,[2] were faltering growth relative to Britain's principal competitors in terms of real GDP per worker and total factor productivity and a declining share in the world market for manufactured goods. The statistical data upon which such generalizations depend are both fragile and contentious. Moreover, as Pollard's survey of British growth performance before 1914 reminds us, the 'economic decline' debate remains inconclusive and unsatisfactory, not least because of 'the fluid nature of the counter-factual assumptions which underlie the notion of blame or failure'.[3] From the perspective of this chapter, it is worth recalling that the analyses of economic growth upon which much of this now familiar debate rests have been premised on the nation state as an economically homogeneous entity capable of investigation. McCloskey's determination to raise industry case studies of entrepreneurial activity, focusing on the opportunities and confines of contemporary costs, resources and market structure, provides a good example of the well documented alternative approach.[4] Yet, as Pollard and Lee in particular have claimed, too little attention has been focused on growth and structural change at the regional level. The obvious manifestations of regional industrialization, such as the boom in cotton manufacture in Lancashire, shipbuilding on the Tyne and the Clyde, and the growth of woollen textiles in West Yorkshire, have customarily been represented merely as adding 'a little local colour' to the overall picture of industrial transformation.[5] But British economic performance in this period can, arguably, only properly be understood if it embraces a regional perspective. When thus perceived, it will defy any easy classification into 'success' or 'failure', or even sustain the primacy of industry in any explanation of national development.

This is not the place to enter the terminological thicket of what is meant by a 'region', suffice to say that the areas delineated for our purpose have a degree of internal homogeneity compared with other regions, have links to a centre of activity, and have well developed networks of internal connections. Of the three most common approaches used to measure the distinctiveness of regions – output, rate of population growth and employment, it is the latter which has been used in the literature to identify the regional measure of British economic and industrial development. Lee's analysis of Census of Employment statistics from 1841 to 1911 groups regions into four major types, a textile-orientated region, a mining and metal working region, a metropolitan region based on London but expanding into contiguous counties, and a slow growing rural peripheral region.[6] The typology of British industrialization conforms to this broad analysis. The first long wave of the Industrial Revolution was heavily associated with the cotton textile industry of the north-west, involving a growth of urban manufacturing centres and a decline of industrial employment in surrounding regions. The Victorian boom and the so-called Great Depression were led by a more diverse combination of heavy industries located around the coalfields of northern England, central Scotland and South Wales. In the third wave leadership passed to the light engineering and metal trades of the West Midlands, accompanied by the beginning of the decline of the northern heavy industries. In all this, there resulted an enhanced spatial division of production between capital equipment and raw material sectors in the north and the southern service sectors and consumer goods manufacturing, finishing and distribution industries.[7]

This is familiar territory, of course, but it is to the more detailed treatment of that spatial divide to which we turn in our search for a clearer regional perspective on British economic performance down to 1914. Few can deny the importance of industrialization in textiles, iron and steel, engineering, shipbuilding and coalmining in Britain's nineteenth-century development, not only as the basis of regionally concentrated industrial growth as such but also as the source of new industrial developments, of which textile machinery manufacture, chemicals and metal manufacture are but three examples, and additionally as a precursor of expanded construction, public utilities provision, and the growth of services such as transport, distribution and varied professional and commercial activities.[8]

But this ready focus on the primacy of provincial industry in economic growth sits uneasily with the available data on regional employment and incomes. The industrial regions make a rather poor showing in terms of nineteenth-century relative incomes. Labour intensive methods of production encouraged the search for competitive low-cost operations based on cheap labour which served to depress income levels in the traditional industrial regions, with concomitant effects on consumer spending and any putative multiplier effects on employment and income growth in the service sector.[9] By contrast, the higher than average level of regional income and wealth in the south-east set it apart from the majority of other regions. Although industrial growth undoubtedly generated the development of service sectors in a number of geographical areas, the comparative advantage of the south-east in particular resulted not from the transfers or spill-over effects from traditional industries such as cotton, heavy engineering, shipbuilding or coal but from a service-orientated regional growth sustained by the income and wealth from trade, finance, investment and the consumer spending of the landed élite. Rubinstein has shown that cotton manufacturing and iron making were not the best avenues to great fortunes in late Victorian Britain; the most important sources came from the metropolitan pursuits of finance and commerce.[10] It was the opportunity provided by the growth of the City of London as an international financial centre down to 1914 that furnished the growth of a complex of financial institutions and international connections. These created the sources of substantial wealth which in turn generated demands for goods and services. The affluent, southern service-orientated economies could to a considerable extent sustain their own well-being.[11] The accumulated returns from trade, finance and the land freed the south-east from the limitations of low incomes. It was there that high levels of service provision, at all levels of skill, fuelled by middle-class and professional incomes engendered an element of self-sustained growth. This structurally different regional economy, in terms of size, wealth and comparative advantage, represents in graphic form the economic and spatial dualism of Victorian and Edwardian England. It is a warning too of the limitation of assessing growth in the period largely in terms of the primacy of industry, whether it be the role of Lancashire textiles or Durham mining. Between 1841 and 1911 66 per cent of all additional jobs created in the south-eastern region, which was dominated by London, were in services alone and most of the others were in consumer-orientated manufactures.[12]

The metropolitan and home counties region emerges as a major growth area larger than either the total mining regions or the total of textile regions whichever statistical approach is adopted, whether population growth, regional structural analysis or income distribution. Service industries, moreover, were highly integrated with each other and were not, as is sometimes presumed, merely a function of manufacturing growth. Moreover, unlike the heavy manufacturing sectors which had low linkages with other industrial orders, the services had several manufacturing sectors closely linked to them, including paper, printing and publishing, timber and furniture, clothing, chemicals and the new instrument and electrical engineering industries.

By 1911 the south-east had 52 per cent of its total employment in the service industries compared to a national average of 41 per cent. Moreover, much of the increase in employment in Britain from 1851 to 1911 had been channelled into this region. It enjoyed for most of that period high activity rates and a large component of high income employment. These developments reinforced the strength of the southern region. Whereas the textile and mining economies depended essentially on demand external to their regions, the metropolitan economy enjoyed internal generation of employment growth sustained by structural diversity, a dense concentration of population, a preponderance of middle-class occupations and conspicuous consumption.[13] 'The South-East', in Lee's phrase, 'appears to have become the world's first large-scale consumer society.'[14]

The comparative advantages of the service-dominated south-eastern metropolitan economy can be viewed from another perspective. The conventional view of the origin of the depressed areas and of the 'regional problem', namely that they were a product of the ravages of the post-First World War economy when an export-orientated high growth northern sector based on engineering, shipbuilding, textiles and mining was decimated by the collapse of export demand, has itself been questioned. Recent estimates of unemployment rates among skilled engineers, carpenters and ironfounders suggest that they were higher before the First World War in the industrial areas of northern England and central Scotland than they were further south. Unemployment among skilled engineers averaged 12.1 per cent in the United Kingdom in April 1909 but reached over 19 per cent in Tyne and Wear, nearly 18 per cent on Clydeside and 15 per cent in West Yorkshire. It was less than 10 per cent in the south and west of England. As Southall puts it:

> Much of Victorian Britain was enmeshed in a pattern of development which created intrinsically unstable regional economies, the benefits of growth being denied to much of the population of such areas by repeated and prolonged episodes of unemployment. . . . This burden was . . . part of the price Britain paid for an apparently prosperous industrial system based on exports rather than

indigenous demand, and it seems that the burden fell most heavily, both then and subsequently, on those regions which created her prosperity.[15]

By bringing a degree of stability to the spatial pattern of regional unemployment into the pre-1914 period, unemployment begins to appear less as a consequence of patterns of secular decline than as a reflection of industrial structure. The interwar regional unemployment problem can thereby be viewed as part of the evolution of late Victorian and Edwardian industrialization, one which contrasts a vulnerable, specialized and export-orientated sector in the north, South Wales and central Scotland with a relatively more affluent and stable south-east orientated towards finance, the professions and government. Thus, when faced with the economic turbulence of the post-1920 period the south-east was able to generate all types of new firms because of the size of its potential market, both regional and European, and its favourable level of local purchasing power.[16]

It is clear from the above that the industry/service dualism of the late Victorian and Edwardian period offers a persuasive case for distancing ourselves from the primacy of industry and for emphasizing the significance of the metropolitan financial/service sector in any assessment of pre-1914 economic change. But the reorientation should not be taken too far. Manufacturing and services were not mutually exclusive; nor is it certain, definitional and data problems notwithstanding, that the productivity performance of the service sector was noticeably superior to manufacturing when viewed in relation to the far from impressive performance of the economy as a whole.[17] Moreover, the existence of a thriving south-east economy able to reap the market and consuming benefits of a concentrated wealthy population should not encourage too stylized a view of industrial performance. The contrasts drawn above with the older established industries could readily portray them as risk-avoiding sectors averse to mass production techniques, wedded to labour intensive manual craft skills, and locked into less than optimum levels of production and efficiency. In Chandlerian terms, the ability of such sectors to expand without much recourse to the financial sector reinforced the survival of the small family firm and the capacity of owners to retain control, thereby denying themselves the advantages of multi-divisional managerial and technical expertise and efficient mass production techniques so ably taken up by America.[18]

The debate on 'industrial decline' before 1914 has continued for so long because of the arguments, counterfactual and otherwise, ranged against such a generalization. There is a further dimension of this now familiar debate between the optimists and the pessimists, however, which deserves greater emphasis, namely the variety and complexity of activity within and between industrial regions. The delineation of regions according to their allegedly 'favourable' or 'unfavourable' industrial structure provides useful evidence of the contrasting experiences of the industrial north and the service-dominated south. But it will not reflect adequately the myriad of industrial activities that contributed to pre-1914 economic success or otherwise. Although the bulk of industrial employment in the nineteenth century was to be found in the north and west of Britain, a clear distinction could be made between the 'industrial periphery' of Wales, Scotland and the northern region and the 'manufacturing heartland' of the West Midlands, north-west and Yorkshire and Humberside regions. The fastest expansion of manufacturing employment during the nineteenth century occurred in the latter regions which went on to increase progressively their share of national manufacturing employment (see Figure 8.1).

The process by which the West Midlands gained its second wind as a leading industrial area illustrates, as a first example, how an apparently 'unfavourable' industrial structure subsequently played a part in encouraging a faster growth of newer sectors of considerable short-term and medium-term significance. In the late nineteenth century the Birmingham region had several industries – cast hollow-ware, buttons, small arms, wrought nails – which were in relative decline. The 'Great Depression' hit the metal trades hard while overseas competition from Europe and the USA encroached similarly upon the region's finished manufactures. Birmingham and its industrial hinterland, however, developed more rapidly than other manufacturing regions down to 1914 because it was able to utilize the factors of production released from its relatively stagnant sectors. The newer industrial sectors of the region such as the cycle and motor trades, heavily concentrated in Birmingham, Coventry and Wolverhampton, emerged out of other lines of production, assembling products which demanded a wide range of components from a variety of metal, leather, woodworking, electrical, rubber, paint, varnish and even textile trades. This type of industrial evolution was enhanced by the fact that the existing forms of industry in the area were relatively unspecialized in plant and tools, permitting the non-specificity of investment, together with the existing pool of skilled labour, to assist the generation of new products and market opportunities. Growth occurred too in sectors such as food and drink not otherwise associated with the traditional industries of the area but able to benefit from Birmingham's excellence as a distributing centre for the home market.[19]

It was of some importance in the long run that if industrial specialisms of a past era should begin to lose their comparative advantage they should do so at a time of new opportunity. In Birmingham's case, it was this process of industrial evolution during the late Victorian and Edwardian period, during which new industries emerged out of the old, which permitted the region to adapt to changing patterns of competition, demand and technology. And it was this process which provided the region with a degree of resilience in the later and turbulent interwar period. It is significant that the expanding industries of the interwar period (electricals, electrical engineering, motor vehicles and cycles amongst others), grew at roughly the same rate in depressed and prosperous regions during the 1920s and 1930s. Differences between regions were due more to their 'initial positions' with respect to the relative importance of expanding and declining industries in the region in the early 1920s. Data on the share of new manufacturing industries in the total of insured persons in regions of Britain in 1923 show that the Midlands region was relatively favoured in its share, reflecting that earlier successful process of industrial evolution and restructuring.

Birmingham weathered the interwar period because adjustment had begun several decades earlier. New and expanding industries, well established in the early 1920s, were able by their absolute size and continued growth to provide a solid economic base for the region, especially in the motor car, cycle and electrical sectors. The combination of non-specificity of investment and high skill in labour proved as favourable for product innovation and the birth of new firms as had been the case in earlier decades. The Midlands in general was able to attract and generate new industries in their early stage of development because of the variety of trades and skills in the region, the resulting growth helping to compensate for declining sectors. It was this cumulative process of growth from the late Victorian and Edwardian periods that enabled the region in the 1920s to be well placed for relative success. Although therefore we must rightly identify the particular strengths and advantages of the south-east services region in the Edwardian period in particular, it is also necessary to seek out cases of flexible industrial adaptation derived from local and regional endowments of capital and labour, not only as evidence of Edwardian successes but also as a more informed way of understanding regional, and with it national, responses to the next significant phase of cyclical fluctuation after 1920.

In recent years the most influential alternative to examining such market relationships has been the 'big business' approach of Alfred Chandler which stresses the ability of the large corporation to achieve economies of scale and scope. Chandler implicitly assumes a uniformity rather than a diversity of business experience based on large organizations making efficiency gains through a combination of technology, investment and bureaucracy, and a causal link between lagging economic performance and the persistence of small-scale personal capitalism.[20] 'Propriety capitalism' is linked directly to the decay of international competitive advantage. What we need by way of counterbalance, however, is greater understanding of the part played by small and medium-sized, often family-run, firms in economic development and here Birmingham's experience is again instructive. The region exhibits for the late nineteenth and early twentieth centuries important evidence of business strategies based on quality production and flexible technology which were sufficient to underpin enterprise and success in the Edwardian period and, as noted already, to enable the region to sustain a measure of stability during the turbulent interwar period.

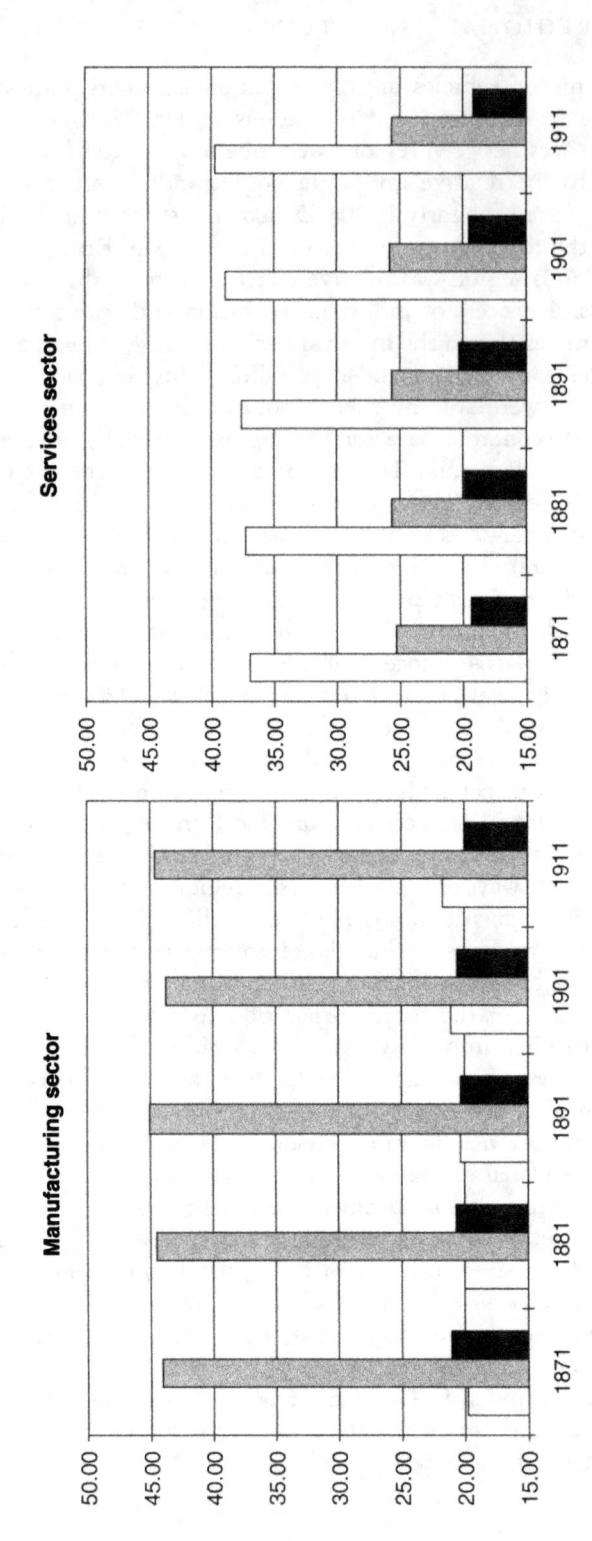

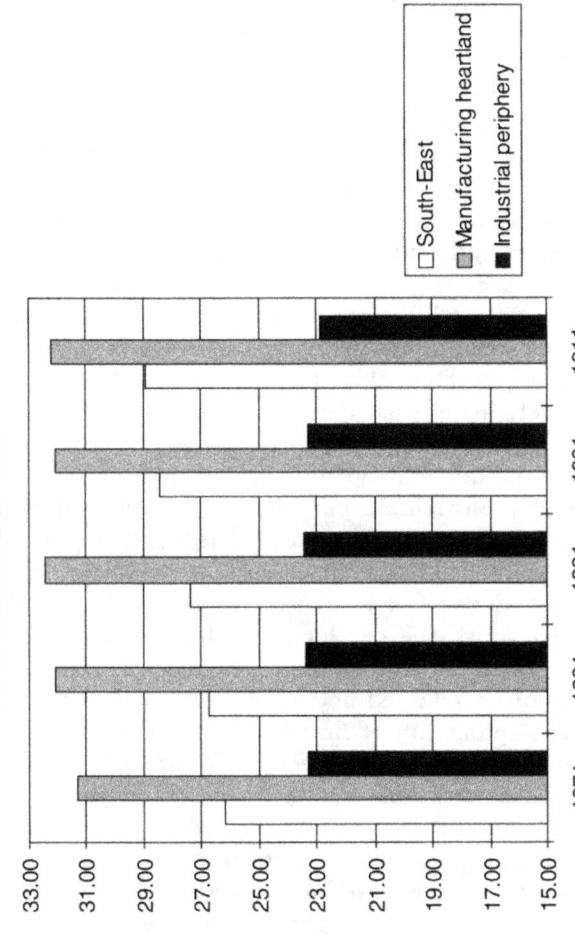

Figure 8.1 Distribution of national employment by major geographical divisions, 1871–1911 (Great Britain = 100%). Calculated from census data in C.H. Lee, *British Regional Employment Statistics 1841–1971*, Cambridge, 1979.

Note: South-East: London, Middlesex, Kent, Surrey, Sussex, Hampshire, Berkshire, Oxfordshire, Buckinghamshire, Bedfordshire, Hertfordshire and Essex.
Manufacturing heartland: West Midlands, North-West, Yorkshire and Humberside.
Industrial periphery: North, Wales and Scotland.
This representation cannot capture the complexity of definitional problems across census years. For a full discussion, see Lee 1979.

And there is a wider dimension to consider. The findings of Storper, Walker and Porter have emphasized the significance of the clustering of small firms in industrial districts which proved capable of providing an alternative pathway to industrial capitalism by the exploitation of flexible specialization and the commonalities of custom, language, dialect and culture.[21] The argument is that spatial dimension is a crucial part of industrialization. Despite the effects of global markets and lower cost transport in reducing the frictions of distance, industries continue to bunch in a highly uneven fashion. The resulting 'clusters' are capable of achieving substantial economies and of sustaining competitive advantage over a long period. Of particular importance is the extent to which intra-industry links within an industrial region develop to make firms interdependent in ways that are stronger than pure market transactions. The traditional emphasis upon the growth of large firms in the twentieth century and the focus of themes such as uncertainty and bounded rationality can blind us to the more subtle forms of industrial collusion and social relationships that help to determine competitive strength and economic resilience. The Chandlerian concentration on the firm and its internal organization neglects relations between firms and the extent to which enterprises of varying size frequently externalized with business communities, sharing a network of information and a business culture based on informal contacts and trust, all within organizational settings infinitely looser than the multi-divisional firm.

Subcontracting, strategic alliance and the use of trade associations to sustain a social culture of production and information exchange are examples of this wider milieu of industrialization.[22] Regions such as Birmingham were adept at developing specialized skills and knowledge. Changing technology was able to be explored through the industrial production process and ideas flowed within and between related activities via buyers, sellers and specialized craftsmen. With the development of a specialized labour market and with skills geared to local industry, educational facilities and the social life of communities reflected and reinforced the needs of local industry. The close spatial proximity of firms created a favourable milieu in which innovation and change became a collective process, with knowledge and skills 'in the air'. Ideas and information flowed freely via personal contacts, both business and social, raising the possibility of new product developments through diversification or the creation of 'spin-off' firms. As an industrial complex developed, resultant advantages became self-reinforcing. Skills and organization were upgraded in ways suited to local industry and critical aspects of the infrastructure were specifically geared to its needs. In effect industrial progress became a social process in which know-how about production processes, machines, tastes and designs were embedded in the local business culture and workplace.

And Birmingham is only one example. Recent work on Sheffield also suggests the emergence in that area from the late nineteenth century of successful innovative firms which based their business strategy on quality production, market niche, flexible technology and consumer-orientated production.[23] Likewise it appears from recent research that an important part of Clydeside's pre-1914 economic success lay in its tightly integrated complex of interdependent firms linking coal, iron, steel, engineering, ships, textiles and chemicals. The links between firms extended beyond raw material exchanges to include familial and financial ties. The region's dominant firms diffused technical innovations rapidly via extensive economic and social networks, enhanced by craft labour markets characterized by high degrees of mobility.[24]

It is interesting, moreover, how exaggerated is the notion that London businessmen overshadowed their provincial counterparts. One consequence, writes Berghoff, 'of emphasising the London–provinces divide over and again is the misconception of provincial entrepreneurs as one grey mass of equally second-rate and uninteresting men'. What he has found in biographical case studies of entrepreneurs in Birmingham, Bristol and Manchester between 1870 and 1914, is a clear domination of industrial over commercial financial wealth, the virtual non-existence of significant drains of business funds on land purchase, as well as a persistent adherence to frugality, self-respect and a strict work ethos.[25]

To conclude: it is pointless attempting to substantiate total failure in the late Victorian and Edwardian economy while Britain retained a leading place among industrialized nations. She was still in 1913 the most productive economy in Europe, and was only gradually beginning to reveal within specific industries and particular regions evidence of relative economic sluggishness, though admittedly in those sectors destined for future development. Britain's lead in export performance was being closed but only slowly; growth rates were understandably faster in countries in those earlier growth stages that Britain had already experienced but few such developers caught up with Britain in absolute terms. Moreover, as one recent commentator has reminded us, for a wide range of manufacturing and service industries over the period 'entrepreneurs were alive to new opportunities and ready to adopt new technologies when it was profitable to do so'.[26] What this chapter has suggested is the need to balance the complex story of aggregate 'failure' and 'success', however defined and elucidated, with a more eclectic approach embracing two principal elements: first, a recognition of the contribution of the service/consumer economy, focused predominantly on London and the south-east, in generating income and employment levels which added considerably to the development of the national economy, and second, an appreciation of the extent of flexible structural adaptation within manufacturing regions which, when more fully researched, may not overturn but could temper the notion of economic (and even political) subordination of industrialists to finance and commerce, however much we acknowledge the structural advantages of London and the home counties. The fact is that in the decades before 1914 there were an enormous number of changes in the balance between different types of economic activity, the consequences of which in terms of flexibility, competitiveness, success and failure were 'scattered patchily over the economy'.[27] Pollard has already reminded us of how the process of modernization and industrialization in Europe appeared, not in a uniform way, but in a regionally concentrated pattern based on localized clusters of industry, transport and social relations. Likewise, the British pattern of economic change down to 1914 was not homogenously reflected in all industries in all parts of the country. Some regions were marked by their relative immunity from long wave fluctuations while others experienced rapid growth in an upward wave, only to suffer an equally sharp contraction in the downswing. Others again enjoyed a buoyant pattern, gaining a share of growth in each wave of development. The service and manufacturing regions of southern England were of a buoyant nature relatively immune from the dramatic swings of fortune felt by their northern counterparts, while the Midlands experienced a succession of industrial transformations in which former leading sectors were replaced by other more dominant activities.[28]

We need therefore more comparative analyses of business strategy and performance in contrasting manufacturing and service regions but also similar studies within economic and culturally similar regions, especially where, as in small-scale manufacture, the key to success often lay in access to market information, in the social, cultural and information environment in which business communities interrelated, in a capacity for strategic flexibility and product innovation, and in the range of networks and looser forms of organization between firms that are far removed from the multi-divisional 'ideal'.

Notes

1 S. Pollard, 'Regional and Inter-Regional Economic Development in Europe in the Eighteenth and Nineteenth Centuries', in *Debates and Controversies in Economic History*, Milan 1994, 78.
2 The debate has ranged over issues of lost entrepreneurial zeal, inadequate industrial management, institutional rigidity, poor take-up of emerging technologies, the predominance of the family firm and the slow development of corporate capitalism. For a review of the themes see S. Pollard, *Britain's Prime and Britain's Decline: The British Economy 1870–1914*, London 1989; J. Foreman-Peck (ed.), *New Perspectives on the Late Victorian Economy: Essays in Quantitative Economic History 1860–1914*, Cambridge 1991; B.W. Alford, *Britain in the World Economy since 1880*, London 1996.
3 Pollard, *Prime and Decline*, 261.
4 D.N. McCloskey, 'Did Victorian Britain Fail?', *Economic History Review*, 23, 1970; 'Victorian Growth: A Rejoinder', *Economic History Review*, 27, 1974; and L. G. Sandberg, 'From Damnation to Redemption: Judgements on the Late Victorian Entrepreneur', *Explorations in Economic History*, 9, 1971/2.
5 C.H. Lee, *The British Economy since 1700: A Macroeconomic Perspective*, Cambridge 1986, 125.

6 C.H. Lee, 'Regional Growth and Structural Change in Victorian Britain', *Economic History Review*, 34, 1981.
7 M. Marshall, *Long Waves of Regional Development*, London 1987.
8 Lee, *The British Economy*, 136.
9 *Ibid.*, 137.
10 W.D. Rubinstein, 'The Victorian Middle Classes: Wealth, Occupation and Geography', *Economic History Review*, 30, 1977; *Men of Property: The Very Wealthy in Britain Since the Industrial Revolution*, London 1981; *Wealth and Inequality in Britain*, London 1986.
11 C.H. Lee, 'The Service Sector, Regional Specialization, and Economic Growth in the Victorian Economy', *Journal of Historical Geography*, 10, 1984.
12 Lee, *The British Economy*, 134.
13 Rubinstein, 'The Victorian Middle Classes'.
14 Lee, 'Regional Growth and Structural Change', 451.
15 H. Southall, 'Regional Unemployment Patterns in Britain, 1851–1914', unpublished Ph.D. thesis, University of Cambridge, 1983, 400; 'Regional Unemployment Patterns Among Skilled Engineers in Britain, 1851–1914', *Journal of Historical Geography*, 12, 1986; 'The Origins of the Depressed Areas: Unemployment, Growth and Regional Structure in Britain before 1914', *Economic History Review*, 41, 1988.
16 J. Foreman-Peck, 'Seedcorn or Chaff? New Firm Formation and the Performance of the Interwar Economy', *Economic History Review*, 38, 1985.
17 Alford, *Britain in the World Economy*, 102.
18 A.D. Chandler, *Scale and Scope: The Dynamics of Industrial Capitalism*, Cambridge, Mass. 1990.
19 G.C. Allen, *The Industrial Development of Birmingham and the Black Country, 1860–1927*, London 1929; A. Briggs, *History of Birmingham*, vol. II, Oxford 1952.
20 See B. Supple, 'Scale and Scope: Alfred Chandler and the Dynamics of Industrial Capitalism', *Economic History Review*, 44, 1991; R. Church, 'The Limits of the Personal Capitalism Paradigm', *Business History Review*, 64, 1990.
21 M. Storper and R. Walker, *The Capitalist Imperative: Territory, Technology and Industrial Growth*, Oxford 1989; M. E. Porter, *The Competitive Advantage of Nations*, London 1990.
22 M. Casson, *The Economics of Business Culture: Game Theory, Transaction Costs and Economic Performance*, Oxford 1994.
23 R. Lloyd-Jones and M.J. Lewis, 'Personal Capitalism and British Industrial Decline: The Personally Managed Firm and Business Strategy in Sheffield, 1880–1920', *Business History Review*, 68, 1994.
24 A. McKinley and A. Slaven, 'Unravelling an Industrial District? The Experience of Twentieth Century Clydeside', unpublished Working Paper, University of Glasgow, Centre for Business History, 1995.
25 H. Berghoff, 'Regional Variations in Provincial Business Biography: The Case of Birmingham, Bristol and Manchester', *Business History*, 37, 1995.
26 R. Floud, 'Britain, 1860–1914: A Survey', in R. Floud and D. McCloskey (eds), *The Economic History of Britain since 1700, Vol. 2: 1860–1939*, Cambridge 1994.
27 Pollard, *Prime and Decline*, 266.
28 Marshall, *Long Waves*.

Part IV

INSTITUTIONS AND CULTURE

9

EDUCATION AND ECONOMIC DECLINE, 1870–1914

An innocent suspect?

Michael Sanderson

There has been a long tradition of associating Britain's supposed economic failure or falling behind new competitors with defects in education. From the Paris Exhibitions beginning in 1867, the Victorian investigations of Bernhard Samuelson and the Duke of Devonshire to the reports of S.J. Prais and the NIESC in our own day it has been a recurrent theme. Indeed a symposium on 'decline' is, to cite a well-known cinematic phrase, something of 'a round up of the usual suspects' with education being regarded as more shiftily suspicious than most. Yet we should be cautious because the issues of the past have become merged with contemporary political attitudes. Criticisms aimed at the Conservative governments about the economy or education in the 1980s or 1990s would be deflected by the reply that such problems are deep seated, long lasting, and go back over 100 or 120 years.[1] Accordingly, such reasoning suggests that the responsibility of present day decision makers, politicians and businessmen is limited because it is shared with an historical tradition of culpable predecessors. The emphasis on education as a factor in decline is also convenient in another way because criticism and blame can thereby be shuffled off not only on to the past but from politicians and businessmen on to (left-wing) school teachers, (trendy) training colleges and (ivory tower) universities and their supposed anti-business ethos. The very purpose of a symposium seeking the roots of decline before 1914 has political overtones possibly clearer to English than to French scholars. The problem is a tangled one with several areas of conflicting debate.

The classic adverse view is that of David Landes who writes of 'an enormous gap between British and German achievements in this area . . . the late and stunted growth of technical and scientific education in Britain . . . the uneven and inadequate provision of facilities'. This he attributes to employers being unwilling to spend money on education because they had little education themselves, they believed that education gave employees an exaggerated sense of their own merit and they feared it could lead to the disclosure of trade secrets. Overall this led to 'Britain's relative lack of skills and knowledge' which contributed to her loss of supremacy.[2] François Crouzet after a more considered discussion likewise concluded that in approaching the transition from the nineteenth to the twentieth century 'the British were badly prepared for it in terms of education and training'.[3] One way or another this theme has run through the influential writings of Derek Aldcroft, Gordon Roderick and Michael Stephens, Correlli Barnett and others.[4] But there are many parts of the education and training system, many linkages or lack of them and many decades in the period 1870–1914. Let us look more closely at some of these.

A peculiar problem is that of the English public school. A familiar argument is that the public schools were inimical to business and industry, their curriculum was focused on the arts and neglected the sciences and technology, and the ethos of the public school produced the gentleman and public servant, not the entrepreneur. Consequently the public schools did not attract sons of businessmen nor did they produce boys for such careers. Accordingly the public schools were either irrelevant to England's industrial competitiveness or positively harmful to it.[5]

Historians have taken several different approaches to this. The first might be regarded as the optimistic view, namely that the public schools adjusted to industrial society successfully. From teaching initially no science in the early nineteenth century many public schools took it up with enthusiasm after the late 1860s. There were various reasons for this. The Clarendon Royal Commission on the public schools, partly influenced by J.M. Winter, the pioneering science master of Rugby, urged schools to teach science. The Clarendon Report (1864) coincided with the Paris Exhibition of 1867 and Samuelson's Select Committee (1868) to investigate the educational background to England's relative lack of success there and also with Matthew Arnold's Report on Prussian education (1868). The concern about public schools was thus drawn into the wider tide of concern about education, science and industrial competitiveness. Even if public school headmasters felt they could ignore that, they had to pay attention to Sandhurst whose entrance examinations required two science subjects from the mid-1850s. The importance of artillery so evident in the Prussian army's victories in the 1860s gave urgency to raising the educational level of British officers after the Crimean War. Headmasters were helped by the new Natural Sciences Tripos at Cambridge (1848) and the Honours School of Natural Science at Oxford (1852) which both provided science graduates who were Anglican and gentlemen and hence suitable as public school masters who in turn could prepare boys for the new science degrees at the ancient universities. The changes at Oxbridge broke a log jam which had dissuaded the public schools from studying science seriously in the early nineteenth century. Some public schools built notable laboratories, F.W. Sanderson at Oundle in the 1890s, Westminster and Rugby in the 1900s, echoing the spate of industrial and university research laboratory building before 1914.

If the curriculum changed so did the hidden curriculum of the values transmitted by the schools to their pupils. In the first half of the nineteenth century the Arnoldian ideal was that of the 'Christian gentleman', the rather academic scholarly boy much concerned about his religious conscience. This was more appropriate for future schoolmasters and clergymen than businessmen. More secular values were introduced into the schools by the encouragement of organized games and athleticism. This made boys fit, of virile physique, developed qualities of character and leadership, encouraged sociability and team working to achieve goals, discouraged bookishness. Alongside games playing came the military corps, some Volunteers others merely rifle clubs. They became popular in the Boer War and crystallized as the Officer Training Corps in Haldane's army reforms in 1908. These inculcated the same secular values as games playing but added an even greater concern for authority, control and order. The secularization of the ethos was matched by a laicization of the schoolmasterly élite. In 1870 54 per cent of the staff of the ten leading schools were ordained, but by 1906 this had fallen to 13.6 per cent. All these changed the ethos of schools from Godliness to manliness and to secular values and qualities of character useful to business no less than to the army and colonial service.

The enhanced attractiveness of public schools led to a sharp increase in businessmen's sons going to public schools before 1914. At Winchester the percentages of boys' fathers in business and industry rose (see Table 9.1).[6] The proportion who were sons of businessmen rose from small single figures in the early part of the century to consistently one-quarter from the 1880s.

Apart from the factors referred to earlier two others increased the attractiveness of the public schools to businessmen. In the 1850s many of the leading public schools (Eton, Winchester, Rugby, for instance) started entrance examinations. This had several effects. It gave rise to a sector of preparatory schools to prepare for entrance. These rose from 20 in 1850 to 400 by 1900. By 1890 Harrow was fed by 134 prep schools.[7] This probably raised the intellectual level of the receiving public schools. But by increasing the overall expense of a preparatory–public school education an advantage was given to wealthy businessmen over clergy, army officers and schoolmasters who wished to place their sons in increasingly attractive public schools.

Table 9.1 Percentage of Winchester boys with a father in business

Birthdates of boys entering school	1850s–1860s	1860s–1870s	1870s–1880s	1880s–1890s	1890s–1900s	1900s–1910s
	13	19	21	24	24	25

Table 9.2 Boys going into busienss and industry (%)[8]

	1860s	1870s	1880s	1890s	1900s	1910s
Winchester	24	29	33	35	37	33
Clifton	9	—	16	—	25	—
Marlborough	17	—	23	—	23	—
Merchant Taylor's	—	13	—	42	—	25
Mill Hill	—	31	—	30	32	—
Harrow and Rugby	6.9	6.9	20.7	20.7	—	—
St Oswalds, Ellesmere	—	—	—	21	—	—
Loretto	—	—	—	36	—	—
Sedburgh	—	30	—	30	—	—

These various factors contributed to increased proportions of public schoolboys themselves choosing careers in business and industry before 1914 (see Table 9.2).

Whereas negligible numbers went into business in the early nineteenth century, from the 1890s fairly consistent proportions of 25–35 per cent of boys were going into business and industrial careers across a wide range of schools studied by different historians.

Such may be regarded as the optimistic view of the public schools – changes in curriculum and ethos stimulating increases in boys from business and industrial backgrounds going into such careers. But thereafter there are shades of opinion and debate. Indeed almost every viewpoint is entertained – that there was a close contact or little contact between the public schools and business and industry and that these had either beneficial or adverse effects.

Bishop and Wilkinson, although showing the sharp increase of boys coming from and going to business, are yet doubtful whether this was beneficial for the economy. They come to the view that boys were returning to family firms and their social origin was more important than their ability. They ask,

> must we take it that in British business before and after World War I high social origin carried more weight than it did in Her Majesty's Forces or in the Foreign Office . . . Perhaps the less formal recruitment and promotion system of private business accommodated greater opportunities for nepotism than did public service bureaucracy. If so it would be an ironic fact that middle class business rationalism, having helped to achieve public service reform, the replacement of patronage by open competition, then turned increasingly from promotion by merit towards patronage.[9]

Charlotte Erickson takes a similar line that there were many public schoolboys in the steel industry but their lack of technical training diminished their value to industry. Only 10 per cent of steel masters in 1865 and 16 per cent in the period 1875–95 and then 31 per cent in 1905–25 had such training. Moreover, their family connections stifled the advancement of those below them with technical expertise but lower social standing.[10]

A contrary view was taken by D.C. Coleman who argued that businessmen sending their boys to public school may have been beneficial since it dissuaded them from industrial careers and thereby cleared them from the path of thrusters from below.[11] But the evidence of Bishop and Wilkinson seems against this ingenious argument as does Coleman's own finding that 50 per cent of Courtaulds directors were public school men by 1914 and 82 per cent by 1938. This argument is in the tradition of David Ward who thought that the public schools caused a 'haemorrhage of talent' away from industry because the irrelevance of their curricula did not prepare the boys for such careers and so provided no reservoir for managerial and technological talent. Yet Ward was among the first to show about one-third of public schoolboys going into industry in the late nineteenth century which was hardly a 'haemorrhage' away.[12] Coleman thought that public schoolboys not going into industry was beneficial, Ward thought it adverse, but their own statistics undermine their arguments.

Hartmut Berghoff argues that we are looking through the wrong end of the telescope. What is significant is not so much the proportion of public schoolboys going into industry but the proportion of businessmen who had been to public school. In his study of Birmingham, Bristol and Manchester he finds

> that the relevance of public schools for a study of the late nineteenth century business community has been gravely exaggerated, for only a mere 18 per cent of all entrepreneurs . . . had attended one of these élite institutes . . . the overall impact of these schools on the entire business class must have been very limited indeed.

This is confirmed by Berghoff's analysis of David Jeremy's *Dictionary of Business Biography* (5 vols, London, 1984) where 12.7 per cent of businessmen born 1840–69 attended a leading public school and 20.6 per cent any kind of public school.[13]

The most important statement of the limited relevance of the public schools to industry is that of W.D. Rubinstein. He is rightly sceptical of Ward's view of the 'haemorrhage of talent'. By use of probate records he finds that the parents of public schoolboys were predominantly professional and middle class. Yet fewer than 4 per cent of the potential middle class attended any public school (still less an élite one) in the 1860s and fewer than 7 per cent by the end of the nineteenth century. The public schools were predominantly for the professional classes whose sons tended to enter the professions. Likewise businessmen's sons followed their fathers and the drift from business to professional far from being a haemorrhage was 'amazingly small'. He suggests that the public schools simply did not produce a haemorrhage of talent away from business life 'too few sons of entrepreneurs attended a public school to make any real difference'.[14]

However, there is agreement that public school men had established a substantial and beneficial presence in banking. Cassis has shown that 44 per cent of London bankers 1890–1914 were public school men but even more significantly 62 per cent of those educated between 1861 and 1880 had been to public schools.[15] Social contacts and social ease at a certain high level, the sense of honour and integrity and discretion that a public school education sought to foster were most appropriate to this sector. The lack of technical education was no drawback and it was a more attractive white-collar clean-hands career for public schoolboys than manufacturing industry.

Public school men going to university would go to Oxford and Cambridge. About half of Winchester schoolboys went there. How valuable would an education received in the ancient universities have been for the economy? In this Oxford and Cambridge were quite different. Oxford had been good at science in the mid-nineteenth century and remained so in medicine. But it became backward in late Victorian times and much inferior to Cambridge. In particular, its chemistry and physics were poor and its engineering non-existent until 1908. Janet Howarth has indicated the factors behind this.[16] William Odling and R.B. Clifton, professors of chemistry and physics respectively, though active in research before their appointments lost interest thereafter. The cultural atmosphere was antagonistic to science, the 'Young Oxford' movement of the 1880s asserting the idea that science had no natural place at Oxford. More important, Oxford was less successful at transferring funds from the colleges to the university for the founding of science chairs. Also Oxford recruited more than Cambridge from the public schools with their bias against science. A third of Oxford students were from Clarendon public schools.

Cambridge by contrast was excellent in science and subjects of potential use to industry. Its physics (with Clerk Maxwell, Rayleigh, Thompson) chemistry (with Sir James Dewar, the inventor of cordite, quinoline and the vacuum flask) engineering and industrial economics (Alfred Marshall) were world class. It is partly a matter of personalities. Oxford had R.B. Clifton and William Odling. Cambridge had Lord Rayleigh (OM, Nobel prize) Sir Joseph Thomson (OM, Nobel prize), Sir James Dewar, James Stuart (PC), Sir Alfred Ewing.[17] At Cambridge the university taxed the colleges and could spend the money on science without reference to the colleges and it could finance new appointments from the Common University Fund. Both universities were badly hit by the decline in rents in the agricultural depression of the 1870s to 1890s, especially Oxford where the depression and a consequent lack of funds 'dictated that scientific research and education continued to be under provided at Oxford'.[18] Cambridge disposed its finances better and more to science, for Cambridge was a stronger, richer, more centralized university and science benefited from this. It was also less tied to the public schools, only about one-fifth of its intake being from Clarendon schools.

And yet a disturbing paradox began to emerge which tells us much about English business recruitment. The intake of students into Oxford from a business background was negligible before 1886 whereas 9–17 per cent of Cambridge students came from this background. When we compare outputs to business for the period 1752–1886 Cambridge remained ahead of Oxford. But Oxford was sending more students out to business than it was receiving while for Cambridge it was the reverse. By the period of the late nineteenth century to 1914, output levels for both Oxford and Cambridge were roughly similar in the 10–15 per cent range. Recent work on Oxford University has shown that between 1900 and 1913 13.89 per cent of Oxford arts graduates and 15.99 per cent of scientists went into careers in business and industry.[19] From another angle Rubinstein found that 6 per cent of his industrialists 1900–19 had been to Oxford but none at all to Cambridge. This was a curious situation. Cambridge had adjusted to develop a range of curriculum and research and a financial structure relevant to science and industry but Oxford had not done so and was virtually useless in this regard. Yet although Cambridge received more students from business families it sent fewer back to business and positively diverted them away from such careers. On the other hand, Oxford sent more to business than it received and sent out proportions surprisingly similar to those of Cambridge while a businessman was more likely to have been an Oxford than a Cambridge man. This tells us something about business recruitment attitudes. It was as if business and industry were ignorant of or indifferent to the dissimilarities between Oxford and Cambridge; they chose to ignore the fact that Cambridge was more suitable for their needs and evidently preferred the former. Some employers rationalized this on the grounds that for general management they were looking for the same sort of man who would enter the Civil or Colonial Service, of good background and generally intelligent but the subject content of whose studies was largely irrelevant. If there is a culpability here it lies with the employers as much as will Oxford, but certainly not with Cambridge.

The system of technical education evolved through this time into a satisfactory even impressive one. Following the shock of the Paris Exhibition of 1867 and reinforced by the eleven-year recurrence of these international expositions in 1878, 1889 and 1900 a system began to be created in five main ways. First, a number of colleges were started in industrial provincial cities which were to grow into civic universities.[20] The virtual reform of Owens College Manchester in 1873 was followed by the Yorkshire College of Science in Leeds (1874), a direct response to the Paris Exhibition of 1867, then Firth College Sheffield (1879), Mason College Birmingham

(1880), Liverpool University College (1881), and before 1914 they were joined by lesser colleges in Southampton (1862), Exeter (1865), Newcastle (1871), Bristol (1876), Nottingham (1881) and Reading (1893). For our present argument three features of these civic universities stand out. They were all created and funded with money from local industrialists often on a substantial scale. By the mid-1900s Manchester, Liverpool, Birmingham and Leeds all had fixed capitals of around £300,000–400,000 and endowment incomes of £8,000–23,000 a year. Secondly, the curricula and research of the civics were closely related to national and regional industrial needs. The creation or development of bearing lubrication, colliery pumps, vanadium steel, chrome leather, gas fires, beer, soap, the quadruple expansion engine, marine radio and much else all benefited from the work of civic university researchers. Thirdly, a high proportion of students came from industrial and business backgrounds and about one-third to one-half of students from Birmingham, Newcastle, Bristol and Manchester took up careers in industry. They were the essential powerhouses creating that human capital for British industrial growth.

The number of students at universities rose from 5,530 in 1871 to 26,432 by 1911 and students in science and technology graduating annually in the civic universities rose from 19 in 1870 to 1,231 by 1910. Their cumulative stock rose accordingly from 127 in 1870 to 14,300 by 1910.[21]

In London a lower level of technical education was created with Quintin Hogg's polytechnics. These provided classes for London artisans and clerks in a whole range of technical subjects and provided an active sporting life. Starting with Regent Street in 1882, these spread in the 1890s to eleven by 1898. By the 1900s they moved into degree work with 500 students studying for London University degrees in 1904. Also in London, the City and Guilds of London was formed in 1879. This was the livery companies' initiative to honour their medieval commitment to craft training by focusing their attention and funds on its contemporary equivalent of technical education. They set up Finsbury Technical College in 1883 and a large Central Technical College in South Kensington in 1884. More importantly, they ran a national system of technical examinations. The massive increase in this examining from 151 passes in 1879 to 14,750 by 1914 is one important indicator of the growth of the technical education movement in these years.[22] This growth is largely explained by the development of the municipal technical colleges in the 1890s following the Technical Instruction Act of 1889. This allowed the new county councils and county borough councils to levy a rate to build colleges and from 1890 the annual windfall of 'whisky money' helped to run them. Some 160 colleges were created in this way by 1898, much of their instruction being evening class work. Finally, the colleges spawned Junior Technical Schools, full time technical education at school level for schoolchildren aged 13+. By 1913 there were 37 schools with 2,900 pupils.[23]

What is often overlooked in addition is a messy undergrowth of technical education. First, there were technical classes in elementary schools encouraged by code changes in 1893–6 allowing science, woodwork and metalwork. Such departments increased from 173 in 1891 to 1,396 by 1895 and from 1904 all training colleges had science departments. Secondly, there were organized science schools supported by the Science and Art Department. These were elementary schools going beyond elementary work. These grew from 600 students in 1860 to 187,000 by 1890. Thirdly, there were older teenagers going to evening classes in technical colleges rising from 120,000 in 1893 to 475,000 by 1900 to 708,000 by 1911. Fourthly, the mechanics institutes revived. It is usually assumed that they died out after the 1850s or declined to sub-educational purposes.[24] However, in the industrial northwest the Union of Lancashire and Cheshire Institutes was established in 1872. A network of institutes provided a post-elementary education in technical and commercial subjects leading to City and Guilds, Society of Arts and Science and Art Department qualifications sufficient for a working class lad to be able to set up as a cotton manufacturer.[25] Sidney Pollard is one of the few participants in the debate to give due recognition to these layers. He notes, 'the rate of expansion was truly breathtaking'.[26] Dintenfass, while criticizing the seeming lack of co-ordination of these parts, likewise has recognized its flexibility and capacity for rapid expansion.[27]

There remains the question of apprenticeship. There was a common belief among pre-1914 commentators of the time that this was declining in the 1900s. This is attributed to the dilution of skills due to the introduction of semi-automatic machines and mechanization, splitting up processes into different jobs. It was claimed that apprentices increasingly were given speedy training on one automatic machine, that they were used as cheap labour with narrowing differentials between first and final year, that they took part in strikes, worked more overtime and attended night school less.[28] Keith McClelland, however, looking at engineering and shipbuilding finds this argument overplayed. In spite of dilution vast numbers of craftsmen were needed to set tools and maintain machinery as well as engage in production. Also, apprenticeship remained a cheap way of training labour. McClelland concludes, 'in the end a shop floor practical training in which apprenticeship remained of central importance continued to be the most favoured means of transmitting skills in the engineering and shipbuilding industries'.[29] Bernard Elbaum likewise finds that what was remarkable about apprenticeship in Britain at this time was its survival not its dwindling; it verified worthiness, was cheap and led to stability of employment.[30] Beyond apprenticeships several firms started their own education classes – fourteen railway companies, Brunners Mond, United Alkali, Crosfields, Lever, Rowntree, Cadbury, Reckitts and several others.[31]

One salient point emerges from our consideration of these developments. First, it is misleading to regard 1870–1914 as one period. Before 1890 there can be little doubt that English education was defective, lacking a proper structure of universities, state and local government finance, technical colleges, free and compulsory elementary education or popular secondary education. The period 1870–90 saw Britain in danger of falling behind. It was the last phase when Britain had modestly good growth rates (1.2 per cent GDP per man year) compared with its competitors while still running a poor educational system. After 1890 the situation was transformed. School education became compulsory from 1891. In the 1900s the secondary system was structured with a scholarship ladder from the elementary school to the grammar school and thence to university. Central schools and Junior Technical Schools (JTS) catered for the commercially and technically inclined. The elevation of civic university colleges into full-scale degree-giving universities, with state grants from 1889, the spread of activity of polytechnics, City and Guilds and the creation of technical colleges needs no reiteration. Whereas an Englishman in 1950 would scarcely recognize the education system of 1880, that of 1910 would be quite familiar.

The 1890s and 1900s are also distinctive in that they saw a positive effort to Germanize and Frenchify the English education system to ensure that those nations did not continue to enjoy competitive educational advantages.[32] The civic universities matched the German Technical High Schools and the 1896 Louis Liard reform of universities in France. Imperial College (1907) was designed as the London Charlottenburg to match the great TH in Berlin just as LSE imitated the Parisian *grandes écoles* for law and politics. The stratification of secondary education in England in the 1900s deliberately imitated in a simplified form the German *Gymnasium-Realschule* division. The JTS part of it was a replication of the German trade schools and French *écoles primaires supérieures*. There were differences of course. Britain never understood the concept of the Ecole Polytechnique, of a layer of higher education based on science and technology superior to the universities. London polytechnics were certainly not in that mould. Also, as Peter Hennock has shown, neither did Britain accept the Germanic system of engineering divided off into a TH stream of education separate from the universities.[33] Also, Britain's wide dispersal of municipal technical colleges was probably superior in dealing with lower levels than the German and French systems, probably reflecting the importance of the apprentice–college linkage in England. By 1914 it is not evident that there were serious gaps in English education that would have put her at a competitive disadvantage.

Thirdly, this break in the 1890s is evident from the statistical trends (Table 9.3). If we take six indicators of expansion across universities, technical colleges, the City and Guilds, the production of engineers, we find growth, respectable between 1870–90 but then very considerable from 1890–1914. This was 'the astonishing and accelerating rate of growth' referred to by Pollard and it conflicts with the 'improvement came slowly' view of Landes.[34]

EDUCATION AND ECONOMIC DECLINE

The question inevitably arises as to why the situation changed so sharply after 1890. A number of factors seem to lie behind this gear shift. Twenty years of government investigations into education and the economy (Samuelson 1868, Devonshire 1871–5, Samuelson 1884) had culminated in the Royal Commission on the Great Depression in 1886 with yet another volume on education, followed by Lord Selbourne's Commission on the University of London in 1889. Between 1868 and 1889 there was scarcely a year in which some government investigation had not been taking evidence on, reporting on and publicizing the issue which was becoming supersaturated in the public mind. Secondly, 1889 was the year of the most spectacular Paris Exhibition hitherto (including the Eiffel Tower), yet again making England defensive about the public display of her industries *vis-à-vis* her Continental rivals. Thirdly, the strong German Patent Act of 1876 encouraged the rapid growth of German research laboratories and employment of graduates in the 1880s. It was manifest in the near trebling of German dye exports in the 1880s and the 'Made in Germany' and 'Charlottenburgitis' scares of the 1890s. Fourthly, the 1880s was the decade when Britain began to lose its world predominance. It was overtaken by the USA in GDP per man year around 1880, and in the virility symbol of steel production by the USA in the 1880s and by Germany in the 1890s. These factors focused around 1890 rather than around 1870 as the turning point.

Let us now consider seven arguments against the culpability of education for economic retardation before 1914. First it is pointed out that concern about education was linked with a belief that specific industries and their entrepreneurs were performing badly. This was the tone of much economic historical writing of the 1960s. Yet revisionism in a range of studies dealing with cotton, steel, coal and machine tools has found that rates of technical change and productivity growth in Britain compared well with the competition. So if the problem does not exist then education can hardly be blamed for creating it. As Stephen Nicholas observes, 'recent work on British growth in productivity found little evidence that the economy experienced failure. As a result, deficiencies in technical and scientific education, if they existed, are cause without an effect.'[35]

Secondly, we may ask who thought that education was an important element in economic retardation before 1914? The technical education lobby were notable figures, linked with each other and pushing the band wagon. If we take twenty of the leading names in the field, fourteen were academics or academic administrators or lawyers, ten were politicians often overlapping academic careers. Only six were businessmen.[36] There was always a suspicion that it was an issue of much greater interest to academics than industrialists. It was one out of which educators could make and advance careers and politicians find a cause rather than one which would enhance the earnings of businessmen. As Sidney Pollard has observed, 'the agitation was clearly

Table 9.3 Student enrolment at universities and in technical education institutes in the UK, 1870-1914

	University students (a)	Students graduating in science and technology in civic universities (b)	Cum. stock of (b)	C & G passes (d)	Students in technical colleges evening classes (e)	Day students in engineering classes in four colleges (f)	Total of six indicators
1870	5,530	19	127	—	—	114	5,790
1879	—	—	—	151	—	—	—
1880	10,573	55	512	515	—	119	11,774
1890	16,013	166	1,447	3,507	—	193	21,326
1893	—	—	—	—	120,000	—	—
1900	17,839	378	4,984	8,114	475,000	376	506,691
1910	26,432	1,231	14,300	14,105	—	613	764,681
1911	—	—	—	—	708,000	—	—
1914	—	—	—	14,570	—	—	—

Sources
(a) Lowe, 'The Expansion of Higher Education'.
(b) Roderick and Stephens, 'Scientific Studies and Scientific Manpower'.
(c) Ibid.
(d) Mills, Technical Education, p. 61.
(e) Pollard, Britain's Prime and Britain's Decline, p. 179.
(f) Guagnini, 'The Training of Mechanical Engineers', p. 33.

self-interested; it came from a lobby of scientists who wanted more status and more resources, and must on that account be suspect'.[37]

Thirdly, it was not self-evident at the time that there was any close connection between the success of certain industries and the extent of their educational support. There is unanimity on the failure to develop a dyestuffs industry in Britain before 1914 and an element in this was undoubtedly the shortage of organic chemists in England. It is the main plank in Julia Wrigley's critical treatment of defects of technical education.[38] Yet when we move away from this safe ground the picture becomes very fractured.

Let us take some undoubtedly successful industries – shipbuilding, metal mining and cotton. Shipbuilding was the British industry most inviolate from foreign competition. Britain made 50–60 per cent of world tonnage, had the largest navy and merchant marine in the world and the only shipbuilding industry large enough to be efficient. The major technical advances, compound engines and the turbine, were British and productivity and real wages rose steadily. Yet Paul Robertson has grave reservations about the relevance of education for this. Entrepreneurs were reluctant to bother with technical education, preferring on the job training, and they neglected the new university departments at Glasgow, Newcastle and Liverpool and only one-fifth of apprentices in the north-east took any technical college evening class examinations. Britain's competitors in shipbuilding paid far more attention to technical education but this did not pay off for them and Robertson takes the view that Britain was right not to invest more in technical education for this industry.[39] A converse situation appertained in metallurgical mining. This very successful industry had good educational support but not enough of it. The British firms would have been eager to employ more British mining and metallurgical graduates had they been available. Yet this did not seem to hold back the industry: 'investment in mining and metallurgical education may have been quite limited before 1914, but this did not significantly frustrate the activities of those intent on grabbing a big share of the world metal mining industry'.[40] The cotton industry was by far Britain's chief export and remained so until the late 1930s. Historians have shown that its technology was appropriate and not backward. Yet here was an industry with virtually no educational back-up at all. Even Manchester University, supported by the industry, had no cotton department. Training was on the job from the age of 12 or 13. So this range of successful industries presents a curious spectrum in their relations with education. One had good education which was neglected, another good education which was insufficient and a third scarcely any education at all.

If we turn to some industries of questionable success we find similar dissonances. Scarcely any industry other than dyestuffs aroused such feelings of guilt as did our steel industry. Britain was overtaken in production by the USA in the 1880s and by Germany in the 1890s and a host of reasons have been advanced for this, including inevitably education. Yet this was an industry very well served in metallurgical education by Sheffield University which was well used and appreciated by local firms and admired by the Germans.[41] Yet Temin has suggested that such were the global problems of the British industry in terms of the location of raw materials and markets that its educational support could not have made any difference, however good or bad.[42] If Temin absolves the enterpreneur at one level so does McCloskey at another.[43] She finds its performance good up to 1900 but diminishing in the 1900–14 period precisely when metallurgical education was at its most effective. Both Temin and McCloskey, contrary to P.W. Musgrave for example, would find education quite marginal to steel's problems.[44] At the local level, Le Guillon likewise finds educational factors irrelevant to the success or failure of the Teeside steel industry at this time.[45] Coal is rather similar, but the converse. This was an industry with good output, profits and exports though criticized for its poor productivity and technical change. Yet at the managerial level this was one of the best educated industries of all. It was the only one where managers were obliged to be qualified (by Acts of 1887 and 1903) and it had many excellent university and college departments of mining (Birmingham, Newcastle, Leeds, Cardiff, Manchester, Nottingham and Wigan Technical College). It was thus an unusual industry with a considerable gap between well-educated managers and an ill-educated labour force, producing in quantity but inefficiently.[46] Accordingly, the expertise of troubled industries was as varied as the successful, both steel and coal paradoxically being well served with education which could do little to offset their problems in other directions.

A fourth argument is that education and training are not acquired uniquely through formal academic institutions and academics, more than most, tend to exaggerate the role of the latter. The role of apprenticeship on the job has been stressed as a distinctive part of the English scene, and preferred to the college-based training of the Continent. This was not only so for the working class but also for upper class entrants to engineering who served as premium paying apprentices in the offices of leading engineers whether university graduates or not. Thus to deplore the fact that England did not adopt extensive systems of publically financed college training is to overlook the role of the workplace as a place of education. Robertson and Guagnini and Floud have stressed this for shipbuilding and engineering. This had wider implications since it placed the cost on the employer and on the apprentice in foregone work and wages. The assumption was that both would recoup themselves through better value work and higher craftsman's wages later on. This contrasted with Continental assumptions of publicly funded college education where the cost was borne by the taxpayer. There was a logic in the English system where the costs fell on employer and employed as producers and as the direct beneficiaries through wages and profits, rather than on the taxpayer as the notional putative future consumer. It has been a false comparison to regard the English system as inferior to the Continental when it is essentially different. Moreover, in areas like shipbuilding and engineering it delivered the goods more effectively. Roderick Floud has shown just how apprentice-based engineering education was. Of 126 members of the Institution of Mechanical Engineers who died in 1890, 1900, 1910 and 1920 (presumably having most of their careers during the period 1870–1914) 119 (94.4 per cent) had served an apprenticeship and only 24 (19 per cent) had any higher education. Yet Floud finds training 'well attuned to the economic environment of the time', and 'the British system was able to supply skilled engineers to man the industry both at home and abroad'.[47]

Fifthly, linked with this, one of the underlying assumptions about the backwardness of English education was a belief in the superiority of the German or Prussian system of the time and since. Yet Pollard has shown how unfounded or exaggerated such beliefs were.[48] In spite of earlier legislation Prussian literacy was not better than English by the late nineteenth century. Prussian emigrants to the USA were less literate than Englishmen. The Gymnasium secondary schools were quite as academic and classically hidebound as English public schools and Oxford and this was where most German businessmen were educated. German universities over-produced theologians, lawyers and philosophers and their product aspired to the Civil Service quite as much as any Oxford high flier. It was true that German organic chemistry relating to dyestuffs and pharmaceuticals was superior but these were unusual and not a large part of the German economy. English physics, mathematics, metallurgy, inorganic chemisty and engineering were quite as good or superior. In any case England rapidly matched the best aspects of the German educational system in the 1890s and 1900s and in the First World War even more rapidly replicated what had hitherto been regarded as uniquely excellent German products – the dyes, drugs, optical glass, magnetos and soap powder. Elsewhere in this volume Robert Millward has shown that output per employee was the same in Germany and the UK in both 1875 and 1937 and was slightly less in Germany in 1899. Total factor productivity, taking account of capital per employee, was identical in both countries in 1899. This was hardly suggestive of the great superiorities of German education and hence 'human capital' which some Victorian–Edwardian advocates claimed. Pollard is scathing: 'altogether it would be hard to maintain that Germany derived much gain and much in the way of superiority over Britain'. If in the 1900s Britain still had a richer economy, identical productivity and a not inferior education system then what is the problem?

Sixthly, the work on growth of Matthews, Feinstein and Odling-Smee views this 1870–1913 period in an optimistic light.[49] They find a growth of labour quality resulting from improvements in education. Annual percentage growth rates rose from 0.3 per cent in the period 1856–73 to 0.5 per cent in the period 1873–1913 and remained at 0.5 per cent or 0.6 per cent thereafter until 1973. Also, education was the most important source of the improvement in the quality of labour. So this period 1873–1913 is not one where education began to fail the economy; on the contrary, it was one where modern levels of contribution were achieved for the first time.

Finally, can defects of education before 1913 really relate to the British decline? Such a proposition depends on the identification of the timing of both decline and educational deficiencies. Before 1914 only the USA overtook the UK in GDP per man year. Britain's real falling behind came between 1955 and 1975 when it was overtaken by France, Germany, Italy and Japan in rapid succession. Is it not stretching it too far to relate educational deficiencies before 1913 to economic lags in the 1960s and 1970s? Children who left school in 1913 would have been born in 1900 and so could still have been around in the workforce in 1965. But how many? Of 3.7 million boys aged 0–4 in 1901 there were 2.7 million as men aged 60–64 by 1966. This made up 10.9 per cent of the total labour force assuming that they were all still in work, which is highly unlikely. Can this 10 per cent realistically be blamed for the falling behind of the sixties and seventies? In any case, it seems the real deficiencies of education relate to the 1870–90 period and all that generation would have left the labour force by the 1940s. Robert Fitzgerald takes a highly critical view of Britain's human resource development which he thinks 'has unquestionably contributed to the country's failure' in the twentieth century; yet he absolves the 1870–1914 period. He finds:

> Whatever the weaknesses in management education and industrial training by 1914, however, there was no general sense of failure or crisis. Exports had reached record levels and industry and business were able to obtain their personnel needs. The demand for managerial and technical staff was easily met and labour skills fulfilled the needs of the economy.[50]

If we look back on the various factors referred to in this chapter they fall into three categories – admirable features, defective features which probably did not matter and matters of concern that may have held Britain back. Of things to admire we may indicate the civic universities and Imperial College, the widely diffused system of technical colleges of various types, the rapid development of this 'undergrowth' of technical classes, schools and examinations especially from 1890, an apprenticeship system which clearly worked, Cambridge science, the public school–Oxbridge ethos in the financial sectors. In defective features which probably did not matter we may place the lack of science in the public schools and at Oxford. But some things are of concern. First, the very slow response to the shocks around 1870. This created a gap in the development of a balance between on the job and formal training provisions between 1870 and 1890. The gap was quickly closed after 1890 and especially from 1900 but those who look for deficiencies have more of a case in the early period. Second, we must put particular blame on employers for this extraordinary feature of their equating Oxford and Cambridge as equally suitable educators of men for business and industry. Ignorance, snobbery or the pursuit of other values, notably those of the public service, may account for this.

But perhaps we should be more concerned about more recent policies as much closer explanations of our present troubles: the abandoning of the Technical Schools in the 1950s, the failure of any schools to deal effectively with technology in the 1960s and 1970s, the 'policy drift' to arts allowed in polytechnics and technological universities, the decline in the attractiveness of the teaching profession since the 1950s. All these underlay Britain's slipping down the league table of economic powers since 1950 more surely than any features evident before 1914. Historians should beware of allowing present day policy makers to avoid responsibility for contemporary failings by shrugging them off on to a conveniently distant Victorian and Edwardian past. Nor should they allow politicians, businessmen and financiers to pass too much of the blame that lies with them on to educators. To return to our cinematic reference, the whole point of Captain Renault's 'usual suspects' was that they were all innocent, but customarily detained to distract attention from the real culprit. This may not be too dissimilar from the role attributed to Victorian–Edwardian education by historians.

Notes

1 Raven, 'British History and the Enterprise Culture'.
2 Landes, *The Unbound Prometheus*, pp. 339–48.
3 Crouzet, *The Victorian Economy*, p. 421.
4 Aldcroft, 'Investment in and Utilisation of Manpower'; Roderick and Stephens, *Education and Industry*; Barnett, *The Audit of War*, chapter 11 'Education for Industrial Decline'.
5 Wiener, *English Culture and the Decline of the Industrial Spirit*.
6 Bishop and Wilkinson, *Winchester*, pp. 104–8.
7 J.R. de S. Honey, *Tom Brown's Universe*.
8 For Winchester: Bishop and Wilkinson, *Winchester*, pp. 64–9; for Clifton: Reader, *Professional Men*, Appendix 2, 'Public Schoolboys' Occupations 1807–1911'; for Harrow and Rugby: Bamford, *The Rise of the Public Schools*; for St Oswalds: Heward, *To Make a Man of Him*, p. 140; for Sedbergh: Ward, 'The Public Schools and Industry'.
9 Bishop and Wilkinson, *Winchester*, pp. 188–9.
10 Erickson, *British Industrialists*.
11 Coleman, 'Gentlemen and Players'.
12 Ward, 'The Public Schools and Industry'.
13 Berghoff, 'Public Schools'.
14 Rubinstein, *Capitalism, Culture and Decline* Chapter 3 'Education, the Gentleman and British Entrepreneurship'.
15 Cassis, 'Bankers in English Society'.
16 Howarth, 'Science Education'.
17 Sanderson, *The Universities and British Industry*, Chapter 2.

18 Jones, 'The Agricultural Depression'; also considers the earlier part of this debate by J.P.D. Dunbabin and Arthur Engel.
19 Harrison, *The History of the University of Oxford*, p. 68.
20 Sanderson, *The Universities and British Industry*, Chapters 1, 3, 4, 7.
21 Roderick and Stephens, 'Scientific Studies'.
22 Mills, *Technical Education*, p. 61.
23 Sanderson, *The Missing Stratum*.
24 Wrigley, 'The Division between Mental and Manual Labour'.
25 Thistlethwaite, *A Lancashire Inheritance*, pp. 59–62.
26 Pollard, *Britain's Prime and Britain's Decline*, pp. 180–1, 193–4.
27 Dintenfass, *The Decline of Industrial Britain*, p. 34.
28 Knox, 'Apprenticeship and deskilling', pp. 1–2.
29 McClelland, 'The Transmission of Collective Knowledge'.
30 Elbaum, 'The Persistence of Apprenticeship'.
31 Fitzgerald, 'Industrial Training and Management'.
32 Sanderson, 'French Influences'.
33 Hennock, 'Technological Education'.
34 Pollard, *Britain's Prime and Britain's Decline*, p. 194; Landes, *Unbound Prometheus*, p. 344.
35 Nicholas, 'Technical Education and the Decline of Britain'.
36 Lyon Playfair, Philip Magnus, T.H. Huxley, Henry Roscoe, Lord Haldane, Bernhard Samuelson, A.J. Mundella, Quintin Hogg, Norman Lockyer, Arthur Acland, Swire Smith, William Garnett, Sidney Webb, Michael Sadler, John Donnelly, Matthew Arnold, John Slagg, Frederick Mappin, H. Llewellyn Smith, William Armstrong.
37 Pollard, *Britain's Prime and Britain's Decline*, p. 122.
38 Wrigley, 'Technical Education and Industry'.
39 Robertson, 'Technical Education'.
40 Harvey and Press, 'Overseas Investment'.
41 Sanderson, 'The Professor as Industrial Consultant'; Eason, 'Education and Training'.
42 Temin, 'The Relative Decline'.
43 McCloskey, *Economic Maturity*.
44 Musgrave, *Technical Change*.
45 Le Guillon, 'Technical Education 1850–1914', p. 183.
46 Church, *History of the British Coal Industry*, pp. 294, 430–1, 458, 774.
47 Floud, 'Technical Education'.
48 Pollard, *Britain's Prime and Britain's Decline*, pp. 143–62; James, 'German Experience' for a critical view of German education.
49 Matthews, Feinstein and Odling-Smee, *British Economic Growth*, pp. 105–13, 211–13, 502, 527–4.
50 Fitzgerald, 'Industrial Training and Management', pp. 86–7.

References

Aldcroft, D.H., 'Investment in and Utilisation of Manpower in Great Britain 1870–1914' in B.M. Ratcliffe (ed.), *Great Britain and her World* (Manchester, 1975).
Bamford, T.W., *The Rise of the Public Schools* (London, 1967).
Barnett, Correlli, *The Audit of War* (London, 1986).
Berghoff, Hartmut, 'Public Schools and the Decline of the British Economy 1870–1914' *Past and Present* No.129, 1990.

Bishop T.H.J.H. and R. Wilkinson, *Winchester and the Public School Élite* (London, 1967).
Cassis, Youssef, 'Bankers in English Society in the late Nineteenth Century' *Economic History Review* Vol. XXVIII, No. 2, May 1985.
Church, Roy, *The History of the British Coal Industry, Vol.3 1830–1913 Victorian Pre-Eminence* (Oxford, 1986).
Coleman, D.C., 'Gentlemen and Players' *Economic History Review* Vol. XXVI, Feb. 1973.
Crouzet, François, *The Victorian Economy* (London, 1982).
Dintenfass, Michael, *The Decline of Industrial Britain* (London, 1992).
Eason, M., 'Education and Training, the Key to Business Success? Human Resource Development at Thomas Firth and Sons Ltd c. 1880–1940' in *Papers of the Economic History Society Conference*, University of Lancaster, 1996.
Elbaum, Bernard, 'The Persistence of Apprenticeship in Britain and its Decline in the United States' in Howard Gospel (ed.), *Industrial Training and Technological Innovation* (London, 1991)
Erickson, Charlotte, *British Industrialists: Steel and Hosiery* (Cambridge, 1959).
Fitzgerald, Robert, 'Industrial Training and Management in Britain' in N. Kawabe and E. Daito (eds), *Education and Training in the Development of the Modern Corporation* (Tokyo, 1993).
Floud, Roderick, 'Technical Education and Economic Performance in Britain 1850–1914' *Albion*, 1982.
Harrison, Brian (ed.), *The History of the University of Oxford. Vol.8 The Twentieth Century* (Oxford, 1994).
Harvey, Charles and Jon Press, 'Overseas Investment and the Professional Advance of British Mining Engineers 1851–1914' *Economic History Review* Vol. XLII No. 1 Feb. 1989.
Hennock, Peter, 'Technological Education in England 1850–1926: The Uses of a German Model' *History of Education* Vol. 19, No. 4, 1990.
Heward, Christine M., *To Make a Man of Him* (London, 1988).
Honey, J.R. de S., *Tom Brown's Universe: The Development of the Victorian Public School* (London, 1977).
Howarth, Janet, 'Science Education in late Victorian Oxford: A Curious Case of Failure?' *English Historical Review*, Vol. CII, 1987.
James, Harold, 'German Experience and the Myth of British Cultural Exceptionalism' in B. Collins and K. Robbins (eds), *British Culture and Economic Decline* (London, 1990).
Jones, Michael John, 'The Agricultural Depression, Collegiate Finances and Provision for Education at Oxford 1871–1913' *Economic History Review* Vol. I, No. I Feb. 1997.
Knox, W., 'Apprenticeship and Deskilling in Britain 1850–1914' *International Review of Social History* Vol. 31, 1986.
Landes, David S., *The Unbound Prometheus* (Cambridge, 1969).
Le Guillon, Michael, 'Technical Education 1850–1914' in G. Roderick and M. Stephens (eds), *Where did We Go Wrong?* (Lewes, 1981).
Lowe, Roy, 'The Expansion of Higher Education in England' in K.H. Jarausch (ed.), *The Transformation of Higher Learning 1860–1930* (Chicago, 1983).
McClelland, Keith, 'The Transmission of Collective Knowledge: Apprenticeship in Engineering and Shipbuilding 1850–1914' in Penny Summerfield and Eric Evans (eds), *Technical Education and the State since 1850* (Manchester, 1990).
McCloskey, D.N., *Economic Maturity and Entrepreneurial Decline: British Iron and Steel 1870–1913* (Cambridge, Mass., 1973).

Matthews, R.C.O., C.H. Feinstein and J.C. Odling-Smee, *British Economic Growth 1856–1973* (Oxford, 1982).
Mills, C.T., *Technical Education: Its Development and Aims* (London, 1925).
Musgrave, P.W., *Technical Change: A Study of the British and German Iron and Steel Industries 1860–1964* (Oxford, 1967).
Nicholas, Stephen, 'Technical Education and the Decline of Britain 1870–1914' in Ian Inkster (ed.), *The Steam Intellect Societies* (Nottingham, 1985).
Pollard, Sidney, *Britain's Prime and Britain's Decline 1870–1914*, (London, 1989).
Raven, James, 'British History and the Enterprise Culture' *Past and Present* No. 123, May 1989.
Reader, W.J., *Professional Men* (London, 1966).
Robertson, P.L., 'Technical Education in the British Shipbuilding and Marine Engineering Industries 1863–1914' *Economic History Review* Vol. XXVII, No. 2, May 1974.
Roderick, G. and M. Stephens, *Education and Industry in the Nineteenth Century* (London, 1978).
Roderick G. and M. Stephens, 'Scientific Studies and Scientific Manpower in the English Civic Universities 1870–1914' *Science Studies* Vol. 4, No. 1, 1974.
Rubinstein, W.D., *Capitalism. Culture and Decline in Britain 1750–1990* (London, 1993).
Sanderson, Michael, *The Universities and British Industry 1850–1970* (London, 1972).
Sanderson, Michael, 'The Professor as Industrial Consultant: Oliver Arnold and the British Steel Industry 1900–1914' *Economic History Review* Vol. XXXI, No. 4, Nov. 1978.
Sanderson, Michael, *The Missing Stratum: Technical School Education in England 1900–1990* (London, 1994).
Sanderson, Michael, 'French Influences on Technical and Managerial Education in England 1870–1940' in Youssef Cassis, François Crouzet and Terry Gourvish (eds), *Management and Business in Britain and France* (Oxford, 1995).
Temin, Peter, 'The Relative Decline of the British Steel Industry 1880–1913' in Henry Rosovsky (ed.), *Industrialization in Two Systems* (New York, 1966).
Thistlethwaite, Frank, *A Lancashire Inheritance* (Cambridge, 1996).
Ward, David, 'The Public Schools and Industry in Britain after 1870' *Journal of Contemporary History* Vol. 2, No. 3, 1967.
Wiener, Martin, *English Culture and the Decline of the Industrial Spirit 1850–1980* (Cambridge, 1985).
Wrigley, Julia, 'The Division between Mental and Manual Labour: Artisan Education in Science in Nineteenth Century Britain' *American Journal of Sociology* Vol. 88 Supplement, 1982.
Wrigley, Julia, 'Technical Education and Industry in the Nineteenth Century' in B. Elbaum and W. Lazonick (eds), *The Decline of the British Economy* (Oxford, 1986).

10
THE VOICE OF INDUSTRY AND THE ETHOS OF DECLINE

Business citizenship, public service and the making of a British industrial élite[1]

Michael Dintenfass

On 13 April 1923, the *Colliery Guardian*, the journalistic voice of the British coal trade, published a short sketch of Joseph Albert Pease, Baron Gainford of Headlam, and above it a formal photograph of the man. This presentation of Lord Gainford to the business world of coal represented a new departure for the paper, the start of an illustrated series devoted to the 'Men of Note in the British Coal Industry'. Appearing in every other issue of the weekly trade journal, the feature ran for six years, coming to an end on 1 March 1929. In this time, the *Colliery Guardian* honoured 155 individuals as 'Men of Note'.

From a journalistic point of view, the *Colliery Guardian*'s Men of Note series was a mundane affair. There was no advance announcement of the column, and at its debut in April 1923 there was no editorial comment about the new feature and no indication of the criteria by which the paper would select its honourees. The *Colliery Guardian* did not name the authors of the profiles, and it never identified the sources of its biographical information about the men it celebrated. Since a seated portrait accompanied each biography, it seems safe to assume that no one appeared in the series against his will. In any event, 'Men of Note in the British Coal Industry' immediately took its place alongside 'Notes from the Coal Fields', 'Current Science and Technology', 'The *Colliery Guardian* Share List' and 'Labour and Wages' as one of the *Colliery Guardian*'s regular features. So routine a part of the journal did it become that after May 1925, when the editors inadvertently dropped C.P. Markham, the chairman of the Staveley Coal and Iron Co., from the list of those already honoured, they misnumbered every single one of the 101 sketches they published.

From the historical perspective, the Men of Note series constitutes a remarkable text. Its authors were men whose business it was to know the trade in which the *Colliery Guardian*'s honourees had distinguished themselves. Their assignment was to profile the most outstanding participants in the industry they were paid to chronicle. Their audience was the Men of Note themselves, their associates and competitors in the coal trade, and their subordinates. Consideration of who the *Colliery Guardian* selected as members of its coal industry élite and the ways it represented them to their mining peers cannot fail to shed light on that much-discussed but still quite obscure domain: the culture of British business in an era of relative economic decline.

This chapter explores the values and ideals – the governing ethos, one might say – that the *Colliery Guardian*'s Men of Note exemplified. Sections I–III examine closely the composition of this industrial élite and the attributes that figured most prominently in the journal's depiction of its members. Part IV locates the values that informed the *Colliery Guardian*'s construction of its coal industry honour roll in the Britain of the Men of Note's day, and it discusses the implications of such ideals for entrepreneurial performance. The argument, in brief, is that the leading journal of the mining and metals trades subscribed to an ethic of civic responsibility that was pervasive in Britain from the middle nineteenth century through the early twentieth century and that this governing ethos militated against the most efficient direction of private enterprises.

I

Let us begin with Lord Gainford or, better still, with the three Lord Gainfords who appeared in the *Colliery Guardian*'s Men of Note profile in April 1923. First there was the industrial statesman who had 'rendered great services to the coal mining industry'. 'A spokesman on behalf of the North of England in connection with the coal industry', Gainford, the journal reported, was now vice chairman of the Durham Coal Owners' Association, a member of the National Board for the Coal Industry and 'a prominent figure on the Central Committee of the Mining Association of Great Britain'. His signal contribution to the fortunes of the coal trade, however, had come four years before during the hearings of the Coal Industry Commission over which Sir John Sankey had presided. Gainford's evidence then had 'turned the tables on Mr. Robert Smillie [president of the Miners' Federation of Great Britain and a member of the commission] and Mr. Sidney Webb [one of the MFGB's nominees to the commission]' and 'made it clear to the world that the prosperity of the industry and the prosperity of the workers depended upon private enterprise and would not be promoted by socialistic nationalisation proposals'.[2]

The second identity with which the *Colliery Guardian* fitted Lord Gainford was that of public servant. His 'career as Patronage Secretary, Chancellor of the Duchy of Lancaster, Minister of Education, and Postmaster-General, during the war', the journal assured its readers, 'is well known', and it reminded them that Pease had received his peerage in 1917. Finally, the *Colliery Guardian* presented its Man of Note as the scion of an industrial dynasty. The second son of Sir Joseph W. Pease, Bart., his family had 'for many years been associated with the coal and iron trades of Durham and Cleveland'. The collieries of Messrs Pease and Partners, of which firm Gainford was vice chairman, along with those of its subsidiaries, produced 'upwards of 80,000 tons a week, whilst the firm is probably the largest coke manufacturing concern in the kingdom'.[3]

Suffice it to say that the portrait the *Colliery Guardian* drew of Lord Gainford was not the kind that would have appeared in *Fortunes Made in Business* or *Millionaires and How They Became So*. Nor was there anything in the journal's sketch that would have qualified its honouree for a place in any series devoted to Britain's wealthiest men or most successful entrepreneurs. There were no heroic tales of businesses built from scratch, no prodigies of technological innovation, no pioneering forays into untapped markets; nor was there anything in the way of corporate consolidation or even the competent stewardship of well-established undertakings. The only business distinction with which the *Colliery Guardian* credited Lord Gainford was that of association. His place in the coal industry was a matter of family ties, and if the firms to which he belonged were prominent by virtue of their size, there was not the slightest suggestion that the Man of Note had had anything to do with their growth.

The conception of industrial noteworthiness that governed the *Colliery Guardian*'s representation of Lord Gainford was thus a civic one and not an entrepreneurial or managerial definition. His identification as an outstanding figure in the coal trade turned on the political service he had performed on mining's behalf and not on his contributions to the output, employment, sales or revenues of the businesses with which he was associated. It was as a statesman representing his industry and a public official filling some of the highest offices of state that Gainford claimed his place as one of the leading lights of one of the largest and most important sectors of the British economy.

II

The civic understanding of industrial distinction that gave meaning to the *Colliery Guardian*'s portrayal of Lord Gainford also informed the selection of the journal's 154 other Men of Note. Thirty-seven (24%) of the individuals the *Colliery Guardian* featured were not businessmen at all, nor even employed on the profit-seeking side of the coal trade, but men engaged in the work of public institutions. Nine were members of HM Mines Inspectorate, including five who rose to the chief inspectorship of mines in the course of their careers.[4] Seventeen Men of Note were mining educators, occupying chairs at Sheffield, Leeds, Glasgow, Armstrong College, Newcastle, and the Imperial College of Science and Technology, among other places. C.H. Lander, director of fuel research under the Department of Scientific and Industrial Research, and Aubrey Strahan, director of the Geological Survey of Great Britain and the Museum of Practical Geology, were research scientists in the service of the government. J.S. Haldane and J. Ivon Graham were the director and assistant director respectively of the Mining Research Laboratory at the University of Birmingham.

The civil service also provided a noteworthy contingent of the *Colliery Guardian*'s coal trade élite. Edward Troup had had much to do 'with all administration and legislation affecting mines' in his fourteen years as the permanent undersecretary in charge of the industrial division of the Home Office.[5] T.A. O'Donahue was the mineral specialist at the Valuation Office of the Inland Revenue. The ranks of the *Colliery Guardian*'s Men of Note also extended to Viscount Chelmsford, the former viceroy of India, who chaired the Miners' Welfare Committee.

What distinguished all of these men was the prominent part they played in the provision of services ancillary to the getting and selling of coal. They monitored the health of Britain's mine workers and the safety of British mines. They researched working conditions underground, and they studied the chemical properties and industrial uses of coal. They developed new mining technologies, they collected and collated the statistical records of the mining industry, and they administered the laws pertaining to coal. Above all, the public officials the *Colliery Guardian* honoured headed the government agencies that discharged these tasks.

Seven trade union leaders joined the thirty-seven public sector Men of Note on the *Colliery Guardian*'s honours list. All of them were men of moderate industrial politics who had worked to preserve the civility of labour relations in the coal industry. Thomas Richards, general secretary of the South Wales Miners' Federation, had been a proponent of the sliding-scale method of wage determination and was, in the words of *The Times*, 'moderate, cautious, and conciliatory'. The *Colliery Guardian* described Frank Hodges, 'the able and energetic secretary of the Miners' Federation of Great Britain', as an 'advocate of constitutional methods and a redoubtable opponent of extremism'.[6]

In presenting these conciliatory trade unionists to the business community of coal the *Colliery Guardian* stressed that their sense of responsibility to the trade extended beyond industrial relations to less contentious concerns about safety and education. According to his profile, Richards was a member of the Safety in Mines Research Board and the Board for Mining Examinations. The general secretary of the Yorkshire Miners' Association, Samuel Roebuck, also sat on the examinations board and on the Miners' Lamps Committee while F.B. Varley, financial secretary of the Nottinghamshire Miners' Association, was a member of the Department of Mines' Committee on Rescue and Aid Regulations.

Altogether, more than one-quarter (44/155) of the men the *Colliery Guardian* featured as notable figures in the British coal trade made their livings outside private enterprise. With the exception of John Cadman, the former mines inspector, professor of mining, and adviser to the Coal Mines Department of the Board of Trade who played a major role in the development of the Anglo-Persian Oil Company, none of these Men of Note would ever have appeared in any compendium of Britain's best businessmen or wealthiest citizens. Like Lord Gainford's, their contributions were to the good of the mining industry and not to the fortunes of any particular firm within it. The very composition of the élite the *Colliery Guardian* identified thus confirms the priority accorded to public service and industrial citizenship in the journal's comprehension of British coal mining.

III

Most of the *Colliery Guardian*'s Men of Note (111/155) belonged to the profit-seeking side of the British coal industry. The proprietors, partners, directors, and general managers of coal mining enterprises accounted for the majority (61/111) of these private-sector Men of Note, but the journal's honour roll also included twenty-eight consulting engineers and mine managers, twelve coal merchants, five permanent officials of coal owners' associations, two manufacturers of colliery plant and equipment, two research scientists in private practice, and one mineral owner and royalty-holder advocate. How did the *Colliery Guardian* represent these individuals to the business world of coal? Were their profiles put together from tales of expanded outputs, increased efficiency, larger revenues, and higher profits? Or did the profitable exploitation of Britain's coal measures occupy a place in the journal's narratives about its private-sector Men of Note subordinate to industrial citizenship and public service?

The Edward Smallwood the *Colliery Guardian* presented to its readers in July 1927 as the 112th Man of Note was far more an accomplished actor on the civic stage than the personification of business vitality. According to the portrait the paper sketched of him, the Derbyshire-born Smallwood had come to London from the Doncaster Grammar School and at 17 commenced what turned out to be a life-long engagement on the distributive side of the coal business. In the course of his time in the capital, he spent nine years on the Islington Borough Council, was appointed a magistrate for the county of London, twice won election to the London County Council, and rose to the vice chairmanship of the LCC's Fire Brigades Committee. Smallwood served nine months in the Royal Naval Air Service during the First World War, and in 1917 he entered the House of Commons as the MP for East Islington. In 1918 he became the first president of the

Coal Merchants' Federation of Great Britain. Lastly, the paper told its audience that Smallwood had 'consecrated thirty years of his life to social work in the Metropolis'.[7]

Readers of the *Colliery Guardian*'s profile of Edward Smallwood would not have been able to form any picture of his place in the coal business. Not only did the journal's account of his life make no claims about the Man of Note's commercial credentials, it did not even identify the coal trading establishments with which Smallwood had been associated or the positions he held with the firms that engaged him. The story the *Colliery Guardian* told about him was almost entirely a story of politics and philanthropy, and the distinction the leading voice of the coal industry bestowed on Smallwood owed nothing to his activities as a coal merchant.

Certainly the *Colliery Guardian*'s complete disregard for the details of Edward Smallwood's career in private enterprise was uncharacteristic. The journal at least identified all of its other private-sector Men of Note with the undertakings at which they worked. The emphases of Smallwood's portrait, however, were quite characteristic of the way the paper construed the attainments of the individuals it placed at the forefront of the British coal industry.

Edward Smallwood was one of two Men of Note to appear in the *Colliery Guardian* as the head of the Coal Merchants' Federation of Great Britain (H. Cecil Rickett, another metropolitan coal dealer, was the other), and the journal described D.T. Hobkirk, managing director of the Newcastle-based coal-exporting firm Wm. Milburn and Co., and the Humberside coal trader H.L. Greig as one-time chairmen of the British Coal Exporters' Federation. Evan Williams, the president of the Mining Association of Great Britain at the time of his *Colliery Guardian* profile in 1923, was one of five Men of Note depicted in that capacity. According to the paper, one of these individuals, the Scottish coal and iron master George A. Mitchell, also presided over the Association of British Chambers of Commerce while the Wearside coal merchant Walter Raine served as a vice president of that body. In addition, no fewer than twenty-two presidents and chairmen of regional coal owners' and exporters' associations appeared among the *Colliery Guardian*'s honourees, as did seven presidents of district chambers of commerce. Altogether, the *Colliery Guardian* described 52 of the 111 Men of Note active in private enterprise (47% of the total) as the leaders of coal trade associations.

The *Colliery Guardian* also emphasized the prominent part that its private-sector Men of Note played in the professional societies of Britain's mining engineers and colliery managers. It identified the Lochgelly Coal Co.'s George A. Mitchell, R.A.S. Redmayne, a consulting engineer and former professor of mining and chief inspector of mines, the Durham coal master W.C. Blackett, and Wallace Thorneycroft, managing director of the Plean Colliery Co., as presidents of the Institution of Mining Engineers, and four of their fellow Men of Note as vice presidents of that organization. Percival Muschamp, agent of the New Hucknall Colliery Co., and H.F. Smithson, the general manager of Airedale Collieries Ltd in West Yorkshire, were notable in the eyes of the journal as presidents of the National Association of Colliery Managers, two of the six of the paper's honourees who had headed the NACM. Taking into account the thirty individuals the *Colliery Guardian* highlighted as the top officers of regional mining institutes and the seven chairs of regional branches of the colliery managers' association, forty-three private-sector Men of Note (39%) appeared in the journal's Men of Note series as the leaders of professional mining bodies.

The *Colliery Guardian* represented thirty-two (29%) of the coal owners, mining engineers and coal merchants whom it celebrated as members of Royal Commissions and departmental committees and as expert witnesses before such bodies. As the journal told it, the membership of the Royal Commission on Mining Subsidence (1923) included M.F. Maclean, the son of a chief justice of Bengal and the chairman of the United Collieries Ltd of Glasgow, and G.A. Lewis, the Midlands mining engineer and coal company director who had been secretary of both the National Association of Colliery Managers and the Midland Counties Institution of Mining Engineers, as well as two Men of Note from the public sector of the coal industry (Professor Henry Louis of Armstrong College and Viscount Chelmsford, who chaired the commission for a while) and the Nottinghamshire trade unionist F.B. Varley. The paper recognized as expert witnesses before this commission Arthur Morton Hedley, mining engineer and agent to Bolckow, Vaughan and Co. and a vice president of the Institution of Mining Engineers, and Arthur Hassam, mining consultant to the Pekin (*sic*) Syndicate in China and a president of the North Staffordshire Institute of Mining Engineers, along with the mines inspector H.M. Hudspeth and T.A. O'Donahue of the Inland Revenue.

These different forms of industrial public service – the direction of trade associations, the leadership of professional societies and the official deployment of coal-related expertise – were among the activities the *Colliery Guardian* used in defining the coal-trade distinction of no fewer than 87 of the 111 private sector figures (78%) on its who's who list. Public office-holding at the national and local levels furnished another strand of half (56/111) of the narratives the paper constructed about the company directors and executives, coal dealers and colliery managers it honoured. The profiles it published identified twelve members of parliament, sixteen municipal and county councillors and alderman, and forty-three justices of the peace. In addition, the *Colliery Guardian* drew attention to one lord lieutenant (Hugh Bell, the iron and coal magnate, held this office in the North Riding of Yorkshire), eleven deputy lieutenants and five high sheriffs in its presentation of the best and brightest of the British coal industry. All in all, statesmanship, whether of the industrial or political sort, proved a constituent element of the distinction with which the *Colliery Guardian* endowed nine-tenths (99/111) of its private sector Men of Note.

Where amidst this celebration of civic activism did the profitable getting and selling of coal fit into the *Colliery Guardian*'s understanding of the distinction of its private-sector Men of Note? What tribute did the journal pay to the development of collieries, the founding or reshaping of mining enterprises, the introduction of new techniques, the raising of outputs, the enhancement of productivity, and the generation of profits? Where, in short, did *business* accomplishments figure in the *Colliery Guardian*'s representation of the most outstanding participants in British coal mining?

Something of the discourse of the industrial titan is apparent in the *Colliery Guardian*'s column about Lord Aberconway, the Scots-born politician-turned-businessman. Here the paper found 'an industrial magnate in the true sense of the word'. 'His lordship is on the board of no fewer than nine colliery companies, and they include some of the most important concerns in the United Kingdom.' 'There is probably no one capable of exerting wider influence in the coal and iron trades than Lord Aberconway.' Its portrait of Samuel Kelly, the proprietor of Coalisland Collieries, County Tyrone, was even more explicit. This Man of Note, it wrote, 'may be said to have a paramount interest in the Irish coal trade, and the companies which he controls do fifty per cent. of the coal trade of all Ireland, with a fleet of 38 steamers'.[8]

These two instances aside, however, the tales the *Colliery Guardian* told about its Men of Note did not touch upon the power and influence that any of them wielded in the coal business. Indeed, the journal's pen portraits only infrequently concerned themselves with achievement in the realm of private enterprise proper. The development of mines, the creation of new undertakings, and the acquisition and rationalization of existing companies provided a part of the plot in just 14 of the 111 stories the paper published about its private sector honourees. The North Eastern coal owner Lord Joicey appeared in the *Colliery Guardian* as the 'leading spirit' in the growth of 'two of the largest colliery concerns in the county of Durham'. The journal credited John Gregory, the chairman and managing director of Sneyd Collieries Ltd, Stoke-on-Trent, with 'the enlargement and modernisation of an old colliery', and it portrayed the coal merchants Daniel Stevenson, Samuel Instone, C.L. Clay, and H.L. Greig as the founders of new trading houses.[9]

Similarly, technological innovation was not often one of the themes the *Colliery Guardian* employed to give meaning to the lives of its Men of Note. The North Staffordshire coal master John Gregory was, according to the paper, 'a pioneer in the application of three-phase power transmission underground and the utilisation of exhaust steam in turbo-generation'. In the eyes of the journal, H.E. Mitton of the Butterly Co. was the man who 'introduced' the Rheolaveur coal washery into the Nottinghamshire coal industry.[10] Even in the portrayal of those Men of Note closest to the coal face, however, industrial citizenship took precedence over the organization of production in the *Colliery Guardian*'s construction of distinction. Of the twenty-eight profiles devoted to mine managers and consulting engineers, twenty-three represented their subjects as individuals who filled leadership positions in professional bodies, supplied expertise to official inquiries, or held public office, while only fifteen defined their Men of Note in terms of achievements specific to the enterprises that engaged them.

Overall, the *Colliery Guardian* depicted just one in four (27/111) of the Men of Note active on the profit-seeking side of the coal business as technological pioneers or organizational innovators. As a device for establishing the distinction of its honourees, business prominence by association, as Lord Gainford exemplified it, served the journal almost as well. The paper identified twenty of the coal company directors and managers it featured in terms of the large or prominent firms with which they were associated or the well-known mining families to which they belonged, without in any single case suggesting that the standing of the undertaking or the clan owed anything to the individual in question. Thus it presented W. Newton Drew, chairman of the South Yorkshire concern Messrs Newton, Chambers and Co., as the great-great-grandson and great-grandson of the firm's founders and the top-ranking figure in an enterprise raising 'upwards of 1½ million tons per annum' and making approximately 250,000 tons of coke annually.[11]

The attributes the *Colliery Guardian* bestowed on the coal owners, colliery managers, mining engineers and coal merchants on its honour roll indicate as clearly as the membership of that honour roll that the industrial élite the journal selected between 1923 and 1929 was a service élite and not an economic élite. However much the Men of Note may have done to promote the efficiency and profitability of British coal mining, it was not accomplishments within the narrow ambit of ordinary business priorities that the paper fêted. Rather, it was as individuals of broader horizons – as the leaders of trade associations, the heads of professional societies, experts at the state's disposal, and members of the country's governing élite – that the *Colliery Guardian* represented its Men of Note to the business world of coal.

IV

The individuals the *Colliery Guardian* presented to the coal trade in the 1920s as mining's most distinguished men were above all paragons of civic virtue. The conduct that won them their places on the journal's honour roll took place outside profit-seeking enterprises and within the realm of voluntary associations, the institutions of higher education and the apparatus of government. The hallmark of their characters was their commitment to the community and not the satisfaction of their self-interest.

Such, of course, was not the reputation that Britain's coal masters of the late nineteenth and early twentieth centuries enjoyed among their contemporaries, even those who earned their livings above ground and out of the sight of winding gear. Nor is it the image that posterity has bequeathed to us, the coal owners' bloody-minded approach to labour relations having given them a uniquely demonic place in a national industrial relations history replete with confrontation, conflict, and villainy. When even a scholar as sympathetic to the owners as Barry Supple can decry the 'obstinately reactionary' nature of their 'political and industrial-relations postures', it is necessary to consider whether there was not some ulterior motive at work in the composition of the *Colliery Guardian*'s group portrait.[12] Might not its Men of Note series have been a public relations effort designed to cleanse a collective reputation besmirched by more than a decade of bitter disputes? Might not the column have been a kind of defence mechanism whereby Britain's coal masters sought psychic compensation for the ferocity with which they had fought the miners and their unions?

Plausible though such arguments are, they don't stand up to close inspection. In the first place, the *Colliery Guardian* commenced the series at a moment of political triumph for the coal owners and at a time, all too fleeting as it proved, of prosperity for the trade — and not, therefore, at a point when mining's leading figures would have felt that they and their less prominent compatriots needed to refurbish their public standing.[13] Furthermore, the journal was quite backward-looking in the depiction of its honourees. The achievements it recalled were very much accomplishments of the past: pre-Sankey Commission, pre-war and, to a very considerable extent, pre-1900. Thus, they did not constitute a record likely to carry much conviction in the present. Finally, the *Colliery Guardian* itself was an unpromising vehicle for the public rehabilitation of the mining industry's entrepreneurs and managers. As the contemporary equivalent of the trade's *Financial Times*, the journal possessed too small a general readership to sell effectively the virtues of coal's leading lights.[14]

It is a further defect of these attempts to cast doubt on the authenticity of the *Colliery Guardian*'s celebration of industrial citizenship that they ignore the power and pervasiveness of the ethic of civic responsibility in the Britain of the Men of Note's time. In the realm of intellectual life and political thought, 'the duty of altruism and sacrifice to others' defined the dominant 'moral sensibility of the Victorian educated classes' — a group in which many of the Men of Note would have to be included. At the heart of the philanthropic tradition in nineteenth and early twentieth-century Britain — a tradition itself very much at the heart of Victorian culture — there was a higher conception of citizenship that enjoined the working and middle classes alike to seek the fulfilment of 'their own best selves by helping those less privileged than themselves to fulfill their best selves, thus realizing the common good'. British thinking about welfare between 1890 and 1940 proceeded very much within the framework set by 'the cultural hegemony of idealism' — 'with its emphasis on corporate identity, individual altruism, ethical imperatives, and active citizen-participation' — and this same cluster of values was the taproot of that dense network of voluntary organizations that proliferated after 1780 as the British wrestled with the social complications that urbanization, industrialization, and political reform wrought. Indeed, Harold Perkin has gone so far as to claim that the development and diffusion of 'the professional ideal of public service, a sense that service to the community should come before the pursuit of profit', has been the central force in British life over the last century.[15]

As the product of a culture thoroughly suffused with a profound commitment to the common good, it is hardly surprising that the *Colliery Guardian* should have emphasized industrial statesmanship and civic activism in the selection and presentation of its 'Men of Note in the British Coal Industry'. Moreover, evidence of this concern for the community that the journal celebrated can be found within the rather negligible body of historical literature that has Britain's coal masters as its subject. In a richly impressionistic but by no means sympathetic essay about the coal owners of South Wales before 1914, L.J. Williams detected some of the very attributes out of which the *Colliery Guardian* fashioned its Men of Note.

The coal masters of South Wales, Williams maintained, had contributed little, the provision of capital aside, to mining, let alone to the principality. They had performed 'no especially crucial function in the industry'. They had done 'very little' to diversify the region 'by investing to establish subsidiary, ancillary or alternative industries'. They had left 'few permanent legacies ... no great architecture, no school of literature or art.... There were no model colliery villages, no hopeful experiments in industrial or social relations.'[16]

Yet Williams also acknowledged that there was 'considerable evidence that the coalowners (not necessarily all of them, of course) made financial contributions towards the social capital and institutions of the coalfield communities' and that at least until the 1880s they were very active in local politics and administration, sitting on 'representative bodies like Boards of Guardians and ... [performing] nominated functions like [those of] the Justices of the Peace'. Furthermore, he took pains to deny that this civic-minded behaviour could be reduced to motives of social control. 'Cultural values', 'religious considerations', a concern with 'moral elevation' and 'some simple benevolence', Williams insisted, were all at work here.[17]

The values to which the *Colliery Guardian* gave expression during the 1920s in its Men of Note series had deep roots in Britain's Victorian past, and the conduct such values engendered was clearly visible in Britain's most rapidly expanding coalfield in the decades before 1914. If this ethic of business citizenship and public service was one of the means by which British industrialists achieved integration into the broader middle-class culture of their day, it also dictated patterns of behaviour that distinguished British entrepreneurs from their continental competitors. Herein lies its relevance to discussions of British economic performance after 1870.

Social and cultural explanations of Britain's relative economic decline have long foundered on the similarities between British and foreign industrialists with respect to social origins, education, marriage patterns, landownership, and lifestyles. We can now see, however, that, for all the similarities of their private lives, the coal masters the *Colliery Guardian* featured and their compatriots in other lines of business conducted their affairs in ways very different from their German rivals. As Hartmut Berghoff and Roland Moller have shown, there were 'clearly perceptible' contrasts between British and German entrepreneurs 'in the sphere of public life'. British businessmen were far more active in local government and parliamentary politics than their German counterparts. British businessmen invested far more time and money in charitable undertakings. Having taken 'over a multitude of public activities' to which German manufacturers and merchants did not attend, British entrepreneurs simply were not able to pursue their 'economic ambitions' as single-mindedly as their competitors.[18]

This is not to say, of course, that British businessmen had no economic ambitions or that they neglected their undertakings. Rather, it is to suggest that they necessarily sought solutions to the dilemmas of their trades that were readily to hand and economical of time and attention. In the particular case of coal, this bred a fixation upon labour costs to the exclusion of the other factors that bore on the profitable getting and selling of coal. Indeed, the sheer force that Britain's mine owners concentrated on questions of wages and hours is exactly what we ought to have expected from proprietors and managers too busy with trade associations, professional societies, local offices, and proceedings in Whitehall to explore the intricacies of cutting and hauling techniques, the economies to be realized in the acquisition and use of materials and stores, and the commercial advantages of rational product lines, carefully cleaned coal, and the routine provision of professional labouratory analyses to their customers.[19]

The origins of Britain's relative economic decline over the last century are thus not to be found in an allegedly unique cultural antipathy to industry but in the country's abiding attachment to an ethos of civic responsibility. The idealistic conception of citizenship that governed British life in the late nineteenth and early twentieth centuries – with its injunctions to duty to others and service to society – did not withhold status and prestige from business activity, as Martin Wiener would have it.[20] Rather, it defined the dignity that attached to industry and commerce as a matter of stewardship on the community's behalf, and not as the pursuit of economic self-interest. The whole ethical tenor of British culture thereby worked against the concentration of entrepreneurial and managerial initiative on profit-seeking activity. By endorsing in its Men of Note series a code of conduct that put the commonwealth before the generation of wealth, the *Colliery Guardian* unwittingly gave voice to the ethos of decline.

Notes

1 I would like to thank Sylvia Schafer and Peter Marsh for their responses to a preliminary draft of this chapter and the participants at the 'Roots of British "Decline"' conference at Montpellier where it was first presented, especially James Foreman-Peck, David Greasley, and Donald McCloskey.
2 *Colliery Guardian*, 13 April 1923, p. 881. Unless otherwise indicated, all the information in this chapter comes from the *Colliery Guardian*'s Men of Note series. Specific references to this source are given only for direct quotations.
3 *Ibid.*
4 A sixth chief inspector of mines, R.A.S. Redmayne, also appeared among the Men of Note. By the time the *Colliery Guardian* featured him, however, he had left government service and become a consulting engineer.
5 *Colliery Guardian*, 14 April 1927, p. 875.
6 *The Times*, 9 November 1931, 14d and the *Colliery Guardian*, 10 August 1923, p. 333.
7 *Colliery Guardian*, 22 July 1927, p. 209. Owing to an editorial error, Smallwood was actually the 113th individual to appear in the series.
8 *Ibid.*, 13 July 1923, p. 83 (Aberconway) and 2 September 1927, p. 47 (Kelly).
9 *Ibid.*, 25 May 1923, p. 1247 (Joicey) and 13 November 1925, p. 1155 (Gregory).
10 *Ibid.*, 13 November 1925, p. 1155 (Gregory) and 2 May 1924, p. 1121 (Mitton).
11 *Ibid.*, 11 May 1928, p. 1849.
12 Barry Supple, *The History of the British Coal Industry*, vol. 4 *1913–1946: The Political Economy of Decline* (Oxford: Clarendon Press, 1987), p. 410.
13 It is instructive here to recall the exultant tone in which the *Colliery Guardian* recounted Lord Gainford's testimony to the Sankey Commission.
14 We might well wonder too whether men renowned for their 'political stupidity and lack of flexibility' (Supple, *History*, p. 424) were capable of the Machiavellian subtlety these arguments ascribe to them.
15 For intellectual and political life see Stefan Collini, *Public Moralists: Political Thought and Intellectual Life in Britain 1850–1930* (Oxford: Clarendon Press, 1991), pp. 62–3 and 87, and more generally chapter 2 on 'The Culture of Altruism: Selfishness and the Decay of Motive'; for philanthropy see Gertrude Himmelfarb, *The De-Moralization of Society: From Victorian Virtues to Modern Values* (New York: Alfred A. Knopf, 1995), pp. 153 and 164, and more generally chapter V on 'Gain All You Can . . . Give All You Can'; and F.K. Prochaska, 'Philanthropy', in *The Cambridge Social History of Britain 1750–1950*, vol. 3 *Social Agencies and Institutions*, ed. F.M.L. Thompson (New York: Cambridge University Press, 1990), pp. 357–93; about the intellectual origins of modern welfare policy see Jose Harris, 'Political Thought and the Welfare State 1870–1940: An Intellectual Framework for British Social Policy', *Past & Present* 135 (May 1992), pp. 123 and 137; and about voluntary organizations see R.J. Morris, 'Clubs, Societies, and Associations', in *The Cambridge Social History*, iii: 395–443. Harold Perkin's position is set out at length in his *The Rise of Professional Society: England since 1880* (New York: Routledge, 1990). The passage cited here can be found on p. 374.
16 L.J. Williams, 'The Coalowners', in *A People and a Proletariat: Essays in the History of Wales 1780–1980*, ed. David Smith (London: Pluto Press, 1980), pp. 102–4 and 112.
17 *Ibid.*, pp. 106–8. Williams argued (p. 107) that from the 1880s the coal owners' participation in local affairs declined 'both relatively and absolutely', but his essay provides no evidence that this was the case.

18 Hartmut Berghoff and Roland Moller, 'Tired Pioneers or Dynamic Newcomers? A Comparative Essay on English and German Entrepreneurial History, 1870–1914', *Economic History Review* XLVII (May 1994), pp. 278–83. While they acknowledge that 'the concept of responsibility for public affairs and the welfare of one's inferiors seems to have been deeply rooted in nineteenth-century English culture' (p. 279), Berghoff and Moller stress the differences between the German and British political systems in accounting for the very different public postures of the two countries' businessmen. My view is that the civic-mindedness of British industrialists was just one possible response to the peculiarities of the constitution and not the inevitable corollary of the political structure. Therefore it is necessary to ask why 'the absence of state-run [insurance] institutions' (p. 279), the genuine decision-making powers of the House of Commons (p. 281), and the relative stability and respectability of British political parties (p. 279) elicited the public activism of British entrepreneurs.

19 For an extended discussion of entrepreneurial opportunities in the interwar British coal industry see Michael Dintenfass, *Managing Industrial Decline: Entrepreneurship in the British Coal Industry between the Wars* (Columbus: Ohio State University Press, 1992).

20 Martin J. Wiener, *English Culture and the Decline of the Industrial Spirit 1850–1980* (New York: Cambridge University Press, 1981).

11
THE CITY OF LONDON, 1880-1914
Tradition and innovation[1]

Peter Cain

Twenty years ago it would have been impossible to construct a history of the City of London in the nineteenth and early twentieth centuries which could in any way have matched the rich and varied accounts of the development of British industry and agriculture. Part of the problem was the traditional shyness of City institutions much of whose success had depended on secrecy or, at the least, discretion. Such inhibitions have now largely vanished; archives have been opened and historical curiosity stimulated. The reasons for this rather sudden desire for exposure are not entirely clear but they may, in an oblique way, reflect economic decline. Despite the City's survival as an international financial centre it is now an offshore island of a global capitalism rather than, as it was in its heyday, the market which expressed the international dominance of British capital and British commercial and financial institutions. For the great names of the City, including the Bank of England itself, the days of supreme achievement are quite obviously over and contemplation of a glorious past may offer some small compensation. Whatever the rationale, the outcome has been a flood of research redressing the previously inevitable overemphasis on the fortunes of industrial capitalism which has distorted historians' perceptions both of the complexity of the British economy and of its evolution.[2] It has also directed attention to the fact that, whatever were the tribulations of industry after 1880, the City of London, like the south-eastern service sector of which it was the core, was a remarkably dynamic and enterprising entity rather than a mere derivative of industrial development. The result is that some traditional judgements which have long associated the service sector with labour intensity and low productivity are being revised and the importance of entrepreneurship and institutional innovation in these areas of the economy more clearly recognized.[3]

I

In what follows, my intent is to make a modest contribution to the debate which has recently arisen about the sources of this dynamism in the Square Mile by looking again at the concept of 'gentlemanly capitalism' formulated by Tony Hopkins and myself some years ago.[4] The notion of gentlemanly capitalism was intended to illuminate the existence of a series of overlapping groups of élite politicians and administrators, professionals and others who had a privileged position at the centre of British social and political life and, it was argued, the City had a significant role within that complex of wealth and power. Despite the claims of various critics, there was never any intention to argue that the whole of the City could be described as gentlemanly capitalist in this sense, only that there was a significant group of merchant houses and merchant bankers, frequently associated with the Bank of England's directorate, who had a differential access to power and to wealth. Indeed, for us, one of the fascinations of the City was that it was simultaneously a meeting point for a ferociously competitive capitalism and a home for a high status élite which had 'made it' to the top of the English social hierarchy as indicated by the frequency of intermarriage between wealthy bankers and financiers and the landed class after 1880.[5] We also suggested, though somewhat obliquely, that the gentlemanly capitalist core was capable of innovative activity and that élites were often at the heart of economic change. In practice, historians of the City have sometimes acknowledged the fact that there was a gentlemanly capitalist element in the City but they have assumed that the gentlemen were no longer the movers and shakers of commercial and financial capitalism but were the remnants of once-dynamic family businesses which had opted now for a life of leisure, social prestige and, occasionally, political influence.

In adopting this stance, historians of the City reflect the conventional wisdom. The Wiener thesis has been criticized on many different grounds, but the critics are generally agreed that the influence of aristocratic or gentlemanly social mores was inimical to entrepreneurial endeavour even when they disagree with Wiener about the actual influence of tradition on industry and the industrial spirit.[6] The most that is conceded is that gentlemanly culture was a contingent factor with no noticeable effect on business performance or attitudes. In the City context, Chapman and Kynaston echo this tradition.[7] Gentlemanly capitalists existed, but they were one-time worker bees now transformed into wealthy drones or, at least, those whose firms were damaged by social success and who had ceased to lead in business. By contrast, the key entrepreneurial figures in the City were new men bringing new ideas and methods. Taking advantage of the openness of the City and Britain's commitment to free trade, many of them came from Europe as well as from the British provinces. Indeed, Chapman sees this ceaseless flow of Continental immigrants as the reason why the City had proved so full of vitality throughout the nineteenth century. As the most successful of them became wealthy and lost their cutting edge, so they were superseded as market leaders by another wave of migrants in a continuous process of renewal which impelled the City forward and kept it at the forefront of innovation. Where there were cases of long-lived and intergenerationally successful groups like the Rothschilds, the argument is that their continued prominence depended far more on their extraordinary international, family-based communications networks than upon the talents of the leaders of the English branch itself whose performance is found wanting in numerous ways.[8] As for the new men, at least in their days of energy and enterprise, many professed a work ethic indistinguishable from that of any prominent Northern industrialist and were as far removed from the social and political world as was the latter.

There is certainly an abundance of evidence demonstrating the huge contribution made to the City by new talent in the period 1880–1914. The rise of Ellerman to the forefront of the shipping world and the great inroads made into the acceptance business by incoming merchant bankers such as Kleinworts, Schroders and the Ralli brothers are indication enough of Chapman's contention. Moreover, the business ethics of these movers and shakers were often worlds away from those of the established set around the Bank of England. This was especially true in the mushroom markets surrounding mining or in certain kinds of company promotion in Britain itself, where the motivators were not so much anti-genteel as positively shady: as witness the career of Edmund Davis, later famous as the creator of the Chrome trust, who in 1906 was described as someone 'who would cheat his blind grandmother at cards'.[9] Equally, it is not difficult to find the decline and even demise of once powerful firms, some of whom had influence at the Bank of England and beyond, but who had dissipated their assets through conspicuous consumption or failed to produce new blood to drive the business on when the changing international environment made adaptation unavoidable.[10] Moreover, there are descriptions of the behaviour of leading members of traditional City firms which, while confirming the status of the leading participants as gentlemen, hardly inspire confidence in the firm's desire to seek out new horizons. Here, for example, is Ronald Palin's description of George Littlehales, the 'titular boss' of the coupon department at Rothschilds during the 1914–18 war who:

> did not spend much time in the office. He lived at Mersea on the Essex coast and could hardly be expected to come in every day from such a distance. When he did turn up it was usually about noon. He would spend the next hour prodding his men into greater diligence; at one o'clock, he went to lunch and at 2.30 he caught his train home from Liverpool Street.[11]

Even for those who turned up regularly the day often began at 10.30. Alfred Rothschild himself would often arrive late in the morning and then spend his afternoon asleep on the office sofa.[12]

Palin himself made a distinction between gentlemen and players in the City and thought that, even in the 1920s, the former were as numerous as the latter.[13] But the distinction can be fatally overdrawn. Consider the activities of Colonel Scott, 'an awe-inspiring but kindly old gentleman' who worked in the cashier's department at New Court in the 1920s and whose responsibility it was to oversee the daily flow of cheques and banker's drafts and 'to get all payments paid into our clearing bank round the corner, balance the cash book and to ascertain how much should be lent to or drawn from the money market':

> he appeared to spend much time gossiping with the elegant and distinguished representatives of the discount houses who, still almost invariably top-hatted, spent their short day walking round the City from bank to bank before catching their afternoon train to Ascot or Sunningdale. How many transactions were actually consummated in the course of these perambulations I do not know; it always seemed to me that most of the business was done on the telephone between two-thirty and three o'clock. But let us live and let live not uncharitably; the system provided a pleasant occupation for some very nice men, and no doubt their conversations all over the City and the views they heard expressed enabled them to feel the financial pulse of the country and to give sound advice to their boards.[14]

The image of the top hat and the mid-afternoon train suggests yet another example of genteel inefficiency but there is a sting in the tail of the quotation. Scott and his business partners were clearly behaving in a gentlemanly manner but in this case they were not simply wasting time. Rather, they were using their cultural networks and their acquired social skills to create a working atmosphere in which confidence was built up, the strengths and weaknesses of situations and persons assessed and their credit – as much a matter of social psychology as economics – accurately gauged, so that bargains and agreements of binding force could be made as informally as possible. Banking was a world in which personal assessment and understanding often had a key role to play in business and Scott, like so many of his gentlemanly companions in the City, was engaged in that elaborate code of social behaviour which made it possible to use such phrases as 'a gentleman's agreement' and 'a gentleman's word is his bond', sentiments which meant a good deal in these circles. They were well paid for their trouble but they were also cheap at the price: without this dense, informal, social web which turned a large part of the City into a commercial and financial village, firms would have had to hire a much larger staff of clerks, buy a great deal more paper and pay for the services of far more lawyers and accountants.

Gentlemen made good players in the City: gentlemanly intercourse kept transactions costs down and helped the City to maintain its competitive edge in the money market. At a more elevated level of social interaction it was these social networks, not just the range of their international contacts, which kept firms like Rothschilds at the apex of the City and maintained their prestige despite the personal limitations of some of the leading family members. New merchant banking firms like Schroders and Kleinworts made big inroads into the bread and butter business of acceptance credits before the war but the traditional names hung on to their position in the new issue market where only Ernest Cassell and Morgans made any serious challenge to the older firms for the most lucrative business.[15] It was in the field of issues that prestige counted for most; and that prestige was sustained in part by the fact that the older firms had ramifying gentlemanly contacts throughout the City and, beyond that, into high politics and London society as well as an extensive range of overseas contacts.

The interlocking groups of gentlemanly 'amateurs' in the City had a still greater significance than that suggested above. The detailed research of Youssef Cassis has revealed that the directorates of a large number of the joint stock or clearing banks – the biggest financial institutions in the country by 1900 – the international banks, the insurance companies and many other leading City firms, including many of those venturing into new types of business, were dominated by the gentlemanly heads of the much smaller merchant banks and merchant houses and by the directors of the former private banks which had often been absorbed by the larger clearing banks. As the directorate, they provided the strategic management of the leading institutions. For example, in the case of the clearing banks, Cassis concludes that

> everything happened as if the primary purpose of the big deposit banks, those immense credit institutions, was to make possible the activities of the private banking and trading firms and the overseas ventures and partners of these firms, by supplying them with cash credit and not by taking any initiatives themselves. This dependent role explains why the professionals were actually the subordinates of the amateurs in this type of company.[16]

Except in rare cases such as Sir Edward Holden whose influence came through his power within a large joint stock bank, the Midland, the controlling elements in City capitalism before 1914 were not the managers of the leading firms but informal groups of capitalists many of which were under the direction of Cassis's 'amateurs'.[17] The latter controlled the flow of credit on which the system depended, frequently heading the firms at the vanguard of the City's overseas activities and the important new institutions and financial groupings which were appearing in the late nineteenth century such as investment trusts, investment groups and free standing companies.[18] The latter are of particular interest and have begun to attract the scholarly attention they deserve in recent years.[19] Largely concerned with organizing mining, transport, plantation agriculture and similar activities, or in providing the finance for these activities on the primary producing periphery, they were one of the City's main innovative reactions to the decline of classic merchanting which had followed the development of the telegraph from the 1870s.[20] Unlike modern multinational companies, free standing companies had their head offices in London but did all of their substantive business abroad. The London base was, nonetheless, crucial not just because of the extent of the funds available there but because of the expertise which could be gathered together through the huge, interconnected social networks of the imperial metropolis with gentlemanly financiers at the centre of them. The City élites and the institutions they guided were the conduit through which thousands of investors put out their capital in quiet, safe portfolio stocks bringing in steady returns to finance genteel lifestyles in the suburbs and small towns of Southern Britain. At the same time, they were also the backers and the directors of shoals of risky ventures across the globe, embodying novel institutional forms many of which failed but some of which were an impressive long-run success.[21]

An excellent example of Cassis's general point and of the importance of a common, traditional culture in breeding this success in the City can be found in the history of the international banks. These were classic free standing companies which sprang up after 1850 to service the financial needs of Britain's trade on the periphery and whose directorates were often drawn from the circles described above. A number fell by the wayside but, in general, the international banks were a considerable success over a long period of time. Their shrewd but conservative lending strategies proved highly profitable and kept many of them afloat in times of acute international depression such as the 1890s when local rivals succumbed to liquidity crises. An equally fundamental cause of their longevity was their reputation for honesty and reliability, qualities which their leading historian attributes to the values inculcated not only into the directorate but into the senior management during their education at British public schools or in colonial institutions which inherited the public school ethos.

> These banks recruited their future managers through their London office, a device which effectively limited staff to British subjects. Recruits were invariably middle class, and normally from the fee-paying public schools. Formal educational attainments were less important than the possession of social and sporting skills, which

ensured that young recruits would conform to the corporate culture, be trusted and perform a proper representational role for a British overseas bank.[22]

They were sent overseas early in their careers, were discouraged from marrying early and shared a common social life for years at a time.

The upshot of these recruitment and career patterns was the creation of strong corporate cultures centred on small management élites of British nationals ... the socialisation strategies pursued by British overseas banks enabled them effectively to manage their branch networks and to limit losses from bad debts and fraud.

The system also 'economised on information and monitoring costs' and limited 'agent–principal conflict'.[23] As such, British overseas banks stayed ahead of the competition until after 1945.

Another institution full of public school men was the Stock Exchange and that was also a highly successful and adaptive organization before 1914.[24] Indeed, as far as the City is concerned, it may be time to look again at the relationship between educational background and occupational attainment. Public schools at one and the same time encouraged a strong sense of corporate solidarity and individual competitiveness, qualities which undoubtedly have no logical connection with each other but which, in banking and finance – as in government, managing an empire and on the sports field – appear to have produced a creative tension conducive to the job in hand.[25] At the individual level, one character who personified this duality was Cuthbert Heath, the highly innovative Lloyd's underwriter who did so much to diversify the insurance business before the war and thus helped to maintain Lloyd's reputation as a world centre.[26] Heath, 'a commanding, rather austere figure, possessed [of] the highest standards' and devoted to the welfare of the institution wherein he practised, was the son of an admiral who began business with a £7,000 loan from his father in 1880. Reacting to the depressed traditional market in marine insurance in the mid-1880s, Heath pioneered insurance for fire, burglary and earthquakes and then moved into credit insurance to safeguard businesses against defaulting creditors besides playing a crucial role in instigating the organizational changes which fitted Lloyd's to enter the twentieth century with confidence. Moreover, one of the leading partners in the first Lloyd's firm to be entirely devoted to non-marine insurance, Matthews, Wrightson and Co., was a Old Marlburian.[27]

II

If the City was a success story before 1914 then gentlemanly financiers had a significant role to play in it, a role which went far beyond providing a charming veil to hide the capitalist indecencies hidden beneath. Capitalist activities arose out of gentlemanly social networks and depended on them to survive and to prosper. However, if success is measured in terms of the impact of City finance on the British economy as a whole, some qualifications might seem to be in order. First, there was a long tradition in Britain, beginning with the Fair Trade movement in the 1880s, associating the City with the promotion of economic policies which enhanced Britain's relative industrial decline. The Fair Trade argument, echoed by the Tariff Reformers twenty years later, was that unilateral free trade exposed British industry to unfair competition, encouraged manufacturing imports from Europe and depressed both profits and domestic industrial investment. Simultaneously, low domestic profits encouraged the export of capital and the fortunes of City financiers were enhanced.[28] It may be true that unilateral free trade harmed some sectors of British industry in the long run but the City did not bear the responsibility for this because it is impossible to argue that free trade was a City policy vainly opposed by industry. Far from being a simple confrontation between protectionist manufacturers and free trade bankers, the Tariff Reform campaign after 1903 split industry down the middle whilst also attracting the support of some prominent City men who could appreciate Chamberlain's concerns about the future of industry.[29] Moreover, the tariff issue was a matter of widespread public concern and attention. It was thus a matter which could only be resolved through lengthy public debate, a process which reduced the influence of particular pressure groups considerably.

Fiscal policy had to be decided under the glare of publicity: in contrast, monetary policy was a more arcane business and therefore one much susceptible to influence by interested groups close to governments. Also, there seems little doubt that the City was almost unanimous in its support for the gold standard. As the price of silver, the monetary base of many Eastern countries, fell in the 1880s and 1890s the leaders of some prominent industrial export industries agitated in favour of bimetallism: but there was never any real prospect of change if only because governments, whether Liberal or Conservative, appear to have taken it for granted that the City understood money best.[30] In consequence, some important British exports, such as the cotton textiles sent to India and other Far Eastern markets, were hampered by an overvalued currency and suffered accordingly, though the exact effects of this handicap are unknown. It must also be recognized that, besides increasing the receipts from invisible income including investments abroad, maintaining the gold standard cheapened raw material and other imports from markets based on silver and this may have enhanced competitiveness in other areas of British industry. Nor can it be claimed that there was ever any general agitation amongst industrialists against the gold standard: though whether this indicated satisfaction with the status quo, deference to City expertise or widespread ignorance about the effects of gold is hard to say at present.[31]

Secondly, there have been a number of attempts by historians to lay the blame for Britain's low rate of industrial investment at the City's door but they have often failed for lack of evidence. In recent times, however, detailed research on the lending policy of the clearing banks and attempts by new industries to raise money in the City in the late nineteenth century have added a new edge to the debate. Capie and Collins' most recent investigation of clearing bank records confirms the banks' distaste for lending long to industry, though they emphasize that the same banks were often happy to renew overdrafts for long periods for trustworthy clients. Established industries usually had little difficulty in raising finance of this kind and, as earlier research shows, were usually well able to finance their long-term capital needs without resort to outside lenders.[32] Traditionally, British industry raised its investment funds through its profits or by a variety of informal, local mechanisms: little happened after 1870 to change this, leaving the City to minister to the needs of government, semi-public utilities such as railways, the finance of international trade via 'bills on London' and the demands of large overseas borrowers. Given a lack of demand for innovative forms of finance from the bulk of British industry and the growing attractions of the overseas market, especially the bill market, it is not surprising that the clearing banks should have become heavily involved in the latter. This involvement in overseas markets also reinforced the banks' traditional caution about long-term domestic lending since success in the bill market depended on high levels of liquidity. The compensation for industry was that the banking system in Britain had a great deal more stability than it did in countries where long-term lending was more pronounced and where liquidity crises were therefore more likely in times of slump.[33]

What recent work does indicate, however, is that new firms – those most likely to be at the pioneering end of the industrial spectrum – did find it more difficult to raise funds on overdraft in a risk-averse banking system whose conservatism may have been reinforced by the tendency, as amalgamation proceeded apace, for decision making on loan policy to become centralized and for local initiative to be reduced.[34] Moreover, Capie and Collins' research has to be put alongside Bill Kennedy's claim that new industry was disadvantaged in the London capital market because firms were frequently let down by poor informational networks and by other organizational failures in the City. Accordingly, the profit potential of firms in pioneering industries was often badly underestimated and they frequently fell into the hands of unscrupulous company promoters who loaded them down with unproductive debt and hampered their profit performance for years afterwards. New industry in Britain was thus hobbled by the City at a critical time in its history when rival firms in Germany and in the United States were taking off in much more propitious environments. On this reading, a considerable percentage of Britain's massive overseas investment was the outcome of systematic market failure.[35]

Kennedy's conclusions have been vigorously contested: it has been argued, for example, that in the case of the electrical and the motor vehicle industries, two of Kennedy's prime examples of City failure, poor growth and investment was actually due to restrictive local and central government legislation which curbed profitability.[36] Moreover, the best documented saga of new industry–City relations before 1914, that involving the Hopper firm, seems to yield ambiguous results on close investigation. Hopper was a brilliant technical innovator in the rapidly growing cycle trade who financed himself originally via personal contributions from the directorate of his firm and from ploughed back profit. Hopper needed outside finance in order to grow faster and, given its level of profitability, his firm was badly undercapitalized. Attempts to use bank overdrafts soon got him into trouble, with his bank, rather revealingly, complaining that the firm 'seem to look upon us not as Bankers, but as financiers, whose bounden duty was to furnish them with such extra capital as they require'.[37] Frustrated by high street banking conventions, Hopper turned to the City, attempting to raise debenture capital in 1907 as a joint stock limited liability company and then, in 1913, hiring a company promoter to refloat the company and release funds for investment. In both cases he failed miserably and had to be content with a larger overdraft obtained by changing his bankers. This may seem to be a classic case of an innovative entrepreneur falling foul of clearing bank conservatism and City ignorance of industry. However, Hopper undoubtedly contributed to his own misfortunes, especially in the City, by giving little substantive information about his company to potential investors. The firm refused to issue proper balance sheets and appears to have offered investors no greater assurance than the boast that the firm was 'as safe as the Bank of England' and 'a first-class security'.[38] Hopper also came to the market the second time when foreign investment was at its height and home industrial stocks severely depressed. In 1913, in investigating his plight, the *Economist* argued that he had come to the market at the worst possible time and that he

> was entirely ignorant of the condition of the money market here as regards flotations, and having an absolute faith in the business itself needed little persuasion as to the furious demand there would be on the part of the public to take shares in such a company, and [his associates] were almost equally simple-minded.[39]

What this episode appears to demonstrate is not just that the City knew little about industry but that industry was equally uninformed about finance. As Hopper's chronicler remarked, if he 'had shown the same flair for finance as he demonstrated in the direction of the technical, manufacturing and sales aspect of the business, many of his problems would never have arisen'.[40]

However, demonstrating a 'flair for finance' was not easy given the historic gulf which existed between City and industry. There was great deal of ignorance and even contempt for British industry in the City.[41] This must have affected the clearing banks as they fell increasingly under City control and it may also have reinforced the tendency within the Square Mile itself to develop non-industrial interests overseas. City attitudes triggered similar responses in the provinces; and, insofar as this made it difficult for industrialists to approach the City or enhanced industry's fears of being exploited and of losing control of their organizations if they ventured too far into the City, it probably added to the influences which made 'personal capitalism' such a strong force within British industry.[42] So, although it appears that British financial institutions met most of the needs of industry after 1870 it is worth remembering that these needs had to some extent already been shaped — and restricted — by the historic divide between City and industry. Both had been set much earlier on development paths which effectively limited the contacts between them.

III

There are a number of conclusions, some more robust than others, which can be drawn from the above discussion. The most obvious one is that it is important to recognize that assessments of business success or failure in Victorian and Edwardian Britain ought to take more account of the service sector, and commerce and finance in particular, than hitherto. In this respect, the prominence of the famous Chandler thesis with its spotlight trained firmly on industrial structures, has not been helpful. Chandler's concern with the origins of the large corporation, and his rather disparaging dismissal of the small firm and of 'personal capitalism' as a promoter of growth, has already come under fire from industrial historians and it is quite inappropriate as far as the Square Mile is concerned since so much of the dynamism and energy displayed has to be understood in these terms.[43] However, one of the responses to Chandler has been to revive the idea of the 'industrial district', first made famous by Alfred Marshall, and, suitably modified, this can be used to suggest a more promising way of understanding the dynamism of the City.[44] Industrial districts are formed out of large numbers of mainly small and medium-sized firms which certainly compete with each other but whose combined activities within a locality generate a series of interlocking relationships (and an 'atmosphere') which are conducive to the spread of ideas, innovation and investment and also prove attractive to skills and capital from outside. This self-generated culture of industrial arts and innovation, reinforced by immigration, is often crucial in helping industrial districts to maintain their competitive edge over rivals long after the initial factors which brought industry to the locality in the first place — such as raw material or energy supplies or easy transport facilities — have ceased to be particularly relevant.[45]

By analogy, it can be argued that the City is the prime example of a commercial and financial district or 'service district'. The original basis of the City's strength lay in Britain's dominant position in international trade and its surplus savings, reinforced in the first half of the nineteenth century by the adoption of free trade and of the gold standard. But by 1870 these advantages were also being constantly reinforced by the synergy released by the interaction of the City's myriad of businesses which created a complex of interlocking services unique on the globe at the time and provided collective benefits which constantly sharpened the edge of its competitiveness. This interactive competitiveness was also enhanced by the enormous geographical concentration of the City's core businesses within the famous 'Square Mile';[46] and by the attraction the City had for hordes of new men, new capital and new ideas from the Continent. In this way, the Square Mile retained what Michael Porter has aptly called its 'competitive advantage'.[47]

What has been said so far is quite compatible with Chapman's analysis of City success with its emphasis on the creative role of the foreigner. But a fuller understanding of the springs of growth, whether industrial or financial, may require a further strand to be added to the argument. In recent years, economists and social scientists have become increasingly interested in identifying the 'social capital' which forms the base upon which economic interaction takes place.[48] Social capital, arising out of 'irrational' sources such as religion, is the fund of ideas, institutions and practices which holds people together in communities and engenders the trust and goodwill that allow markets to operate effectively. Whether this social glue holds together only family networks, or whether it extends to involve ever-wider groups beyond the level of kin, can determine not only the structure of enterprise within particular nations but also influence its rate of growth and overall development. The argument here is that gentlemanly capitalists, with their extensive familial, educational and cultural networks within the City and their equally extensive contacts outside the City's walls, helped to provide a crucial form of social cement within the commercial and financial community at a time of rapid change. They offered strategic leadership and a social and cultural network which increased efficiency: they also brought an element of stability amidst the chaotic dynamics of City life. Gentlemanly capitalism may seem to be a contradiction in terms, an awkward and unhelpful attempt to straddle the divide, recently neatly anatomized by McCloskey, between the traditionally heroic activities of warfare, governance and religion, and the bourgeois virtues associated with market rationality.[49] But sometimes more can be learned about economic growth and structural change from observing the fertile interaction between the old and the new than is possible simply by emphasizing the differences between them.

If the evidence adduced above is correct, gentlemanly capitalism seems to have been a force holding together a range of financial enterprises which helped Britain to become the pre-eminent market for international services. The interaction between gentlemanly capitalists and 'new men' also made for a creative tension in the City which allowed for innovation without undue instability.[50] At the same time, the fact that City leaders and captains of industry drew their inspiration from different wells of social capital and formed different 'trust communities' may have brought long run harm to both the City and industry by preventing co-operation and thus thwarting mutually advantageous developments. From our present perspective, strongly influenced as it is by the recent rapid decline of manufacturing capacity, Britain's peculiar drift from industry towards services after 1880 may seem to have brought more problems than benefits, as the Tariff Reformers predicted would be the case: but this is a highly contentious matter, and should not prevent us from recognizing that services were far more important components of the economy than has usually been allowed and that gentlemen may sometimes have earned their keep in promoting them.

Notes

1 I would like to thank Roger Lloyd-Jones for reading a draft of this chapter and for his perceptive comments.
2 The best introductions to City history are David Kynaston's volumes: *The City of London: A World of its Own, 1815–90* (London, 1994) and *The City of London: Golden Years, 1890–1914* (London, 1995) which give a largely chronological account of City development; and R.C. Michie, *The City of London: Continuity and Change, 1850–1990* (Basingstoke, 1992) which has a more analytical approach. Also valuable is Y. Cassis, *La City de Londres* (Paris, 1987).
3 On the service sector the pioneering work is C.H. Lee, *The British Economy: A Macroeconomic Survey* (Cambridge, 1986). See also the same author's 'The Service Sector, Regional Specialisation, and Economic Growth in the Victorian Economy', *Journal of Historical Geography* 10 (1984). For a recent affirmation of the importance of services in enhancing productivity growth see J. Bhagwati, 'Splintering and Disembodiment of Services and Developing Nations' in Lee, *Essays in Development Economics*, vol. 1 (Oxford, 1985).
4 The most recent statement is in P.J. Cain and A.G. Hopkins, *British Imperialism: Innovation and Expansion, 1688–1914* (London, 1993).
5 On intermarriage between bankers and aristocracy see Y. Cassis, *City Bankers, 1890–1914* (Cambridge, 1994), ch. 6.
6 M.J. Wiener, *English Culture and the Decline of the Industrial Spirit, 1850–1980* (Cambridge, 1981). For informed commentary see B. Collins and K. Robbins (eds) *British Culture and Economic Decline* (London, 1990).
7 S.D. Chapman, *The Merchant Bankers* (London, 1984) and Chapman, *Merchant Enterprise in Britain from the Industrial Revolution to World War One* (Cambridge, 1992). Chapman's pathbreaking article 'Aristocracy and Meritocracy in Merchant Banking', *British Journal of Sociology* 37 (1986) should also be consulted here. Kynaston's thoughts on gentlemanly capitalism are in *The City of London: Golden Years*, pp. 322–39.
8 See Kynaston's remarks on the English branch of the Rothschilds in *The City of London: Golden Years*, pp. 271–4.

9 I.R. Phimister, 'The Chrome Trust: The Creation of an International Cartel, 1909–38', *Business History* 38 (1996), p. 79. Shady company promoters are dealt with by J. Armstrong, 'The Rise and Fall of the Company Promoter and the Financing of British Industry', in J.J. van Helten and Y. Cassis (eds) *Capitalism in a Mature Economy: Financial Institutions, Capital Exports and British Industry, 1870–1939* (London, 1990).
10 For example, M. Daunton, 'Inheritance and Succession in the City of London in the Nineteenth Century', *Business History* 30 (1988).
11 R. Palin, *Rothschild Relish* (London, 1970), p. 91.
12 *Ibid.*, pp. 43, 90.
13 *Ibid.*, p. 95
14 *Ibid.*, p. 49.
15 This point has been emphasized by Y. Cassis, 'Merchant Banks and City Aristocracy', *British Journal of Sociology* 39 (1988). It should be noted here that Morgans' access to power in London was facilitated by their alliance with the Grenfell family which had connections into the British aristocracy and into high political circles. See K. Burk, *Morgan Grenfell, 1838–1988: The Biography of a Merchant Bank* (Oxford, 1989). See also R.C. Michie, 'The Social Web of Investment in the Nineteenth Century', *Revue internationale d'histoire de la banque* 18–19 (1979).
16 Cassis, *City Bankers*, p. 180.
17 *Ibid.*, pp. 178–81.
18 For investment groups see Chapman, *Merchant Enterprise in Britain*, ch. 8.
19 M. Wilkins, 'The Free-Standing Company: An Important Type of British Foreign Investment', *Economic History Review* XLI (1988).
20 On this theme, besides Chapman, *Merchant Enterprise* see also C.A. Jones, *International Business in the Nineteenth Century: The Rise and Fall of a Cosmopolitan Bourgeoisie* (Brighton, 1987).
21 A debate about the purpose and management structures of free standing companies can be found in *Business History* 36 (1994). See J.-F. Hennart, 'International Financial Capital Transfer: A Transactions Cost Framework'; M. Casson, 'Free Standing Companies: Their Financing and Internalisation Theory'; T.A.B. Corley, 'Free Standing Companies: Their Financing and Internalisation Theory'; and Hennart's reply 'Free Standing Firms and the Internalisation of Markets: A Reply to Casson'. The high proportion of British overseas financial flows which were direct rather than portfolio investment has recently been emphasized by T.A.B. Corley, 'British Overseas Investment in 1914 Revisited' in the same issue of *Business History*.
22 G. Jones, *British Multinational Banking, 1830–1990* (Oxford, 1993), p. 50.
23 *Ibid.*, pp. 51–2. For a recent example of the criteria used by an overseas bank in recruiting new staff, see S. Muirhead, *Crisis Banking in the East: The History of the Chartered Mercantile Bank of India, London and China* (London, 1996), pp. 143, 148–9, 150.
24 On the Stock Exchange see Kynaston, *The City of London: Golden Years, passim*; and R.C. Michie, 'The Stock Exchange and the British Economy' in van Helten and Cassis, *Capitalism in a Mature Economy*.
25 A very high proportion of City bankers were educated at public school: Cassis, *City Bankers*, pp. 98–106. By contrast, between 1870 and 1914, only 18 per cent of Berghoff and Moller's sample of English industrialists were so trained. H. Berghoff and R. Moller, 'Tired Pioneers and Dynamic Newcomers? A Comparative Essay on English and German Entrepreneurial History', *Economic History Review* XLVII (1994), p. 269. The fact that a public school education went well with City avocations was noted by D.C. Coleman in his pioneering 'Gentlemen and Players', *Economic History Review* XXVI (1973), pp. 92–116.

26 R. Straus, *Lloyd's: An Historical Sketch* (London, n.d.), pp. 254–6; Kynaston, *The City of London: the Golden Years*, p. 22; R.C. Michie, 'The Finance of Innovation in Late Victorian and Edwardian Britain: Possibilities and Constraints', *Journal of European Economic History* 17 (1988), p.500.
27 Kynaston, *The City of London: Golden Years*, pp. 221–2.
28 One of the most brilliant expressions of this is by Ritortus, 'The Imperialism of British Trade', *Contemporary Review* 76 (1899), pp. 132–52, 282–304.
29 For the City's views on Tariff Reform see Kynaston, *The City of London: the Golden Years*, pp. 375–85; Cassis, *City Bankers*, pp. 301–7. See also A. Marrison, *British Business and Protection, 1903–1932* (Oxford, 1996), ch. 1.
30 For an example, see A.G. Gardiner, *Life of Sir William Harcourt*, vol. II (1923), p. 614.
31 On bimetallism see: M. Collins, 'Sterling Exchange Rates, 1847–1880', *Journal of European Economic History* 15 (1986), pp. 521ff.; E.E.H. Green, 'Rentiers versus Producers? The Political Economy of the Bimetallic Controversy', *English Historical Review* 103 (1988); and the exchange between Green and A. C. Howe in the *EHR* 110 (1990).
32 F. Capie and M. Collins, 'Industrial Lending by English Commercial Banks, 1860–1914: Why Did Banks refuse Loans?' *Business History* 38 (1996). There is a useful summary of previous research in M. Collins, *Banks and Industrial Finance in Britain, 1800–1939* (London, 1991).
33 F. Capie and M. Collins, *Have the Banks Failed British Industry?* (London, 1992), ch. 5.
34 Capie and Collins, 'Industrial Lending by English Commercial Banks', pp. 42–3.
35 W.P. Kennedy, *Industrial Structure, Capital Markets and the Origins of British Economic Decline* (Cambridge, 1987). See also his article 'Capital Markets and Industrial Structure in the Victorian Economy' in van Helten and Cassis, *Capitalism in a Mature Economy*.
36 R.C. Michie, 'The Finance of Innovation in Late Victorian and Edwardian Britain', pp. 510–16. Also M. Edelstein, 'Foreign Investment and Accumulation, 1860–1914' in R. Floud and D. McCloskey (eds) *The Economic History of Britain since 1700, Vol. 2: 1860–1939* (Cambridge, 1994), pp. 187–92.
37 A.E. Harrison, 'F. Hopper and Co. – The Problems of Capital Supply in the Cycle Manufacturing Industry, 1891–1914', *Business History* 24 (1982), p. 15.
38 *Ibid.*, p. 13.
39 *Ibid.*, p. 19.
40 *Ibid.*, p. 20.
41 See D. Kynaston's article in the *Guardian*, 10 June 1995, p. 38.
42 On personal capitalism see A. Chandler, *Scale and Scope: the Dynamics of Industrial Capitalism* (Cambridge, Mass., 1990), pt. III.
43 For an example of where personal capitalism appears to have been vibrant and innovative, see R. Lloyd-Jones and M. J. Lewis, 'Personal Capitalism and British Industrial Decline: The Personally Managed Firm and Business Strategy in Sheffield, 1880–1920', *Business History Review* 68 (1994).
44 A. Marshall, *The Economics of Industry* (3rd edn London, 1919), pp. 153–4.
45 The idea of an industrial district is developed in Lloyd-Jones and Lewis, 'Personal Capitalism and British Industrial Decline', pp. 394–405.
46 P. Ferris, *The City* (London, 1960), p. 10.
47 M. Porter, *The Competitive Advantage of Nations* (Basingstoke, 1990).
48 On this theme see M. Casson, *Entrepreneurship and Business Culture* (London, 1995); J. Brown and M. Rose, *Entrepreneurship, Networks and Modern Business* (Manchester, 1995); J. S. Coleman, 'Social Capital in the Creation of Human Capital', *American Journal of Sociology* 94 (1988); and F. Fukuyama, *Trust: The*

Social Virtues and the Creation of Prosperity (London, 1995).
49 D. McCloskey, 'Bourgeois Virtue', *American Scholar* 63 (1994).
50 In chaos theory (which in its economic extensions has strong affinities with the Hayekian approach to markets) a central concept is that of 'bounded instability' which expresses the paradox that effective organizations need to be both stable and unstable simultaneously. See D. Parker and R. Stacey, *Chaos, Management and Economics: The Implications of Non-Linear Thinking* (London, 1995). As they put it, the paradox is:

> that the efficient conduct of day to day business ... requires that people share a culture and have the same values. But ... creativity requires that these cultures and values must be constantly questioned. Policies or business structures and systems that make it impossible for differences between people to flourish, that prevent a creative tension, block adaptability and innovation. (p. 64)

Part V

A FRENCH PERSPECTIVE ON THE BRITISH DECLINE

12

FRANCE'S EXPERIENCE OF INDUSTRIAL RETARDATION DURING THE *BELLE EPOQUE*[1]

Jean-Pierre Dormois

Economic historians of France should be to some extent familiar with the criticisms levelled at the late Victorian economy: they are in substance similar in content to those directed at its French counterpart in the nineteenth century, and a generation of historians struggled for decades to explain French industrial 'retardation' in the period up to the Second World War. Recently, however, a 'revisionist' approach has set out to rehabilitate the French record during the period of industrialization: no, France's nineteenth-century economic growth was not dismal compared to other industrializers; no, French firms were not unprofitable because too small; no, French entrepreneurs were not timid and conservative rent-seekers. Given the renaissance of France's economy and its promotion to fifth rank among industrial nations after 1945, there must have been, so it is argued, solid foundations in her recent past to explain this belated vitality.

The purpose of the present chapter is not to attempt to survey the arguments or settle the disputes that have developed over the French 'path of industrialization' (French historians having always been adamant that their country was 'special'). Rather, it will focus on the period that was early defined as the *locus* of alleged British industrial retardation or slowdown, the 'Edwardian era', a period that came to be known in retrospect, after the ordeal of the Great War, as the *Belle Epoque*. France's overall economic growth in the period 1870–1914 is remarkably parallel to that of the UK (see Figure 12.1). How can these apparent similarities be explained? Were comparable forces at work that account for the parallel downgrading of the two economies in the face of more dynamic competitors? Can it be said that the two economies followed an essentially 'idiosyncratic' path of development that was all their own?

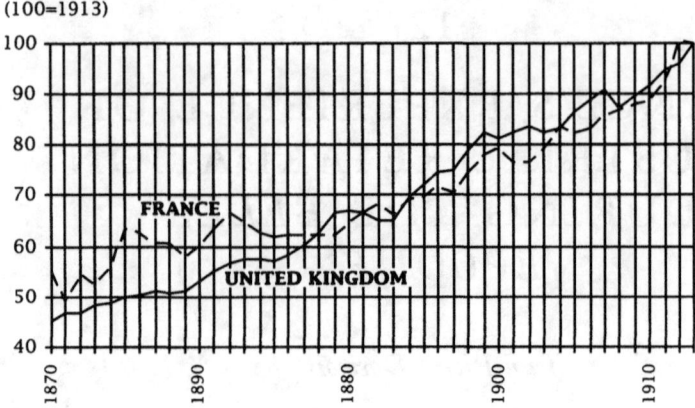

Figure 12.1 Growth of national income, UK and France 1870–1913.
Sources: Feinstein (1972); Lévy-Leboyer and Bourguignon (1990).

Leisurely pace and the business cycle

In the period 1870–1914, France and Britain fall into the category of the slow growers; the French economy grew at an average rate of 1.6% per annum compared with 1.9% for the UK (Maddison, 1995). Moreover, the growth pattern is almost strictly parallel between the two countries. There is indeed ample evidence of a marked slowdown in French economic growth after 1870. In this respect the use of per capita figures could be misleading: French population in its characteristic pattern reached virtual stability after 1880 while other countries' dynamic economies were partly fuelled by sustained population growth.

In a sense Britain has at least the 'excuse' of maturity for this slowdown compared not only to its earlier performance record, but also to that of the late industrializers. France reached the 'plateau' of maturity at a much lower level of development, begging the question: why didn't it join this group of dynamic countries that were entering the process of catching up with the UK economy? Could there be a similar logic at work in the case of France and Britain which explains this parallel evolution?

The problem of 'retardation' in the French case develops therefore from different premisses. The nineteenth-century French economy borrows, it seems, features from both the group of early industrializers (of which Britain was, for a time, the 'paradigm') and from that of late industrializers catching up with the advent of the 'second industrial revolution'. With hindsight, the 'take-off' phase of French industrialization – if indeed there was one – was short lived (a bare twenty or thirty years) and ushered in a period of slower growth after 1860, except that growth now was not so slow compared with the earlier period (Marczewski, 1963). At any rate, the path of French economic development appears very early to have slowed down compared to other advanced economies to the point where its business cycle has sometimes seemed erratic or its effects singularly muffled (Lévy-Leboyer, 1971). This finding took much time to gain acceptance. After all, industrialization, so far as one could judge, had proceeded steadily under the Third Republic and, contemporary public opinion remained unconvinced of its beneficial effects. Besides nineteenth-century French mainstream economists had hinted that recessions were deeper in Britain but relatively mild in France, cushioned as they were by the country's large agrarian economy.

Marczewski probably had in mind La Fontaine's fable of 'The hare and the tortoise' when he stressed there was no discernable 'take-off' of industrialization in France during the whole period 1700 to 1913. The proposition was taken up by revisionists who argued that France had achieved overall the same level of welfare as Britain in the course of the century without going through the 'tribulations' of 'mass' industrialization. This is indeed the picture which the ISEA series constructed in the 1960s (and later those of Toutain) reflect. O'Brien and Keyder (1978) upheld this rehabilitation of French economic performance in the nineteenth century, a view which rested on two premises: a steady rate of economic growth and a very high base in income generating potential from the outset, i.e. the eighteenth century.

From the view that the French economy had grown steadily albeit unimpressively over the whole century, it is highly improbable that a 'climacteric' can be identified. Roehl (1976) thought a climacteric of sorts had occurred after the Napoleonic wars, but it turns out that it was mainly because industrial performance before that period had been grossly overestimated. With regard to the *Belle Epoque*, the identification of a climacteric is highly improbable, essentially because, after the lengthy depression of the 1870s to 1890s, the economy resumed an ascendant path during the first decade of the twentieth century, a period which witnessed a record rate in industrial growth. Crafts has recently dispelled the last suspicions about the location of a climacteric in France as in Britain during the late Victorian or Edwardian era (Crafts, Leybourne and Mills, 1989).

France's standing in the material welfare league

In the light of recent comparisons, there is in fact little doubt left that the level of development attained by the British economy on the eve of the First World War was substantially superior to that achieved by its French counterpart, be it in terms of performance or of welfare. This last consideration was not necessarily held to be true by contemporaries. National accounting techniques were then in their infancy. While French observers readily acknowledged British superiority in terms of efficiency and mechanization, for instance, they did not necessarily link it to superior final disposable income per capita. The extent of the modernization achieved by the British economy did not strike contemporaries because visitors moved in an environment enjoying the same living conditions as those existing in the rest of Europe. Judged solely from the faded daguerrotypes left by the *Belle Epoque*, we cannot see any visible difference between an English village and a French one.

As often happens, the Great War acted as a revelator. French political decision-makers did not vent their dismay (for obvious political reasons), but all the same, they were astonished by the power of the German invasion which forced them to overstretch France's meagre industrial resources to counter it. The government's statistical office had discontinued industrial surveys since the Second Empire. In 1918, for the first time, director-general Dugé de Bernonville had, using material from the 1906 census, hypothesised the French lag behind the British in terms of output and productivity to be of the order of one third (Dugé, 1918).

Before the war, not one observer raised the point that France's 'overcommitment' to the primary sector (see Table 12.1) had constituted a handicap which had put a powerful brake on industrialization. This particular feature was merely perceived as a different specialization, resulting from a different set of preferences in the respective ways of life of France and the UK (this is the thrust of O'Brien and Keyder's argument). Furthermore, numerous politicians embraced the cause of a 'return to the land', arguing that industrialization was not France's real calling, that it had gone too far and that steps had to be taken to offset the 'desertification' of the French countryside (Méline, 1892). A broad consensus existed to blame modern forms of 'capitalist industry' for the ills of the present age (the pressing 'social question'). Verdict and diagnosis on the sluggishness of French economic growth and its possible source were therefore delayed until the 1930s.

Recent measurements of the gap in terms of income per capita as well as productivity (at purchasing power parity) suggest a 30% difference for the year immediately preceding the Great War (virtually Dugé's exact prewar hypothesis). Maddison's (1995) calculations establish it (by backwards extrapolation) at a little over 30% (see Table 12.2).

Table 12.1 Labour-force distribution across three sectors in 1913 (%)

	Primary	*Secondary*	*Tertiary*
France	41.1	32.3	26.6
UK	11.7	44.1	44.2
Germany	34.6	41.1	24.3
US	27.5	29.7	42.8

Table 12.2 Income per capita in selected industrial countries 1870–1913 (UK = 100)

	1870	1900	1913
1. France	57	62	69
2. Germany	59	68	76
3. US	75	89	106
4. Italy	45	38	50
5. Average Europe	61	63	69

Source: Maddison, 1995, p. 20.

Benchmark-year comparisons of GNP at current prices tend to diverge according to the evaluation and the monetary converter used: Toutain's (1987) figures yield a more favourable picture than Lévy-Leboyer and Bourguignon's (1990) series. Neither of them can be said to be immune of possible biases, but, for the purpose of cross-country comparisons, very long time series are notoriously hazardous. Despite claims by revisionists about nineteenth-century French 'robust' economic growth, the evidence available in the present state of the art points towards a substantial French lag in terms of income per capita as well as productivity (Dormois, 1997). Maddison's latest results seem in any case an acceptable compromise.[2]

Present-day economists usually assume that the latest calculation has an *a priori* greater quality than its immediate predecessor. Historians, by contrast, tend to shun long-term extrapolations and like to think that eyewitnesses may have, at least in theory, a soundness of judgement superior to that of remote observers. Despite their well-known pitfalls, it is not proven that the statistical surveys of the beginning of the twentieth century are intrinsically inferior in quality to present-day ones, not to an extent that should reduce them to insignificance.

The long depression

Taken as a whole, the period 1870–1914 represents, from the viewpoint of the volume of production and trade, a 'golden age', coming only second in terms of performance, as Maddison remarks, to the post-Second World War 'miracle'. How did this general expansion seem to have left France behind, relegating her to what North and Thomas called an 'also ran'?

There has been a consensus recognizing, in the premature 'slowing down' (*décélération*) of French economic growth, the Gallic version of a wider European phenomenon. But the careful observation of output indices behaviour has revealed that the slowdown had already set in by the early 1860s, much earlier than in neighbouring countries (Lévy-Leboyer, 1971). Clearly, from the 1870s 'French industry found itself ill-adapted to new world economic conditions' (Caron, 1992, p. 91). To explain this, great emphasis has been laid upon the costs of the Franco-Prussian war and the subsequent annexation by Germany of the industrial Alsace-Lorraine area. Thus, the dramatic fall in the world prices of foodstuffs and raw materials hit some already weakened economic sectors. However, most of the policies deployed by successive governments to counter the Depression only contributed to dragging into the twentieth century some of the economy's most damaging structural weaknesses.

In Britain, the Great Depression was mainly agricultural, the final stage in the specialization process of an industrial society started a century earlier. The government, with public opinion behind it, remained faithful to its free-trade commitment of 1846 and accepted the traumatic transformation brought forth by the termination of independent farming. With hindsight the political establishment *de facto* accepted the undermining of the wealth and power basis of its main constituency, the landed classes (via the depreciation of rents).

In France by contrast, the free-trade policy inaugurated by the Cobden-Chevalier agreement of 1860 did not hold in the face of adversity. As in the UK the landed interest held considerable influence in the political process even if sections of it were progressively estranged from the centres of political power (like the rural nobility). But the decisive discriminating factor between France and Britain was that a somewhat larger share of French households depended on agriculture (with the consequent well-known feature of smaller average landholdings). In the face of growing calls for protectionist legislation, universal suffrage made a 'stalling' policy untenable for a democratically elected government (Smith, 1980). In order to protect agricultural incomes, tariffs had to be raised repeatedly as the gap in production costs between French and overseas agriculture was widening.

As Figure 12.2 makes clear, there were several alarms (1871, 1879, 1891, 1898, 1911) when cheaper grain imports threatened to swamp the domestic market. On each occasion, the government reacted by passing a bill to raise import duties (a hike evidenced on Figure 12.2 by the drop in the price differential). Indeed, protectionism became, from 1892 onwards, part and parcel of the Republican agenda which hardly any political party, be it left or right wing, dared to question. The artificial support of agricultural prices had far-reaching and lasting consequences. It of course contributed to maintaining the urban cost of living at a higher level than elsewhere; it slowed down emigration from the countryside to the cities (one of the avowed objectives of the government anyway) and it kept the price of real estate artificially high, thereby discouraging investment outside the primary sector.

Protectionism backfires

Protectionist measures could stand accused as one of the prime suspects responsible for the slowing down of industrialization. But with the exception

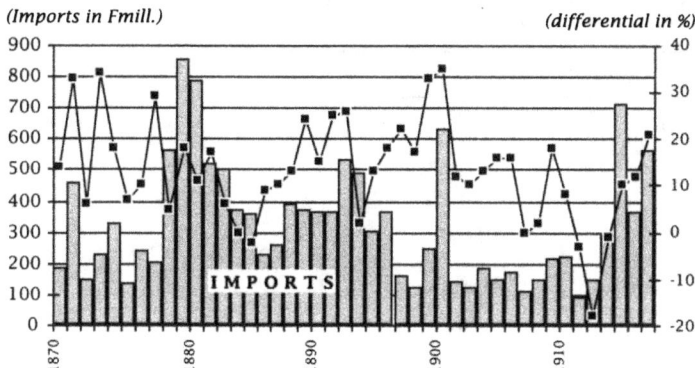

Figure 12.2 France–world price differential for wheat and French grain imports 1870–1913.
Surce: Lévy-Leboyer and Bourguignon (1990), Table A-VI.

of Golob (1944), this obvious scenario has usually been played down by the historiography. Echoing contemporary protests by manufacturers in traditional sectors hit by the Depression and denouncing the 'Napoleon III coup of 1860', some historians have blamed France's, as well as other 'follower-countries" difficulties on Britain's self-interested promotion of *laissez-faire* (Bairoch, 1972).

But attention has recently shifted back to the damage caused by government initiatives to smooth out the hardships of the Depression. Commercial policy was the main policy instrument in the hands of nineteenth-century governments, and the one which also had the widest-ranging effects. Thanks to a high price elasticity of supply, French farmers had for half a century ignored most attempts to rationalize production and compress costs. The policy adopted as early as 1880 with the passing of the first tariff maintained food as an artificially larger proportion of the cost of living.[3] Elementary arithmetic shows that, for foodstuffs and raw materials, relatively high nominal protection translated into disproportionately higher effective protection (because inputs were supplied by the primary sector where value added represents a lower share of output than in manufacturing).[4]

At the other end of the spectrum, manufacturers of more sophisticated products, especially in engineering, faced a handicap because of the tariff pattern of imposing heavy *per valorem* duties on raw materials and semi-finished goods. As shown in Table 12.3, tradable commodities fell into three easily distinguishable categories: (1) those enjoying quasi-discrimination (top three); (2) those enjoying higher effective protection than the nominal rates

Table 12.3 Nominal and real effective rates of protection of manufactures France, 1911–12 (%)

	(1)	(2)
Cast iron, iron & steel	24.4	57.8
Woollens	17.6	51.7
Cottons	14.4	40.7
Fuel (coal)	4.5	14.5
Wine	5.9	11.5
Furniture	6.0	10.9
Chemicals	10.9	9.9
Clothing	8.3	9.7
Food products	4.5	9.0
Pottery, glass, crystal	8.8	7.5
Leather articles	10.2	6.3
Tools & instruments	13.5	0.6
Paper, cellulose	6.3	– 2.2
Vehicles	15.5	– 7.2
Machines & engineering	11.0	– 11.4

Source: Tableau du Commerce général de la France, 1913, p. 212.
Notes: (1) nominal rate of protection; (2) real effective rate.

would suggest, and finally (3) those actually suffering from lack of protection or even supporting negative protection: this policy placed them in an inferior position to their competitors.

France therefore offers a counter-example to British classical *laissez-faire*, and its governments were sometimes blamed by contemporary observers for having let the Great Depression spread far and wide in the countryside. Although adherents to *laissez-faire* in theory, Third Republic governments, perhaps because they were more dependent for their political survival on pressure groups, took several initiatives the logic of which ran contrary to liberal economic principles.[5] It is easily recognizable that trade policy benefited essentially traditional or basic industries and those with most leverage in political circles (particularly large or long-established firms which had preferential access to government officials). Thus, the policy was shaped as the result of the activism of the various lobbies described by Lebovics (1988), especially the Comité des Forges.

Apart from the management of several public monopolies (in tobacco manufacture, telegraph and telephone operation) and state owned enterprises (ranging from matches and ordnance to tapestries), the French government held a vital stake in transport, via regulation of traffic and maintenance of canals and railway infrastructure. As the slump spread from the agricultural to the industrial sector, calls were made for the government to intervene. The Freycinet Plan (1877–83) was designed to provide relief through price support measures to hardup manufacturers in traditional sectors, essentially metallurgy and transport. Over the first three years, the government laid out a total 8 billion francs (from the 4 billion initially earmarked) for the extension of the railway network, intended to keep up orders to the metal and engineering trades. The operation was discontinued due to a dangerously widening budget deficit but the experiment was repeated in 1903. France ended up with a substantially longer railway network. The merchant navy was also among the beneficiaries (along with inland shipping); it received over half of the total government subsidies until 1914 (Dormois, 1998b).

There is, however, convincing evidence that the short-term benefits of these measures were outweighed by long-term costs. The intense public borrowing of these years drained the liquidity markets, increasing the public debt dramatically (up to 125% of GNP by 1913) and crowding out other investment opportunities. Overinvestment in 'public interest' railway lines generated diseconomies of scale, mounting inefficiency and falling profitability (Lévy-Leboyer, 1991, p. 160) which was solved by more government handouts and finally bailing out bankrupt companies (in 1909 the government was managing a quarter of the railway lines in operation). Overcapacity in railway transport resulted also in slowing down migration to the cities, transferring private benefits (of rural residents) into public costs. It is estimated that a solid 25 billion francs was swallowed up by the 'remedies' introduced by successive Third Republic administrations. Because of the time-lag between the diagnosis, the decision to subsidize, and the actual impact on the production line, government intervention also contributed to 'disarticulate' the business cycle. French industry thus found itself on several occasions on an upward course as other industrial economies were in recession, and conversely entering a slump as the world economy was expanding. This pattern is noticeable through the Second World War.

Government intervention could be deemed successful when measured against the government's own objectives, both avowed and unavowed: to protect farmers' (and landowners') incomes, slow down urbanization and ward off 'proletarianization', and to maintain a 'balanced' (i.e. essentially agrarian) economy (Méline, 1892). But it entailed substantial costs, not only to the consumer and taxpayer, but also to politically weaker groups and sectors. Mention has already been made (by Lebovics) of the existence of an 'objective' pact of alliance between large landowners and manufacturers of iron and steel, similar to that found in Imperial Germany at the same time. To be sure, the 'Republican' consensus eventually embraced a much larger constituency, including *fonctionnaires* and railwaymen but conspicuously excluding the industrial working classes (Friedman, 1995); it succeeded in making the preservation of the status quo the rallying banner of large sections of French society.

JEAN-PIERRE DORMOIS

Rent-seeking or risk-averting entrepreneurs?

Commercial policy quite naturally produced a realignment of sheltered and unsheltered sectors and firms. In fact it discriminated against some key industries: those producing consumer goods and those relying on imported semi-finished goods. In the worst cases these faced higher costs of production resulting in more competitive conditions. Facing these odds, it is therefore hardly surprising that the new branches of the chemical industry and several engineering firms lost ground to luckier and more dynamic rivals; neither the Swiss nor the Germans faced such handicaps. Bankruptcy statistics for these sectors offer only part of the story; the numbers of new entrants were also always very modest. The machine-tool and the railway equipment industries are cases in point. The German general staff who ordered in 1916 a survey of industrial establishments in the French occupied territory found (to their astonishment) that, in addition to the frequency of German or Swiss subsidiaries among chemical firms, machine-tools and industrial equipment were invariably of German origin.

For a long time the dim presence of French industrialists in the key industries was attributed to psychological factors: their alleged 'conservatism' and rent-seeking attitude. Parallel in many respects to its British counterpart, the debate opposed the prosecutors of business incompetence to the advocates of French entrepreneurship. Socialists figured prominently among the first group, which later included the partisans of modernization and planning in the 1930s. As early as 1910, Victor Griffuelhes, a leading Socialist, argued that 'French industrialists were intrinsically of an inferior quality compared to their European counterparts.' Theories on 'Malthusianism' (Alfred Sauvy) and *la société bloquée* (Stanley Hoffmann) took over from early critics, giving rise to the type of psychological explanations of inferior French entrepreneurship developed by Landes (1954). Over recent decades, monographs of a 'revisionist' persuasion have highlighted examples of entrepreneurial acumen and attempted to dispel the allegations of the pessimists. It is worth noticing, however, that a number of entrepreneurial successes are attributable to talented managers of well-established, already quite large corporations. Both parties tend to treat managers as a homogenous group regardless of whether they are at the helm of already powerful firms or true entrepreneurs. Are there really sufficient grounds for inferring, however, that 'French firms had proven by 1914 that they dominated the process of innovation' (Caron, 1992, p. 95)? Why this capital of innovation never translated for the most part into actual market shares remains unexplained. In truth, the examples and counter-examples amount to a disappointing draw.

The Malthusian creed, in its basic creed, is naturally untenable: there is no apparent reason to suspect *a priori* French entrepreneurs of congenital incapacity. And now that giant world conglomerates are breaking up into specialized companies, some of the more powerful arguments against the family firm (also used as ammunition against British capitalists) have lost some of their weight. But, if, as the motorcar or pharmaceutical industries, then in their infancy, to some extent illustrate, ingenuity and workmanship were not in short supply, it is in general conditions of the domestic market that obstacles to their full development must be found. It is therefore more relevant to judge from the competitive situation of the markets whether entrepreneurs behaved rationally or not. An examination of French pre-war market conditions shows a striking contrast between the obstacles placed before potential entrants into new industries on the technology frontier and the facilities (including financial) extended to long-established industries with organized pressure groups, i.e. privileged access to political power, large numbers of employees and a strong incentive to continue production processes as long as possible and regardless of competitive conditions. As Adam Smith remarked, 'The interest of manufacturers is always in some respects different from, and even opposite to, that of the public. To widen the market and narrow competition is always in their interest.'[6]

The collusion between industrial pressure groups and government is particularly to be expected in democratic-type regimes, like that of the Third Republic, and to be reinforced by its very endurance. The Republican personnel were not impervious to corruption or bribery as the numerous financial scandals of the period showed. The introduction of price cartels in several branches of industry, even if it was far from being absolutely effective, is further evidence that preference was given to powerful and long-established activities at the expense of new entrants (Aftalion, 1908).

A once powerful argument about British retardation was the contention that industries, especially the most innovative ones, had been starved of venture capital. British bankers, it was argued, had been excessively conservative in their strategies, favouring safe as opposed to risky investments. Can a similar case be brought against French bankers? As the second largest overseas investor during that period, France lends itself, it seems, to this accusation.

Without attaining the volume of British securities placed abroad, French banks handsomely contributed to the 'imperialist' stage of capitalism, coming only second in terms of volume to the UK (Table 12.4). As with its British counterpart, there is evidence that private returns in the French colonial empire were obtained at substantial public cost (Dormois, 1998a). In some cases, merchant bankers hitherto deaf to calls from ingenious innovators channelled investment enthusiastically to foreign firms, sometime grossly miscalculating their expected profitability (most notably in Russia). But on the whole, assessments converge to deny the presence of systematic biases to the disadvantage of domestic manufacturers (Hautcoeur, 1995). Compared to 'capital diversion', the high level of public indebtedness had

Table 12.4 Nominal gross value of overseas investment, 1914 (current $mill. at official exchange rate)

	Total assets	% GNP
Great Britain	18,311	250
France	8,647	115
Germany	5,598	140
United States	3,514	110
Belgium, Netherlands, Switzerland	5,500	n.a.
Rest of Europe	2,200	n.a.

Source: Feis, 1965, p. 66.

much more damaging effects. Bankers in fact chose to support the firms and activities that they had been used to: their only fault was that deriving from 'path dependence'.

Overcommitment

In spite of ventures into promising new fields of production, French industry appears to have been, at least in part, unreceptive to signals of changing competition patterns, and resisted changing comparative advantage induced by the technologies of the 'second industrial revolution'. This structural 'sclerosis' can in fact be perceived as the consequence of a series of policies aiming at preserving the status quo. Thus, the privileged protection enjoyed by traditional industries hampered to some extent any substantial transfer of resources to the areas of technologically innovative activities. By 1910, the textile trades were still France's major industrial employer, like in the UK, but, whereas in the latter their share of manufacturing value-added was halved from 43% to 24% between 1870 and 1914, they held faster in the case of the former where their share of output decreased from 65% to 44% (see Figure 12.3). As a result, while productivity in textile manufacturing reached 77% of the British performance, French clothing had the lowest productivity of industry. The metal trades (metallurgy and engineering) had meanwhile risen to prominence in Britain (with 48% of aggregate value-added) while in France their contribution to industrial output was limited to 25% (Lévy-Leboyer, 1968a, p. 293).

France's performance is particularly surprising since the discovery of the Briey ore-fields in Lorraine promoted it to third world producer of iron-ore. However, by 1913, half of its production was still exported raw. France's domestic resources in iron-ore had been multiplied by a factor of 4.63 (to over 16 million tons) but its production of cast-iron only developed by a factor of 2.33. Britain's output of iron-ore was 10% inferior to France's by 1913, but its manufacturing capacity was 110% larger for cast-iron and 66% for steel (Pohl, 1989, p. 130).

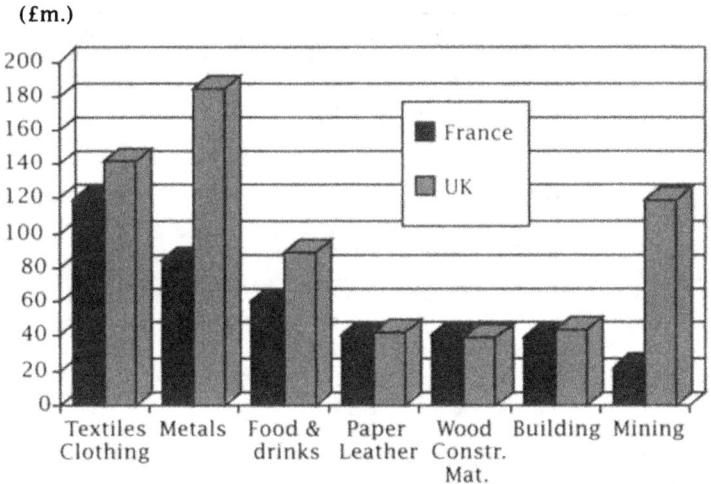

Figure 12.3 Comparative shares of value-added in French and British industries 1906/7
Source: Dormois (1997).

Textiles (including leather goods) made the largest contribution to France's trade balance in manufactures with a F 850 million surplus.[7] By contrast, engineering, clothing and more surprisingly food production ran a chronic deficit. The protectionist machinery designed to support the price of French food and to protect the income of French agricultural producers clearly had failed to build up the kind of self-dependence that the political decision-makers were avowedly pursuing. The deficit of the trade in food-stuffs reached for 1913 an astonishing F 905 million (10% of the value of the aggregate domestic arable product). Besides, if France had held an advantage in luxury and semi-luxury goods for a part of the nineteenth century, this had been eroded by the beginning of the twentieth. The country found itself dependent on foreign suppliers for a whole array of consumer and semi-durable goods. O'Brien and Keyder's 1978 contention that French industries specialized 'towards the finishing end of the assembly line' (in contrast to British manufacturers producing and selling semi-finished staples) must therefore be corrected. This still held true after the Great Depression but it accounted for a shrinking share of French exports, the bulk of which consisted of common semi-finished goods. (See Table 12.5.)

The strengths and shortcomings of France's industrial performance translated naturally into its trade structure. Comparative advantage analysis reveals that, except for carmaking and the film industry (then still in their infancy), firms were most competitive in relatively traditional and technologically backward branches of industry. Compared to the technological

Table 12.5 French trade balance in finished manufactures 1910–13 (Fm.)

	Average imports	Average exports	Trade balance
Mining	719	46	–673
Food products	466	49	–417
Engineering	510	280	–230
Clothing	32	227	–195
Chemicals	529	340	–188
Iron and Steel	313	210	–103
Other	220	170	–50
Glass, pottery	168	123	–44
Paper	81	133	+52
Wood	332	478	+146
Leather	431	819	+388
Textiles	235	1,082	+847
Total	4,036	3,957	–79
Total (finished and semi)	5,844	4,268	–1,576

Source: Dormois, 1996.

leader, and unlike UK firms which had retained a competitive edge in several areas (machinery, iron and steel, mechanical and electrical engineering), all but two of the innovative industries found themselves in the bottom half of the classification (Table 12.6).

France's aged industrial structure before 1914 lies at the heart of her demotion among industrial powers and world exporters. Between 1870 and 1939, France's share of world manufactured exports dwindled from 14.7 to 5.8%.

Table 12.6 Revealed comparative advantage in 1913: France and the US

Rank	France	US
Alcohol and tobacco	1	15
Cars and aircrafts	2	4
Clothing	3	14
Books and films	4	10
Fancy goods	5	13
Wood and leather	6	7
Textiles	7	16
Chemicals	8	12
Brick and glass	9	11
Non-ferrous metals	10	1
Metal manufactures	11	6
Iron and steel	12	9
Electricals	13	5
Industrial equipment	14	3
Rail and ship	15	8
Agricultural equipment	16	2

Source: Crafts, 1989, p. 132.

INDUSTRIAL RETARDATION IN FRANCE

New wind and change of pace

The French economy finally came out of depression in the middle of the first decade of the new century, though there were successive jolts until 1908. Many revisionists have emphasized the vitality of this spurt, which gathered momentum after 1909 to be abruptly interrupted by the outbreak of the war. But to a great extent, France was merely responding (with a time lag) to the expansionary trend affecting the world economy. Between 1900 and 1913 world trade grew at its fastest pace ever (4.75% per annum, almost doubling over this period), pushing world industrial production to unprecedented heights (Kuznets, 1971, p. 306). In this regard France's growth path, again, is remarkably similar to that of all the Western economies (including Great Britain). Industry in particular underwent a 'leap forward' in terms of volume, exhibiting the highest annual growth rates since the beginning of industrialization (4.2% between 1905 and 1913). By most accounts industrial output probably jumped by over a third during this period. But upon closer inspection, this trend appears to have concentrated upon the later years of the *Belle Epoque*. The years 1905 and 1906 were quite normal years and the country went through a recession in 1907–8 (accompanied by a record number of strikes and unrest in the mining north and wine-growing south which spearheaded the working-class movement). The boom spanned therefore the period 1909 to 1913, evidence of 'overheating' already surfacing in the last year.[8] A prominent role is alleged to have been played in this context by the new industries, harbingers of the French economic 'miracle' of the 1950s: the automobile and aircraft industries as well as the public utilities. Certainly they were then the most publicized, and to some extent the breakthroughs accomplished by pioneers in carmaking and related products (bicycles, tyres) put France on the podium for a while. But, what is striking, to repeat, is that despite the boost given to several carmakers during the Great War, French manufacturers had to yield to foreign manufacturers who were quicker to go into standardized production during the interwar period. Similarly, the Lumière brothers' momentous invention – in 1895 – thrust the domestic photography and later film industry to the forefront. The record of French technological success in those years encompasses aluminium technology and the liquefaction processes of natural gas as well.

These innovations, however ingenious, were not of a size to sustain the 'modernization process' that is alleged to have occurred then nor account for the increase in output observed over the period. Apart from the bicycle, the heyday of which was already drawing to a close, these innovations did not reach the mass production stage. They were clearly labelled as luxury products reserved for and sponsored by a limited élite. Not more than a total of 15,000 workers were employed in car and aircraft making. In many respects, the new entrepreneurs had the traditional reflexes of their counterparts in

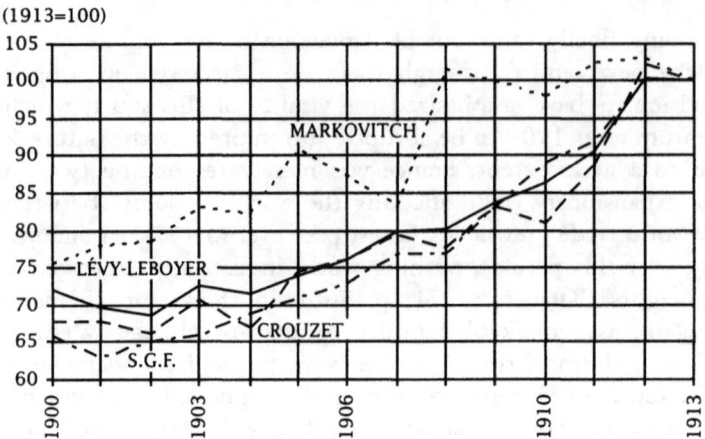

Figure 12.4 French industrial production indices 1900–1913.

Sources: Lévy-Leboyer (1991); Crouzet (1970); Markovitch (1965); S.G.F.: Statistique Generale de la France.

established industries: they relied for production too heavily (?) on family capital, scattered units of production, and high levels of skill and craftsmanship. However technically sophisticated these 'beautiful machines' appeared to be, they could not constitute by themselves the stuff of an industrial spurt.

Disaggregate output growth indices do show that 'new industries' (in their broadest sense) contributed disproportionately to the short spurt of the *Belle Epoque*. They accounted, in the most favourable view, for 25% of that spurt which would, however, not have occurred without the healthy contribution of the more traditionally organized sectors of metallurgy and engineering as well as chemicals (Table 12.7).

There is a strong suspicion, in fact, that the 1908–13 spurt was as much the result of a catching up process after a long period of recession as the outcome of a modernizing wave in French industry. Historians insist on the far-reaching effects of long-term processes, like that of economic development, but this insistence can sometimes prove a blind alley. Carré, Dubois and Malinvaud (1975) entertained the idea that the roots of the French postwar economic 'miracle' were to be found in the *Belle Epoque* because they had been able to bring their series back to 1896. With hindsight they came to regard the 1908–13 boom as the starting point of French modern economic growth. Most business histories of large twentieth-century corporations have taken this stance.

But the long-term view, while stressing the undeniable strength and endurability of certain economic assets, tends to ignore synchronic solidarities. Their legacies do not account for all the late success or expansion of

Table 12.7 Indices of manufacturing output by sector, 1905–13

	(1)	(2)	(3)
Mechanical engineering	220.3	9.2	5.0
'New' industries	202.4	8.2	9.0
Iron and Steel	176.7	6.6	6.4
Engineering and metal trades	176.4	6.5	23.8
Chemicals	142.9	4.0	4.8
Industry as a whole	134.9	3.4	100
Mining	123.0	2.3	8.5
Textiles	118.9	1.9	34.9

Source: Crouzet, (1970), Appendix.
Notes
(1) 1913 index (100=1905).
(2) Growth rate per annum (%).
(3) Share of total industrial value-added (%).

early firms, and the permanence of corporate names and trade marks can be deceptive: what does a 1970s carmaker like Peugeot SA have in common with its earlier incarnation as a textile mill or hardware factory?

Far from being the beacon of distant developments, the short-lived 1908–13 boom was mostly engineered along more familiar lines, those which made up the strength of French exports, for instance. The extension of 'network industries' can hardly count as the hallmark of success; gas and water distribution in large cities as well as tramways were, after all, captive markets where tenders seeking concessions were selected and granted monopolies by political authorities.

Welfare and the 'condition of France'

Turn-of-the-century public opinion in the United Kingdom was beset with worries about the social outcomes of industrialization, the fate of the poor and social surveys. These worries can be rightfully perceived as forming one of the early components of the British 'decline' debate.

In France, the 'revisionist' attack on the pessimist thesis resulted in the proposition that the French economy achieved by the end of the nineteenth century a comfortable standard of living, on a par with Great Britain, and, some said, without having gone through the traumatic upheavals of mass industrialization (Roehl, 1976; O'Brien and Keyder, 1978). More recent reworking of the statistical record has invalidated this proposition and brought to light a gradual but nonetheless evident fall in relative performance and income. If the country held its own on the world stage, its power was no longer commensurate with the wealth creation it commanded earlier. As a world manufacturer, France saw its market share drop from 8.6 to 5.8% between 1880 and 1913.

On the eve of the Great War, the French achieved in terms of income per capita only a fraction of what the other leading economies achieved and came tenth in the league table, behind most Western nations. Had demographic growth not slowed down to the extent it did, the fall would have been even more dramatic. How does one account for this contrast between France's economic and political power and the fall in relative terms of the French standard of living?

A first answer lies with hidden unemployment or widespread underemployment. Official statistics (the 1911 Population Census) record only a handful of people out of work, and contrary to the US and UK censuses, there is no separate entry for the 'hand trades' in industry – propertyless (and sometimes homeless) casual daylabourers (Dormois, 1997, p. 144). This category numbered over 3 million people in the primary sector alone. Like its British counterpart at the time, the French economy had a number of sizeable pockets of underemployment, but these tended to be less conspicuous than across the Channel because they were found in rural areas where casual labour had always been an essential part of everyday life. The *Ancien Régime* pattern of keeping the poor on the land was still, but more informally, in force.

The outcry caused by the 'discovery' of 'dearth in the midst of plenty' in the East End slums had spearheaded the contemporary malaise of British society. But likewise French public attention focused on urban disamenities and the industrial worker's plight, not on the rural constituencies where the real sources of greater distress probably were.[9] Thus, the debate as well as the measures taken by public authorities dealt essentially with the urban disamenities generated by industrial development. Rural destitution was therefore, if not completely ignored, at least given second place in the order of priorities of politicians and philanthropists.[10] The statistical information designed to feed social surveys was collected mainly from the large urban centres (like those on the cost of living) and it is important to keep this restriction in mind when applying comparisons.

How did the standard of living of French (urban) workers compare with their British counterparts during the *Belle Epoque*? The statistical office of the British Board of Trade conducted in the first decade of the century a number of very detailed comparative surveys to document the living standards of Continental workers relative to those prevalent in the UK. The survey regarding France, conducted during the course of 1907, offers prima facie evidence for a sizeable gap in living conditions between French and British urban dwellers. The report (which was later used by a US Senate committee) points to French average weekly wages being on average 25% lower than their British equivalent, the gap rising to 34% when it was taken into account that 'French workers work 17% longer hours than their British counterparts.' Conversely, the survey found that food prices were 'on the whole distinctly higher than those ruling for the same commodities in England and Wales'. In addition, French working-class dwellings did not compare favourably with Britain's and the surveyors found a high proportion (22%) of one-room apartments, a category almost unknown in England (or Germany).

Some critics of this seemingly obvious inferiority have stressed that the gap expressed in money terms could probably be filled if one used purchasing power parities instead of official exchange rates and took account of differences in tastes. Concerning the first disclaimer, it must be noted that purchasing parities would if anything enlarge the gap rather than reduce it; the French currency was overvalued during the *Belle Epoque vis-à-vis* the pound sterling.[11] As far as the second is concerned, it can be pointed out that diets when broken down into protein, vitamin and carbohydrate content, were not that different on either side of the English Channel.

The chasm between lower industrial wages and higher food prices (the direct consequence of the protectionist measures described above) is the single most potent observation barring the possibility of quasi-equivalence of French and British standards of living at the beginning of the twentieth century. The first factor alone casts serious doubt on the possibility of similar levels of productivity performance per worker as O'Brien and Keyder (1978) ascertained.[12] My latest computations of productivity levels agree with the per capita income levels mentioned earlier: overall the gap must have been of the order of 34–35% of the British performance.

This gap was probably larger when one takes into account rural rather than urban areas. Taking the sectoral distribution of the labour force, it can be estimated that while French urban incomes could attain about 75% of their British counterparts, they could have been of the order of 55% in the countryside. Paradoxically, therefore, while British farm incomes clearly grew throughout the Great Depression despite the downward spiralling of foodstuff prices (O'Grada, 1994), in France, where the government extended a protective safety net, farmers' income and production stagnated. By contrast, little was attempted to alleviate the hardships of industrial workers, whose plight had attracted so much public attention. On most counts, the French government resisted longer plans for welfare measures of the type introduced in Germany in 1890 and in Britain from 1906. Most pension schemes (the first introduced in 1898) were almost entirely financed through employees' contributions and health insurance was essentially left in the hands of government regulated charities. Gerald Friedman explains this essentially French characteristic as the result of the relatively small size of the labour constituency, the division of the labour movement and the success of employers' organizations in warding off the forced participation of business in employees' insurance schemes (Friedman, 1995).

Concluding remarks: of the good use of a parliamentary democracy

Critics of the late Victorian and Edwardian economy have suggested that some of the obstacles to improved performance could have been removed through subtle intervention by the British government. These initiatives, it is alleged, would have spared Britain difficult choices later on (Kennedy, 1982, p. 105). This proposition is made in connection with two of the most damning charges against the late Victorian economy: excessive overseas investments and overcommitment to staple industries.

The French economy of the *Belle Epoque* presents to some extent an example of what a nineteenth-century government could do to alleviate the most strident structural rigidities and regulate demand and sometimes supply, and the consequences it had. Evidence has accumulated that the initiatives taken by the Third Republic during this period had little positive effect in the short term and almost systematic negative effects in the medium and long term.[13] Resources were not only massively (and repeatedly) diverted from profitable uses but wasted outright. Cameron (who has since defected to the revisionists) rightly remarked some forty years ago: 'In its attempts to help industrialists overcome their problems, the government with few exceptions did more to hinder than to promote economic growth' (Cameron, 1958, p. 57).

Subsidies direct and indirect served to strengthen old-timers, yield to pressure groups, and consolidate monopolies through restrictive legislation, thereby making it harder for competitors to break even and new entrants to break in. Typically, breakthroughs occurred on the margins, in luxury goods with a very low price elasticity of demand (including motorcars, aeroplanes, films and guns). As soon as the price component became decisive for sales, manufacturers were faced with escalating costs due to the protective cost structure of intermediate inputs. France, which had to import over 80% of its consumption, was the only country in Europe (apart from Spain) to impose an absurd duty on coal. Among those longer and more deeply penalized by the 'Alliance of Wheat and Iron' were (apart from the consumer) the engineering and chemical industries 'which would have competed in the world market, had they been allowed to purchase raw materials at world prices' (Cameron, 1958, p. 55).

The probable lag suffered by these two sectors as a result of the supply constraint certainly handicapped the French wartime economy. French decision-makers, political and other, were in fact especially complacent about and blind to the weakness of the country's industrial capacity to sustain the kind of conflict that would draw on all the country's resources. In this way, France bears many similarities to Austria. Like Cisleithania (the western part of the Habsburg empire) she had a large, Continental and predominantly agricultural economy (and therefore stakes in agricultural protection); industrial activities were concentrated in a few peripheral centres. Moreover, at roughly similar income levels, their regimes had imperial aspirations (albeit of a different kind). In the pre-war framework of defensive alliances, they were supposed to serve as agricultural seconds to the industrial and maritime powers that were Great Britain and Germany. This reminds us how, in view of the abysmal catastrophe and horrendous waste of resources into which Europe descended in August 1914, the ill-conceived manoeuvres of government and business alike sink into insignificance.

Notes

1 The author wishes to thank Terence Lewis and Marjorie Woods who proofread an early draft of this chapter.
2 Maddison has constructed for the nineteenth century a compound GNP series from Toutain (1987) and Lévy-Leboyer.
3 Thiers had already suspended the 'free-trade' agreement of 1860 in 1872. But that was mainly in response to protests by textile and other manufacturers.
4 For more specific details, see Dormois (1996). In the same vein, Toniolo investigated the consequences of the 'under' protection of Italian mechanical engineering in the Giolitti era (see Toniolo, 1977).
5 Pouyer-Quertier, a textile manufacturer from Normandy, is a case in point. As finance minister in the early years of the Republic, he was responsible for the first duty hike after the Anglo-French treaty of 1860.
6 Adam Smith (1776/1976, centenary edition), *The Wealth of Nations*, Book I, XI, London, Penguin, p. 358.
7 The arithmetic covers only *finished* products to the exclusion of raw materials (raw cotton essentially) and intermediate inputs (thread). When these are taken into account, the deficit is of the order of F 650 million.
8 That defence spending may have helped sustain demand (the so-called rearmament bonanza) has been disproved (Crouzet, 1974).
9 By 1906, the rural population of France still accounted for well over 50% of the total, and that is by the definition of the French census, according to which an urban community's lower bound was set at 2,000 residents (compared to 10,000 in the UK and Germany).
10 A prominent exception to the trend was Michel Augé-Laribé, *L'Evolution de la France agricole* (Paris, A. Colin, 1912).
11 Only two series of PPPs exist for this period, those computed by O'Brien and Keyder (1978, p. 47) and those of Dormois (1997, p. 219). They are both expenditure PPPs generally used for comparing levels in income.
12 Colin Clark had in fact based his comparative surveys of labour productivity on the observed levels of wage income (Clark, 1955, 4th edn).
13 By today's standards, the French government, commanding a mere 11% of GNP through taxation, would not be classified as 'interventionist'. By contemporary standards, however, its regulatory and discretionary powers gave it ample room for manoeuvre in areas of economic activity (Lévy-Leboyer, 1991).

References

Aftalion, Alfred (1908), 'Les Kartells dans la région du Nord de la France', *Revue Economique Internationale* vol. 4/1, pp. 144–65.

Alroy, Gil C. (1962), *Radicalism and Modernization: The French Problem*, Ph.D. dissertation, University of Princeton.

Bairoch, Pierre (1972), 'Free Trade and European Economic Development in the Nineteenth Century', *European Economic Review* vol. 3, pp. 211–45.

Board of Trade (1909), *Report of an Enquiry into Working Class Rents and Retail Prices and Rates of Wages . . . in France*, London, HMSO (Cd. 4512).

Cameron, Rondo (1958), 'Economic Growth and Stagnation in France, 1815–1914', *Journal of Modern History* vol. 30, pp. 43–59.

Carré, Jean-Jaques, Paul Dubois and Edmond Malinvaud (1975), *French Economic Growth*, Stanford, Stanford University Press.

Caron, François (1992), 'L'economie française dans les anneés 1900: Dynamismes et blocages', in P. Milza and R. Poidevin, eds, *La Puissance Française à la Belle Epoque*, Brussels, Complexe, pp. 89–108.

Clark, Colin (1955) *The Conditions of Economic Progress*, London, Macmillan.

Crafts, N.F.R. (1983), 'Gross National Product in Europe 1870–1910: Some New Estimates', *Explorations in Economic History* vol. 20, pp. 387–401.

Crafts, N.F.R. (1984), 'Economic Growth in France and Britain, 1830–1910: A Review of the Evidence', *Journal of Economic History* vol. 44 (March), pp. 49–67.

Crafts, N.F.R. (1989), 'Revealed Comparative Advantage in Manufacturing, 1899–1950', *Journal of European Economic History* vol. 18, pp. 127–35.

Crafts, N.F.R., S.J. Leybourne and T.C. Mills (1989), 'The Climacteric in Late-Victorian Britain and France: A Reappraisal of the Evidence', *Journal of Applied Econometrics* vol. 4, pp. 103–17.

Crouzet, François (1970), 'Un essai de construction d'un indice annuel de la production industrielle française au XIXè siècle', *Annales E.S.C.* vol. 25/1, pp. 56–99.

Crouzet, François (1974), 'Recherches sur la production d'armement en France (1815–1914)', *Revue Historique* vol. 251, pp. 45–85; 409–22.

Dormois, Jean-Pierre (1992), *Etude des différentiels de productivité entre la France et le Royaume-Uni à la veille de 1914*, Ph.D. thesis, University of Paris-IV.

Dormois, Jean-Pierre (1993), 'Late-Victorian British Economic Performance in the Continental Mirror', *NEHA Bulletin* vol. 7, pp. 107–22.

Dormois, Jean-Pierre (1996), 'Nominal and Effective Protection Rates for Ten European Countries before 1914', 2nd Congress of the European Association of Historical Economics, University of Venice, January.

Dormois, Jean-Pierre (1997), *L'economie française face à la concurrence britannique à la vielle de 1914*, Paris, L'Harmattan.

Dormois, Jean-Pierre (1998a), 'The Significance of the French Colonial Empire for French Economic Development (1815–1960)', *Revista de Historia Económica* (April).

Dormois, Jean-Pierre (1998b), 'A Century of French Industrial Policy' in J. Foreman-Peck and G. Federico, eds, *A Century of European Industrial Policy*, Oxford, Oxford University Press (forthcoming).

Dugé de Bernonville, Louis (1918), 'Essai d'évaluation de la production industrielle en France avant la Guerre', *Bulletin de la S.G.F.* vol. 8, fasc. 1, pp. 71–92.

Feinstein, Charles (1972), *National Income, Expenditure and Output of the United Kingdom 1855–1965*, Cambridge, Cambridge University Press.

Feis, H. (1965), *Europe: The World's Banker 1750–1914*, New York, Norton.

Friedman, Gerald (1995), 'Revolutionary Unions and French Labor: Were there Rebels behind the Cause?' University of Massachusetts, Amherst, mimeographed.

Golob, Eugene (1944), *The Méline Tariff: French Agriculture and Nationalist Economic Policy*, New York, Columbia University Press.

Gonjo, Yasuo (1972), 'Le Plan Freycinet (1878–1882): un aspect de la grande dépression en France', *Revue Historique* vol. 249/3, pp. 49–79.

Griffuelhes, Victor (1910), 'L'infériorité des capitalistes français', *Le Mouvement Socialiste* vol. 226, pp. 330–7.
Hautcoeur, Pierre-Cyrille (1995), 'Le marché financier français entre 1870 et 1900', Ecole Normale Supérieur, DELTA working paper no. 95–02.
Kennedy, William (1982), 'Economic Growth and Structural Change in the United Kingdom, 1870–1914', *Journal of Economic History* vol. 42, pp. 105–14.
Kuznets, Simon (1971), *Economic Growth of Nations*, Cambridge, Mass., Harvard University Press.
Landes, David S. (1949), 'French Entrepreneurship and Industrial Growth in the 19th Century', *Journal of Economic History* vol. 9/1, pp. 45–61.
Landes, David S. (1954), 'Social Attitudes, Entrepreneurship and Economic Development', *Explorations in Entrepreneurial History* vol. 6/4, pp. 245–72.
Lebovics, Hermann (1988), *The Alliance of Wheat and Iron in the Third Republic 1860–1914*, Baton Rouge, Louisiana State University Press.
Lévy-Leboyer, Maurice (1968a), 'Le processus d'industrialisation: le cas de l'Angleterre et de la France', *Revue Historique* vol. 236, pp. 281–98.
Lévy-Leboyer, Maurice (1968b), 'La croissance économique en France au XIXè siècle', *Annales E.S.C.* vol. 23/4 (July), pp. 788–807.
Lévy-Leboyer, Maurice (1971), 'La décélération de l'économie française dans la deuxième moitié du XIXè siècle', *Revue d'Histoire Economique et Sociale* vol. 49/4, pp. 485–507.
Lévy-Leboyer, Maurice (1991), 'L'intervention de l'Etat: Mythes et réalités', in M. Lévy-Leboyer and J.-C. Casanova, eds, *Entre l'Etat et le marché*, Paris, Gallimard, pp. 251–87.
Lévy-Leboyer, Maurice and François Bourguignon (1990), *The French Economy in the Nineteenth Century*, Cambridge, Cambridge University Press.
Maddison, Angus (1995), *Monitoring the World Economy, 1820–1992*, Paris, OECD.
Marczewski, Jan (1963), 'The Take Off and French Experience', in Walt W. Rostow, ed., *The Economics of Take Off into Sustained Growth*, London, Bowes & Bowes.
Markovitch, Tihomir (1965), 'Le produit de l'industrie française de 1789 à 1962', *Cahier de l'ISEA*, series AF No. 4.
Méline, Jules (1892), *Le retour à la terre et la surproduction industrielle*, Paris, Hachette.
North, Douglas C. and Robert P. Thomas (1973), *The Rise of the Western World: A New Economic History*, Cambridge, Cambridge University Press.
O'Brien, Patrick and Caglar Keyder (1978), *Economic Growth in Britain and France: Two Paths to the Twentieth Century*, London, Allen & Unwin.
O'Grada, Cormac (1994), 'British Agriculture 1860–1914', in Roderick Floud and D. McCloskey, eds, *The Economic History of Britain since 1700*, Cambridge, Cambridge University Press.
Olson, Mancur (1990), 'Is Britain the Wave of the Future? How Ideas Affect Societies', in M. Mann, ed., *The Rise and Decline of the Nation State*, Oxford, Oxford University Press, pp. 91–113.
Perrens, Fernand (1910), *La révision douanière du 30 mars 1910*, Doctoral Law Thesis, Bordeaux, A. Destout.
Pohl, Hans (1989), *Aufbruch der Weltwirtschaft: Geschichte der Weltwirtschaft von der Mitte des 19. Jahrhunderts bis zum Ersten Weltkrieg*, Stuttgart, Steiner.
Roehl, Richard (1976), 'French Industrialization: A Reconsideration', *Explorations in Economic History* vol. 13/4, pp. 233–81.
Smith, Michael S. (1980), *Tariff Reform in France 1860–1900: The Politics of Economic Interests*, London, Cornell University Press.
Toniolo, Gianni (1977), 'Effective production and industrial growth: the case of Italian engineering 1898–1913', *Journal of European Economic History* vol. 6, pp. 659–73
Toutain, Jean-Claude (1987), 'Le produit intérieur brut de la France 1789–1982', *Economies & Sociétés* AF Series vol. 21.

INDEX OF NAMES

Aberconway (Lord) 182
Abramowitz, M. 33
Aftalion, A. 217
Aldcroft, D. 7, 8, 9, 11, 12, 14, 15, 16, 19, 22, 156
Alford, B.W.E. 3, 12
Allen, R.C. 122
Andrews, D.W.K. 68, 69, 71, 74, 79, 80
Arnold, M. 156
Ashworth, W. 72
Auden, W. H. 29
Augustus, 32
Austin, H. 134

Bacon, F. 28, 31
Bairoch, P. 76, 213
Barnett, C. 3, 10, 12, 16, 19, 114, 156
Bell, H. 181
Bellow, S. 34
Berghoff, H. 159, 186
Bernard, A.B. 70, 77, 78
Birdzell, L.E. 35
Bishop, T.H. 158, 159
Blackett, W.C. 180
Bloom, A. 30
Bourguignon, F. 211
Bowden, S. 134
Broadberry, S.N. 49, 51, 54, 72, 88, 89, 119, 121
Brown, W. 135
Burn, D. 37
Byatt, I.C.R. 130

Cadman, J. 179
Cain, P.J. 2, 4, 47
Cameron, R. 226
Capie, F. 197
Caron, F. 211, 216

Carré, J.C. 222
Carty, J.J. 132
Cassis, Y. 193, 194
Chandler, A.D. 1, 49, 119, 123, 134, 145, 199
Chapman, S.D. 190, 200
Chelmsford, 178
Chevalier, M. 212
Christiano, L.J. 68
Church, A. 30
Clay, C.L. 182
Clifton, R.B. 160
Cobden, R. 108, 212
Coleman, D. C. 159
Collins, B. 1, 2
Collins, M. 197
Coppock, D.J. 11
Crafts, N.F.R. 51, 67, 209
Crompton, R.E. 127
Crouzet, F.M. 76, 156

Daems, H. 1
Dante Alighieri, 28
Davis, E. 191
Dicky, D.A. 67, 69, 77
Devonshire (Lord) 155, 165
Dewar, J. 160
Dormois, J.P. 1, 4, 211, 215, 217, 224
Dowie, J.R. 72
Drew, W.N. 183
Dubois, P. 222
Dugé de Bernonville, L. 210
Dunlop, J.P. 123
Dunsheath, P. 127, 130
Durlauf, S.N. 70, 77, 78

Edison, Th. 128, 131
Eichengreen, B. 72

INDEX OF NAMES

Elbaum, B. 1, 2, 10, 12, 13, 16, 19, 49, 114, 115, 122, 163
Engels, F. 36
Ennius, 29
Erikson, C. 158
Ewing, A. 160

Feinstein, C.H. 13, 52, 57, 65, 66, 67, 70, 169
Ferranti, S. 118, 128
Feynman, R. 31
Floud, R.C. 9, 10, 12, 13, 15, 16, 17, 21, 65, 168, 169
Ford, H. 28, 119
Foreman-Peck, J. 2, 3, 13, 54, 57, 58, 126, 130, 133, 134
Fowler, 118
Freycinet, Ch. 214
Friedman, G. 215, 225
Fuller, W.H. 66, 69, 77

Gainford (Lord) 175, 176, 177, 183
Garside, W.R. 2, 3
Gibbon, E. 114
Godel, K. 30
Gordon, J.E.H. 128
Graham, J.I. 178
Greasley, D. 2, 3, 65, 66, 67, 68, 72, 74, 76, 78, 81
Gregory, J. 182
Greig, H.L. 180, 182
Grifuelhes, V. 215
Griliches, Z. 58
Grimstead, W.H. 132
Guagnini, 168

Habbakuk, H.J. 49, 121
Haldane, J.S. 157, 178
Handfield-Jones, S.J. 11, 65
Hassam, A. 181
Hautcoeur, P.C. 217
Hawafuji, M. 133
Heath, C. 195
Hedley, A.M. 181
Herlihy, D. 35
Hobkirk, D.T. 180
Hodges, F. 178
Hoffmann, S. 216
Hofman, A.W. von 125
Hogg, Q. 162
Holden, E. 193
Homer, 27
Hopkins, A. 47, 190

Howarth, J. 160
Hudspeth, H.M. 181
Hume, D. 31, 35
Hume, J.D. 39

Instone, S. 182
Isocrates, 29

James, B.G. 125
Jeremy, D. 159
Joicey (Lord), 182

Kelly, S. 182
Kelvin (Lord) 120, 128
Kennedy, P. 40
Kennedy, W. P. 34, 197, 198, 226
Keyder, Ç. 209, 210, 219, 225, 223
Keynes, J. M. 37, 72
Kirzner, I. 33, 34
Kitchener (Lord), 105
Kuznets, S. 221
Kynaston, D. 190

Laidlaw, J.V. 125
Lanchester, F. 134
Lander, C.H. 177
Landes, D.S. 7, 8, 9, 11, 14, 15, 16, 19, 22, 37, 114, 119, 120, 122, 129, 155, 164
Lawson, H. 134
Lazonik, W. 1, 2, 10, 12, 13, 16, 19, 49, 114, 136
Lebovics, H. 214, 215
Lee, C.H. 140
Lever, W. 28
Lévy-Leboyer, M. 209, 211, 215, 218
Lewis, G.A. 181
Lewis, W. A. 91
Leybourne, S.J. 67, 209
Liard, L. 164
Liebenau, 124
Liebig, J. von, 125
Lindert, P.H. 115
Littlehales, G. 191
Lloyd George, D. 105, 106, 107, 109
Lombardi, V. 38, 39, 41
Louis, H. 181

Macaulay, T.B. 32, 36, 39, 40
McClelland, K. 163
McCloskey, D.C. 1, 2, 3, 8, 9, 10, 12, 13, 15, 16, 17, 18, 19, 20, 21, 49, 65, 122, 140, 168, 200.
McIntyre, M. 30

INDEX OF NAMES

McKinley, A. 134
MacLean, M.F. 181
Maddison, A. 41, 49, 208, 210, 211
Malinvaud, E. 222
Marconi, G. 133
Marczewski, J. 209
Markham, C.P. 175
Marshall, A. 160, 199
Marx, K. 36
Matthews, R.C.O. 57, 66, 67, 70, 76, 169
Maxwell, C. 160
Méline, J. 210, 215
Mills, T.C. 67, 209
Millward, R. 2, 3, 13, 52, 130, 169
Milward, A.S. 72
Mitchell, G.A. 180
Mitton, H.E. 182
Moss, S. 27
Muller, R. 186
Musgrave, P.W. 168
Musson, A.E. 11

Nelson, C.R. 66
Nelson, R.R. 119
North, D.C. 211

O'Brien, P.K. 209, 210, 219, 223, 225.
O'Donahue, T.A. 176, 181
O'Grada, C. 225
Odling, W. 160
Olding-Smee, J.C. 57, 66, 67, 169.
Olson, M. 135
Oxley, L. 2, 3, 66, 67, 68, 72, 74, 76, 78, 81.

Palin, R. 191
Parsons, C. 129, 136
Pavarotti, L. 27
Pericles, 32
Perkin, H. 185
Perkin, W. 125
Perron, P., 68, 69, 74.
Phelps-Brown, E.H. 11, 65
Picasso, P. 28, 30
Plato, 27, 28, 31
Plosser, C.I. 66
Poccock, R.F. 133
Pohl, H. 218
Pollard, S. 9, 12, 52, 65, 123, 139, 140, 163, 164, 169.
Popper, K. 30
Porter, M. 200
Prais, S.J. 155

Preece, W.H. 132
Proust, M. 34

Raine, W. 180
Rappoport, P. 68
Rayleigh, 160
Reader, W.J. 125
Redmayne, R.A.S. 180
Reed, P. 123
Reich, R.B. 40
Richards, T. 178
Richlin, L. 68
Rickett, H.C. 180
Robertson, P. 167
Robbins, K. 1, 2
Roderick, G. 156
Roebuck, S. 178
Roehl, R. 209, 223
Rosenberg, N. 35
Rothschild, A. 192
Rubinstein, W.B. 9, 10, 13, 47, 48, 53, 159

Samuelson, B. 155, 156, 165
Sandberg, L. 8, 12, 13, 15
Sanderson, F.W. 157
Sanderson, M. 2, 3
Sankey, J. 176
Saul, S.B. 76, 115
Sauvy, A. 216
Schumpeter, J. 31
Scott, J.M. 131, 132
Sheard, S. 52
Siegfried, A., 1
Sinclair, D. 131, 132
Smallwood, E. 179, 180
Smillie, R. 176
Smith, A. 35, 108, 217
Smithson, H.F. 181
Socrates, 27, 28, 29
Solomou, S. 66, 67
Solow, R. 33
Southall, H. 142
Starley, J.K. 133
Stephens, M. 156
Stevenson, D. 182
Stewart, J. 160
Strahan, A. 178
Supple, B.E. 13, 15, 16, 20, 21
Swan, J.W. 124, 127

Temin, P. 168
Thales of Millet, 29

INDEX OF NAMES

Thomas, R.P. 211
Thomson, J. 160
Thomson, W., *see* Lord Kelvin
Thorneycroft, W. 180
Thurow, L. 40
Toutain, J.C. 209, 211
Trace, K. 115
Troup, E. 178
Turing, A. 30

Ushida, H. 118
Uzawa, T. 118

Vallin, J. 52
Varley, 178, 181

Ward, D. 159

Ward, R. 57
Weale, M. 67
Weber, M. 31
Wiener, M. 2, 4, 9, 12, 13, 19, 39, 185
Wilkinson, 158, 169.
Williams, E. 180
Williams, L.J. 185
Williamson, J.G. 52, 79
Wilson, Ch. 8, 11, 14, 15, 115
Wilson, J.F. 128, 30
Winter, J.M. 156
Wolcott, S. 74
Wright, G. 119
Wrigley, J. 167

Zivot, E., 68, 69, 71, 74, 79, 80

For Product Safety Concerns and Information please contact our EU
representative GPSR@taylorandfrancis.com
Taylor & Francis Verlag GmbH, Kaufingerstraße 24, 80331 München, Germany

www.ingramcontent.com/pod-product-compliance
Lightning Source LLC
Chambersburg PA
CBHW051055230426
43667CB00013B/2310